Palgrave Macmillan Studies in Banking and Financial Institutions

Series Editor: **Professor Philip Molyneux**

The Palgrave Macmillan Studies in Banking and Financial Institutions are international in orientation and include studies of banking within particular countries or regions, and studies of particular themes such as Corporate Banking, Risk Management, Mergers and Acquisitions, etc. The books' focus is on research and practice, and they include up-to-date and innovative studies on contemporary topics in banking that will have global impact and influence.

Titles include:

Elisabetta Gualandri and Valeria Venturelli (*editors*)
BRIDGING THE EQUITY GAP FOR INNOVATIVE SMEs

Kim Hawtrey
AFFORDABLE HOUSING FINANCE

Otto Hieronymi
GLOBALIZATION AND THE REFORM OF THE INTERNATIONAL BANKING
AND MONETARY SYSTEM

Munawar Iqbal and Philip Molyneux
THIRTY YEARS OF ISLAMIC BANKING
History, Performance and Prospects

Sven Janssen
BRITISH AND GERMAN BANKING STRATEGIES

Kimio Kase and Tanguy Jacopin
CEOs AS LEADERS AND STRATEGY DESIGNERS
Explaining the Success of Spanish Banks

M. Mansoor Khan and M. Ishaq Bhatti
DEVELOPMENTS IN ISLAMIC BANKING
The Case of Pakistan

Mario La Torre and Gianfranco A. Vento
MICROFINANCE

Philip Molyneux and Eleuterio Vallelado (*editors*)
FRONTIERS OF BANKS IN A GLOBAL WORLD

Anastasia Nesvetailova
FRAGILE FINANCE
Debt, Speculation and Crisis in the Age of Global Credit

Anders Ögren (*editor*)
THE SWEDISH FINANCIAL REVOLUTION

Dominique Rambure and Alec Nacamuli
PAYMENT SYSTEMS
From the Salt Mines to the Board Room

Catherine Schenk (*editor*)
HONG KONG SAR's MONETARY AND EXCHANGE RATE CHALLENGES
Historical Perspectives

Noël K. Tshiani
BUILDING CREDIBLE CENTRAL BANKS
Policy Lessons for Emerging Economies

The full list of titles available is on the website:
www.palgrave.com/finance/sbfi.asp

Palgrave Macmillan Studies in Banking and Financial Institutions
Series Standing Order 978–1–4039–4872–4

You can receive future titles in this series as they are published by placing a standing order. Please contact your bookseller or, in case of difficulty, write to us at the address below with your name and address, the title of the series and the ISBN quoted above.

Customer Services Department, Macmillan Distribution Ltd, Houndmills, Basingstoke, Hampshire RG21 6XS, England

Mergers and Acquisitions in European Banking

Franco Fiordelisi
Professor of Banking and Finance, University of Rome III, Italy

© Franco Fiordelisi 2009

All rights reserved. No reproduction, copy or transmission of this publication may be made without written permission.

No portion of this publication may be reproduced, copied or transmitted save with written permission or in accordance with the provisions of the Copyright, Designs and Patents Act 1988, or under the terms of any licence permitting limited copying issued by the Copyright Licensing Agency, Saffron House, 6-10 Kirby Street, London EC1N 8TS.

Any person who does any unauthorized act in relation to this publication may be liable to criminal prosecution and civil claims for damages.

The author has asserted his right to be identified as the author of this work in accordance with the Copyright, Designs and Patents Act 1988.

First published 2009 by
PALGRAVE MACMILLAN

Palgrave Macmillan in the UK is an imprint of Macmillan Publishers Limited, registered in England, company number 785998, of Houndmills, Basingstoke, Hampshire RG21 6XS.

Palgrave Macmillan in the US is a division of St Martin's Press LLC, 175 Fifth Avenue, New York, NY 10010.

Palgrave Macmillan is the global academic imprint of the above companies and has companies and representatives throughout the world.

Palgrave® and Macmillan® are registered trademarks in the United States, the United Kingdom, Europe and other countries.

ISBN: 978–0–230–53719–4

This book is printed on paper suitable for recycling and made from fully managed and sustained forest sources. Logging, pulping and manufacturing processes are expected to conform to the environmental regulations of the country of origin.

A catalogue record for this book is available from the British Library.

A catalog record for this book is available from the Library of Congress.

10 9 8 7 6 5 4 3 2 1
18 17 16 15 14 13 12 11 10 09

Printed and bound in Great Britain by
CPI Antony Rowe, Chippenham and Eastbourne

To Patrizia
for her continuous encouragement, support and love.

To Anna
Welcome!

Contents

Tables

Figures

Preface

This book proposes an independent assessment of the effect produced by Merger and Acquisition (M&A) transactions on bank efficiency and shareholder value. M&A deals have usually been justified to increase the company efficiency and, eventually, create shareholder value, but very few studies have analyzed the overall result of M&A deals to support these motivations, especially in European banking. We first substantiate that our research aims are worthy M&A phenomenon by showing that:

1. M&As are an important phenomenon worldwide;
2. M&As are particularly important in banking;
3. the M&A phenomenon is particularly exciting in European banking.

The book answers three fundamental questions: Why do banks merge? Do M&As create value for shareholders in the short-term? Do M&As create value for shareholders in the long-term? To answer the first question, we firstly provide a theoretical analysis of M&A motives. Next we critically analyze seven of the largest merger deals in European banking (that is, the Royal Bank of Scotland, leading a consortium comprising also Fortis and Banco Santander) and ABN AMRO in 2007, the UniCredit bank and Capitalia in 2007, BNP Paribas and Banca Nazionale del Lavoro in 2006, the Unicredito Italiano and Bayerische Hypo und Vereinsbank in 2005, Banco Santander Central Hispano and Abbey National plc in 2004, HSBC Holdings and Crédit Commercial de France in 2000. To answer the second question, we analyse a large sample of M&As between 1991 and 2005 within the EU 27 (almost 300 deals) running an event study method. To answer the third question, we compare the efficiency levels and the EVA created by the banks in a moment that precedes M&A operations with those obtained in a following moment. The sample used is among the largest adopted until now and it focuses on the four European banking markets (France, Germany, Italy and United Kingdom) mainly interested by the M&A phenomenon. One of the merits of the present book is to combine different investigation methods such as business cases (by reviewing the most recent M&A cases), the event study methodology and the stochastic frontier methods to assess the effects (both in the short and medium term) of M&A deals on banks' shareholder value and efficiency by examining a large sample of M&A deals in Europe. Overall, this text provides an extensive coverage of M&A issues in European banking and it will be of use to financial sector practitioners as well as academics and students interested in measuring the effects produced by M&A deals from a stockholder perspective.

Acknowledgements

I started writing this book in the Winter of 2006 during my visit to the Department of Accounting, Finance and Management at the University of Essex, UK. It was finished at the University of Rome III three years later. I am gratefully thankful to my colleagues for their forbearance and, especially, I would like to thank David Marques-Ibañez, Claudia Girardone, John Goddard, Marcello Pallotta, Ornella Ricci, Paola Schwizer, Jon Williams, for their comments, support and advice covering many areas in the text. Over the years, I have been fortunate to be close to my teachers, colleagues and students, who provided decisive stimulus to my work. I would like to convey special thanks to the Bocconi University Research Centre on Financial Innovation (Newfin), the Essex Finance Centre of the University of Essex and the Bangor Business School for the assistance and collaboration constantly supplied. I am also very grateful to Patrizia Vigliotti for the valuable proof reading. Last but not least, I am most grateful to my teachers and mentors, Alessandro Carretta, Phil Molyneux and Daniele Previati who greatly influenced my understanding of financial institutions and markets.

FRANCO FIORDELISI
University of Rome III, Rome

1
Why Study M&A in Banking?

1.1 Introduction

This book deals with the analysis of Mergers and Acquisitions (M&As) in the European banking markets. One might address the following four questions:

1. Why a book on M&A?
2. Why banks?
3. Why in Europe?
4. Is it necessary to have another contribution to the M&A debate?

With regard to the first question, the M&A is an important phenomenon worldwide. M&A deals are the two most visible expressions of the functioning of the corporate control market. These are often perceived by companies' stakeholders (and, especially, by workforce) as dramatic events since the ownership of an entire company changes hands in a single transaction. In a merger deal, two separate companies agree to combine and form a single corporate entity rather than remain separately owned and operated. This is done by issuing stock of the controlling corporation to replace most of the other company's (or companies') stock.

In some cases, a company acquires all the assets and liabilities of another firm, which ceases to exist after the merger is completed, and retains its name and often most of its top management. In other cases, two separate companies create a completely new firm and both firms cease to exist. In acquisition deals, a company (labelled as "bidder") acquires control of another firm (labelled as "target") by stock purchase (i.e. either through an agreed-upon deal or a hostile takeover) or stock exchange. Acquisitions are also known as takeovers and usually involve big companies acquiring a smaller one. Although Merger and Acquisition refer to different concepts, these terms are often used interchangeably.

The volume of M&A transactions has boosted over the last few years. According to the Thomson Financial (2007), the volume of worldwide M&A declared during 2007 reached US$4.5 trillion in announced deals and US$3.8 trillion in completed deals – that is, 24% increase over the previous record set in 2006. From 2000, the volume of M&A deals has increased by 32%, despite the fall off during the third quarter of 2007 caused by concerns in the credit markets. The M&A phenomenon concerns all countries worldwide (see Table 1.1): in 2007, M&A deals increased by 25% in North America (reaching a volume of almost US$2.0 trillion over 2007 – that is, 52% of M&A deals value worldwide), by 18% in Europe (reaching a volume of almost US$1.3 trillion over 2007 – that is, 34% of M&A deals value worldwide) and they strongly increased also in the Asian-Pacific area by 61% (reaching a volume of almost US$0.4 trillion over 2007 – that is, 10% of M&A deals value worldwide). Regarding the type of deals, the M&A cross-border activity accounted for 47% of worldwide

Table 1.1   Worldwide completed M&A in 2007

Region	Rank value (in USD billion)	No of deals	Change in rank value (in %)
America	1,979.3	11,567	27.1
North America	1,862.1	10,575	24.7
Central America	49.7	181	404.7
South America	58.1	707	41.3
Caribbean	9.3	104	−26.3
Africa/Middle East	39.9	443	−27.6
Asia – Pacific	378.4	5,504	61.1
Europe	1,298.7	9,915	18.2
Eastern Europe	112.4	1,212	21.1
Western Europe	1,186.3	10,575	18.0
Worldwide	3,784.1	28,729	23.9

Source: Thomson Financial (2007, p. 3).

activity in 2007 as global consolidation continued to drive activity in various sectors.

Why banks? This book analyzes the M&A phenomenon focusing on the banking industry since the consolidation in that industry was particularly important worldwide. Although the growth of the consolidation process concerns almost all industries,[1] most deals take place in the financial, materials and energy power industries. In banking, the consolidation process is particularly important: in 2007, M&A transactions among financial institutions worldwide were more than 7,000 for an overall value of more than USD 700 billion (see *Thomson Financial*, 2007, p. 2).

Regarding the third question, the M&A phenomenon is particularly remarkable in the European banking. While over the 1990s most M&A transactions involved North American banks and the European banking consolidation process was minor, the number and the value of deals within the European banking industry has currently a magnitude similar to that of the US banking (see Figure 1.1). Namely, in terms of number of transactions completed over 2005, the European financial institutions were involved as targets for 32% of transactions (EU-15 banks account for 27%) and for 31% of transactions as acquirers (EU-15 banks account for 28%). In terms of value of the deals completed over 2005, the European financial institutions were involved for 40% of transactions as targets (EU-15 banks account for 36%) and for 36% of transactions as acquirers (EU-15 banks account for 32%).

These data provide evidence that the M&A phenomenon is particularly relevant and it is thus an important research area. Given the importance of the M&A phenomenon, this is one of the most investigated areas in finance. To have an idea, we simply searched the Google scholar website (www. scholar.google.com, accessed on 16 May 2008) and found 14,800 papers showing the term "Merger and Acquisition" in the title and 53.600 papers having the word "M&A" quoted in the title. We also searched the Amazon website (http://www.amazon.com, accessed on 16 May 2008): 4,314 pieces of works quote "M&A," 23,803 researches include "Merger and Acquisition."

These data lead us to ask one final question: is it necessary to have another contribution to the M&A debate? May further studies on these topics add to the existing literature? In our opinion, they may do so. Previous books deeply analyzed the M&A phenomenon with

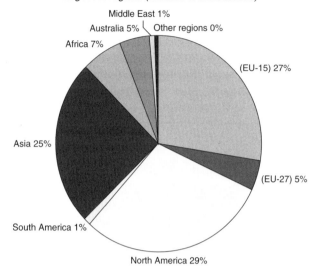

Target F.I. regions (Number of transactions)

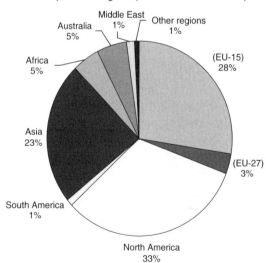

Acquirer F.I. regions (Number of transactions)

Figure 1.1   Continued

Target F.I. regions (Overall value of transactions)

Acquirer F.I. regions (Overall value of transactions)

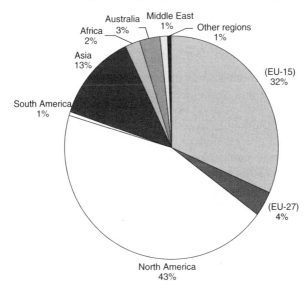

Figure 1.1 Number and value of M&A deals among financial institutions in 2005 for country regions

Source: Thomson ONE Banker database.

regards to management, organizational structure, corporate finance, taxation issues, especially in the US market. Our book aims to advance prior literature focusing on some specific aspects, which have been investigated by only limited number of studies. Namely, this text proposes an independent assessment of the effect produced by M&A transactions on bank efficiency and shareholder value. M&A deals have usually been justified to increase the company efficiency and, finally, create shareholder value, but few studies have analyzed the overall result of M&A deals to support these motivations, especially in the European banking.

In final, we searched the Amazon website using the words "bank" and "Europe" with "M&A" either "Merger and Acquisitions" to verify the number of books dealing with this topic. Overall, we found 15 pieces of work having also "M&A" in the book description and 16 having also "Merger and Acquisition" jointly with "Europe" and "Bank." This research comprises some books, but also special issues of academic journals and digital books. On the whole, we found that none of these was a specific research within European Banking aiming to verify the effects produced by M&A transactions on bank performance and check if M&A motivations have been really achieved.

1.2 Structure of the text

The book combines various investigation methods including business cases (a review of the most recent M&A cases), the event study methodology and the stochastic frontier methods to assess the effects (both in the short and medium term) of M&A deals on banks' shareholder value and efficiency. It is organized into nine chapters. In Chapter 2, we provide a framework for analyzing the M&A phenomenon by discussing some peculiar features of the European banking industry and analyzing recent trends of the consolidation process. Since the 1990s some of the most important M&A deals worldwide have involved European banks (for example, there have been six big mergers from 2006 for an overall value of more than 170 euro billion) and M&As are certainly one of the main bank responses to higher competitive pressures in European banking. New forces of changes are mainly related to structural deregulation and prudential reregulation, competition enhancement, technology developments, globalization, and so forth have occurred. Especially, regulatory changes

played a major role; that is, the structural de-regulation and prudential reregulation processes.

In Chapter 3, we answer to a simple question: why do banks merge?
While it is evident that European banks have increasingly merged
over the 2000s, these operations have various motives. Generally,
M&A deals aim to create shareholder value and, among all possible drivers, we discuss revenue enhancement, cost reduction and
new business opportunity reasons. We also analyze seven cases of
big merger deals in European banking: the Royal Bank of Scotland
(leading a consortium comprising also Fortis and Banco Santander)
and ABN AMRO in 2007, the Unicredit bank and Capitalia in 2007,
BNP Paribas and Banca Nazionale del Lavoro in 2006, the Unicredito
Italiano and Bayerische Hypo und Vereinsbank in 2005, Banco
Santander Central Hispano and Abbey National plc in 2004, HSBC
Holdings and Crédit Commercial de France in 2000.

In Chapter 4, we review the literature dealing with the M&A phenomenon in the financial service industry. Although the number
of studies is very large, there is a mixed evidence about the M&A
effects on the participating financial firms, bank customers and
societal risks. Overall, studies investigating the M&A effect over the
medium-long term in European banking are more homogenous than
the US banking. They show that M&A deals lead European banks to
enhance their performance and productive efficiency. However, the
number of studies investigating the M&A effect on operating performance (especially in Europe) is limited and it is not possible to draw
definite conclusions.

Next, we make various empirical investigations in order to measure the effect produced by M&A transactions. Namely, analyzes of
M&A deals in both the short term by using the event study analysis
(see Chapter 5), and the medium-long term by estimating bank's efficiency and shareholder value changes (see Chapters 6 and 7, respectively) are provided. In Chapter 5, we run an event study finding that
M&A deal created, on average, substantial shareholder value for the
target companies, while the estimated mean Cumulative Abnormal
Returns (CAR) for bidder companies are, on average, negative. The
analysis of the combined entity provides evidence that the "entire"
M&A transaction created (taken as a whole) shareholder value, rather
than simply transfer wealth from the bidder banks' shareholders to
the shareholders of the targets.

In Chapters 6 and 7, we analyze the M&A results in the medium and long term by comparing the levels of efficiency and the value created by banks in a moment that precedes M&A operations to those obtained in a following moment. In the light of the results obtained, the M&A operations analyzed do not seem to have had very significant results on the efficiency of European banks: on a time horizon of five year, the acquiring bank improves its efficiency of 0.67% on average, while the bank resulting from the merger seems to face an average worsening of 0.54%. In terms of value created for shareholders, the effect produced by M&A operations seems to be better: the relative capacity of creating value (given by the ratio between EVA and invested capital) increases by 0.23% in the five year following the operation of aggregation in case of acquisitions and of 0.41% in case of mergers. Further contributions to the analysis on this theme may focus on the analysis of possible benefits in terms of the opportunity cost of the capital invested by banks in consequence of M&A operations, which may determine, *ceteris paribus* – a higher capacity of creating value.

Finally, we analyze the post-acquisition integration phase in Chapter 8. Banks often fail to achieve the expected M&A benefits because of the bad management of the post-acquisition phase. Every acquisition target has unique benefits (for example, operating scale economies, geographical coverage, access to technology, management talent) and each of them is valued differently by individual stakeholders. As such, the integration of two merging banks involves the integration of the banks' systems, processes, procedures, as well as of strategy, reporting system, incentives and, especially, of people. Conclusions are in Chapter 9.

2
Merger and Acquisition Trends in European Banking

2.1 Introduction

A large part of the research undertaken to evaluate the effects produced by Merger and Acquisition (M&A) transactions has been analyzed primarily within the US banking and only a small number of studies have focused on European banks. As shown in Chapter 1, after a simple search on the Amazon website, we found just 15 pieces of work having "M&A," "Europe" and "Bank" in the book description and 16 having "Merger and Acquisition". Recently, Goddard et al., (2007, p. 1720) state "further research is needed in order to identify the types of consolidation activity that yield the highest diversification benefits, and to identify the implications of domestic and cross-border bank mergers for systemic risk." The need for further research in European Banking is quite surprising since there has been a large number of M&A transactions in European banking from 2000 onwards. Recent years have seen the emergence of several large cross-border institutions within the EU: in 2005, the 14 largest cross-border banking groups accounted for almost one-third of total EU bank assets (see Papademos, 2005). In 2007, the largest ever financial services M&A occurred between the Royal Bank of Scotland – leading a consortium of banks – and ABN AMRO. Over the same year, the merger between Unicredit bank and Capitalia created the world's fifth largest bank by market capitalization.

M&A deals have been changing the structure of the European banking and the intense consolidation trend over the 2000s is one of the main bank responses to higher competitive pressures (see Carretta,

2008). Since the 1990s, the European banking has experienced substantial changes and new forces of changes have taken place, such as structural deregulation and prudential reregulation processes (e.g. the Financial Services Action Plan, aiming to create a true Single European banking market), competition, technological developments, globalization, etc. M&A deals are one of the main responses to new force of changes in the banking sector.

This Chapter is organized as follows. Firstly, we analyze the evolution of the European banking markets over the last two decades by discussing the main force of changes. Secondly, we illustrate the structural features of the banking industry; then, we analyze how banks work in this new environment and consequently bank's interest on M&A to respond to the new force of changes. Finally, the M&A phenomenon is analyzed in depth by discussing most recent trends (e.g. number and value of deals, type of transactions) and cases.

2.2   The evolution of the banking market

The European banking experienced substantial changes over the last two decades, since new forces of changes such as structural deregulation and prudential reregulation, competition, technology developments, globalization, etc. have occurred. Banking has traditionally been one of the most heavily regulated industries in all countries. Until the late 1980s, most European Banks were subject to heavy structural regulatory rules in order to inhibit competition, such as having to enter the rationing of banking licences, branching restrictions (for example, the prohibition of interstate banking and branching in the US), credit ceilings, regulatory segmentation between financial activities (for example, between commercial and investment banking), geographic segmentation of the markets (for example, in some countries, banks were restricted to lending only limited amounts of money outside the area where they had their headquarters). In many cases, supervisors were entitled to screen a very large range of bank transactions and each transaction of this kind had to be explicitly authorized. These rules were adopted in most countries as a response to the banking crises of the 1930s. The aim was to constrain competition so as to preserve the stability of the financial industry. The underlying idea was that "competition is dangerous," while banks could enjoy extra-profits in an oligopolistic market in order to foster the stability of individual banks and the overall banking system.

Between the mid-1970s and the mid-1980s, most countries realized that structural and conduct rules protected the banking environment and achieved the goal of guaranteeing the stability of the overall financial system. Nevertheless, they did not supply real incentives to banks to work effectively and achieve the allocative efficiency. Berger and Humphrey (1997, p. 190) note: "Deregulation is typically undertaken to improve the performance of the industry being deregulated. If efficiency is raised, the improvement in resource allocation will benefit society and may lead to price reductions and/or service expansion for consumers if competition is sufficient." In Europe, the Cecchini Report (1988) was the first to assess the benefits of a deregulated market showing that

1. the European domestic banking systems were fragmented and characterized by relatively small size, high concentration, excess capacity, and lack of competition;
2. banks could achieve both economies of scale and scope by increasing their size and expanding the products and services offered;
3. and banks could also achieve gains in efficiency if there were incentives for them to adopt best practices.

Overall, the benefits to consumers were estimated to range between 4–7% of GDP for the nations under study, in the case that the economies of scale and scope, increased efficiency and enhanced competition.

In the 1970s and 1980s, most countries went through a regulatory change; they moved from structural and conduct rules to a prudential regulation framework. Under the new prudential regulation framework, supervisors follow objective rules, which have been set in the banking system to induce banks to adopt prudential behaviours. The new regulatory approach in banking is a real turnaround from the past as summarized by Padoa Schioppa (2001, p. 15):

Supervision is, as we are now in the habit of saying, 'market friendly'. It relies very much on the idea that if banks were strengthened by the gymnastics of competition, the banking system would be stronger and more resilient to shocks. Of course, competition means selection. Hence, such an attitude also implies that authorities must be ready to let the weakest banks leave the market. To the extent that competition is not enough to enhance the robustness of the banking system, supervisors need to step in by resorting to instruments that are themselves 'market friendly'. Capital requirements, for example, are more respectful of entrepreneurial choices than procedures for directly allowing or forbidding the extension of particular loans, which are too risky or not sound according to the supervisors' judgement [...] Competition policy is actively applied to the banking industry and the security supervisors treat banks just like any other listed or limited company. (Schioppa, 2001, p. 15)

Over the 1990s, most of these structural and conduct restrictions were removed in order to allow financial intermediaries to compete more freely (deregulation). Prudential regulation consists of a mixture of regulatory monitoring (on bank's asset quality and effectiveness of monitoring), capital adequacy requirements, other portfolio restrictions (for example, large exposures), fit and proper managers and entry restrictions. Since the 1990s, various changes in the systems of prudential regulation have occurred. First, there has been greater emphasis on monitoring banks' risk management systems given the increased number and complexity of transactions, and less emphasis on monitoring individual transactions. Secondly, in the wave of the financial market liberalization, interest rates have been deregulated and restrictions on the asset choices of banks have been lifted. Thirdly, weight has been placed on capital requirements, typically following the Bank for International Settlements standards of the Basel Capital Accord.

The structural deregulation and prudential reregulation processes were lead by various factors such as globalization and technological developments. In Europe, the regulatory change was also led by the integration of the various domestic banking markets in order to create a single European Banking Market. The actions taken by the European Commission and the Council of Ministers can be divided into five steps:

1. deregulation of entry into domestic markets from 1957 to 1973;
2. various attempts toward harmonization of regulations from 1973 to 1983;

3. the "1992 directives regarding single banking license, home country control, mutual recognition, and freedom of cross-border services;
4. the creation of the single currency in 1999;
5. the introduction of the Financial Services Action Plan (FSAP) from 2001 onwards, which consists of various initiatives to ensure the creation of a fully integrated and competitive market for financial services in Europe.

In 2007, two crucial FSAP initiatives were implemented. The first is the Markets in Financial Instruments Directive (MiFID), which came into effect in November 2007. The second initiative is the Capital Requirements Directive (CRD) which implements the "International Convergence of Capital Measurement and Capital Standards" (labelled as Basel II) for credit institutions and investment firms[1] set by the Basel Committee on Banking Supervision. The CRD aims to create a comprehensive and risk-sensitive framework and to foster enhanced risk management amongst financial institutions.

1977	First Banking Directive: Removed obstacles to the provision of services and establishment of branches across the borders of EU member states, harmonized rules for bank licensing and established EU-wide supervisory arrangements
1988	Basle Capital Adequacy Regulation (Basle I). Minimum capital adequacy requirements for banks (8% ratio). Capital definitions: Tier 1 (equity); Tier 2 (near-equity). Risk-weightings based on credit risk for bank business
1988	Directive on Liberalization of Capital Flows. Free cross-border capital flows, with safeguards for countries having balance of payments problems
1989	Second Banking Directive. Single EU banking licence. Principles of home country control (home regulators have ultimate supervisory authority for the foreign activity of their banks) and mutual recognition (EU bank regulators recognize the equivalence of their regulations). Passed in conjunction with the Own Funds and Solvency Directives, incorporating capital adequacy requirements similar to Basle I into EU law

---

Figure 2.1 Continued

1992	Large Exposures Directive. Banks should not commit more than 25% of their own funds to a single investment. Total resources allocated to a single investment should not exceed 800% of own funds
1993	Investment Services Directive. Legislative framework for investment firms and securities markets, providing for a single passport for investment services
1994	Directive on Deposit Guarantee Schemes. Minimum guaranteed investor protection in the event of bank failure
1999	Financial Services Action Plan (FSAP). Legislative framework for the Single Market in financial services
2000	Consolidated Banking Directive. Consolidation of previous banking regulation
2000	Directive on e-money. Access by non-credit institutions to the business of e-money issuance. Harmonized rules/standards relating to payments by mobile telephone, transport cards, and Basle payment facilities
2001	Directive on the Reorganization and Winding-Up of Credit Institutions. Recognition throughout the EU of reorganization measures/winding-up proceedings by the home state of a EU credit institution
2001	Regulation on the European Company Statute. Standard rules for company formation throughout the EU
2002	Financial Conglomerates Directive. Supervision framework for a group of financial entities engaged in cross-sector activities (banking, insurance, securities)
2004	New EU Takeover Directive. Common framework for cross-border takeover bids
2005–2010	White paper on Financial Services Policy. Plan to implement outstanding FSAP measures, consolidation/convergence of financial services regulation and supervision
2007	Markets in Financial Instruments Directive
2007	Capital Requirements Directives (i.e. the Directives 2006/48/EC and 2006/49/EC) implement the "International Convergence of Capital Measurement and Capital Standards" (labelled as Basel II) for credit institutions and investment firms set by Basel Committee on Banking Supervision from 2008.

Figure 2.1   Legislation impacting the EU banking and financial sectors

Source: Adapted from Goddard et al., (2007, p. 1915), quoting *ECB* (2005, Table 2), and author's updates.

These rules intend to maximize the effectiveness of the capital rules in ensuring continuing financial stability, maintaining confidence in financial institutions and protecting consumers. The CRD came into force in January 2007 for the credit institutions and investment firms opting for the simpler approaches, whereas the most advanced approaches became available from 2008. Figure 2.1 sums up the evolution of the legislation impacting the EU banking and financial sectors.

Analyzing the efficiency gains following the creation of a single European financial service market, Berger (2003) expects modest revenue gains (from diversification in universal banking), small cost scope economies gains, and, perhaps, scale diseconomies due to organizational problems in managing different types of financial institutions.

2.3 The structural features of European banking

The banking sector has completely evolved in most advanced economies and there is no doubt that competitive pressures on banks have increased over the last 20 years. Berger et al., (2005, p. 2180) state that "the developed nations of North America and Western Europe witnessed a tremendous number of domestic bank mergers and acquisitions and foreign acquisitions in response to deregulation, technological advances, and the globalization of non-financial economic activity." Focusing on Europe, this section analyzes the current situation of the banking industry by examining its structural features and bank performances.

In April 2008, there were more than 10,000 Monetary Financial Institutions (MFI)[2] in the European Union (see Table 2.1). MFI in the Euro-area countries are 78% of the overall number. Germany, France, Italy and Austria have the largest number of MFI (respectively, 21%, 13%, 8.45% and 8.16% of the whole number). Overall, these countries represent 50% of the European MFIs and 65% of MFIs in the Euro area. Germany and France account for 43% of all Euro-area MFIs.

Most MFIs are credit institutions[3] (that is, 82%), while the others are Money Market Funds.[4] However, the proportion is not constant in all countries: for example, the proportion of money market funds is larger in France, Ireland, Luxemburg and Slovakia (that is, 44%,

Table 2.1   Number of monetary financial institutions in Europe

	Credit institution	Money market fund	Other institution	Total
Austria	806	19	0	826
Belgium	107	15	0	123
Cyprus	191	0	0	192
Finland	359	35	0	395
France	741	591	1	1,334
Germany	2,025	70	0	2,096
Greece	65	26	0	92
Ireland	82	263	0	346
Italy	818	36	0	855
Luxemburg	155	467	0	623
Malta	22	5	0	28
Netherland	331	7	2	341
Portugal	175	3	0	179
Slovenia	28	2	0	31
Spain	359	102	0	462
Euro Area Total	6,264	1,641	3	7,924
Bulgaria	29	3	0	33
Czech Republic	55	10	0	66
Denmark	189	2	0	192
Estonia	18	1	13	33
Hungary	206	34	0	241
Latvia	32	3	35	71
Lithuania	81	2	0	84
Poland	715	3	0	719
Romania	48	3	0	52
Slovakia	26	13	0	40
Sweden	201	32	1	235
United Kingdom	392	32	0	425
Other European countries	8,256	1,779	52	10,115

This shows the absolute number of MFIs at the second last working day of April 2008.
Source: *ECB* (2008a); MFI statistical report, update April 2008.

76%, 75% and 33% of all MFI, respectively), and smaller in Germany, Italy, Cyprus, Netherland, Austria and Portugal (that is, 3%, 4%, 2%, 2% of all MFIs, respectively).

Over the period May 2007–08, the total number of MFIs decreased by 101 units in the EU-12, 106 units in the EU-15, 251 units in the

Table 2.2   The evolution of credit institutions in Europe

	2000	2001	2002	2003	2004	2005	2006	2007	2008	Change 2000–08 (%)
Belgium	118	116	111	108	107	103	103	107	107	−9.32
Denmark	210	207	198	178	203	198	189	192	189	−10.00
Germany	2968	2701	2507	2332	2210	2132	2083	2039	2025	−31.77
France	1136	1083	1027	975	928	875	852	818	740	−34.86
Greece	59	58	62	61	60	61	62	63	65	10.17
Ireland	82	86	86	83	80	80	79	80	81	−1.22
Italy	876	849	842	815	800	785	802	816	819	−6.51
Luxemburg	211	197	185	185	167	160	151	154	154	−27.01
The Netherlands	604	565	543	503	472	424	376	345	330	−45.36
Portugal	222	213	209	199	201	194	182	176	175	−21.17
Spain	384	369	365	358	345	347	347	355	361	−5.99
United Kingdom	488	485	447	445	417	403	398	394	392	−19.67
EU-12 Total	7358	6929	6582	6242	5990	5762	5624	5539	5438	−26.09
Austria	873	849	835	823	813	798	818	809	806	−7.67
Finland	346	366	371	366	368	363	363	360	359	3.76
Sweden	148	147	213	222	225	201	207	202	201	35.81
EU-15 Total	8725	8291	8001	7653	7396	7124	7012	6910	6804	−22.02
Czech Republic	N/A	N/A	N/A	N/A	71	57	56	57	55	−22.54[+]
Cyprus	N/A	N/A	N/A	N/A	408	399	375	336	191	−53.19[+]
Estonia	N/A	N/A	N/A	N/A	7	9	14	14	18	157.14[+]
Hungary	N/A	N/A	N/A	N/A	221	214	214	209	206	−6.79[+]
Lithuania	N/A	N/A	N/A	N/A	73	76	78	79	82	12.33[+]
Latvia	N/A	N/A	N/A	N/A	23	23	25	28	32	39.13[+]
Malta	N/A	N/A	N/A	N/A	12	16	18	20	22	83.33[+]
Poland	N/A	N/A	N/A	N/A	658	732	724	721	714	8.51[+]
Slovenia	N/A	N/A	N/A	N/A	26	24	25	27	25	−3.85[+]
Slovakia	N/A	N/A	N/A	N/A	21	22	24	25	26	23.81[+]
EU-25 Total	8725	8291	8001	7653	8916	8696	8565	8426	8175	−6.30
Bulgaria	N/A	N/A	N/A	N/A	N/A	N/A	N/A	30	29	−3.33[*]
Romania	N/A	N/A	N/A	N/A	N/A	N/A	N/A	39	48	23.08[*]
EU-27 Total	8725	8291	8001	7653	8916	8696	8565	8495	8252	−5.42

[+] The rate of change is calculated over the period 2004–08.
[*] The rate of change is calculated over the period 2007–08.
This table shows the absolute number of credit institutions at the second last working day of May.

Source: *ECB*; MFI statistical report; annual reports from the 2000 to the 2008.

EU-25 and 243 units in the EU-27 (see Table 2.2). Between May 2000 and 2008, the number of MFIs has decreased by 5.42% in the EU-27, despite the enlargement of EU to many countries. Focusing on the EU-12, the number of MFIs reduced by 26% over the period 2000–08.

The drop in the number of MFIs was substantial in most EU-15 countries: for example, Netherlands –45%; France –35%; Germany –32%, Luxemburg –27%. However, it was small in few countries (Italy –6.5%, Spain –6%, Ireland –1%). This drop is also a common trend in the 12 countries that have joined EU since 2004; that is, 149 units from the 2004 figure, which comes down to 10%.

The reduction of the number of credit institutions from 2000 onwards has increased the EU banking market concentration (see Table 2.3, Panel A). Despite the drop in the number of MFIs, the overall importance of the banking systems in the EU has increased in the 2000s (see also Gandolfi, 2008). Firstly, the number of employees has been kept constant (around 2,2 million people) and the total credit institution branch assets have been of 25 Euro trillions (increasing by 65% from the 1999 level). The European banking market seems to be still a "EU domestic market" since the overall asset quota held by non-EU credit institutions branches and subsidiaries has been constantly lower than 2% from 1999 to 2006.

Over the period May 2007–08, the total number of MFIs decreased by 101 units in the EU-12, 106 units in the EU-15, 251 units in the EU-25 and 243 units in the EU-27 (see Table 2.2). Between May 2000 and 2008, the number of MFIs has decreased by 5.42% in the EU-27, despite the enlargement of EU to many countries. Focusing on the EU-12, the number of MFIs reduced by 26% over the period 2000–08. The drop in the number of MFIs was substantial in most EU-15 countries: for example, Netherlands –45%; France –35%; Germany –32%, Luxemburg –27%. However, it was small in few countries (Italy –6.5%, Spain –6%, Ireland –1%). This drop is also a common trend in the 12 countries that have joined EU since 2004; that is, 149 units from the 2004 figure, which comes down to 10%.

The reduction of the number of credit institutions from 2000 onwards has increased the EU banking market concentration (see Table 2.3, Panel A). Despite the drop in the number of MFIs, the overall importance of the banking systems in the EU has increased in the 2000s (see also Gandolfi, 2008). Firstly, the number of employees has been kept constant (around 2,2 million people) and the total credit institution branch assets have been of 25 Euro trillions (increasing by 65% from the 1999 level). The European banking market seems to be still a "EU domestic market" since the overall asset quota held by non-EU credit institutions branches and subsidiaries has been constantly lower than 2% from 1999 to 2006.

Looking at Europe (see Table 2.3, Panel B), smaller countries tend to have more concentrated banking sectors, with the notable exceptions of Austria (having a strong savings and cooperative banking sector) and Luxemburg (hosting a large number of foreign credit institutions). The market quota held by the five largest banks (CR-5) is substantial only for "small" banking industries: for example, the CR-5 is higher than 50% in Hungary, Romania, Bulgaria, Slovenia, Sweden, Denmark, Cyprus, Czech Republic, Latvia, Greece, Portugal, Slovakia, Malta, Finland, Belgium, Netherlands, Estonia. All these countries account (overall) for 34% of EU total assets and 33% of total EU number of employees.[5] The situation is different for largest countries: German banks account for 18% of EU total assets and 22% of total EU number of employees and have a CR-5 ratio of 22%; in France, banks account for 16% of EU total assets and 14% of total EU number of employees and have CR-5 ratio of 51.8%. Small CR-5 ratios are also found in Italy (8% of EU

Table 2.3   Structural indicators for credit institutions (CIs) in Europe
Panel A – Whole European banking

Year	Number of employees of CIs[#]	Asset of CIs[*]	Asset of branches of CIs from non-EU area countries[*]	Asset of subsidiaries of CI from non-EU area countries[*]	Concentration of banking sector across euro-area[+]
1999	2,191	15,167	107	183	0.0062
2000	2,196	16,241	113	211	0.0066
2001	2,273	17,561	107	247	0.0068
2002	2,247	18,069	86	234	0.0067
2003	2,200	18,888	71	242	0.0070
2004	2,189	20,430	66	221	0.0072
2005	2,192	22,641	86	288	0.0078
2006	2,199	24,928	99	382	0.0078

[#] *Values are in thousands.*
[*] *Outstanding amounts in EUR billions.*
[+] *Herfindahl Index (i.e. 1 = Monopoly; 0 = Perfect competition).*

Source: ECB (2008a, p. 31).

Continued

Panel B – Domestic banking in European countries

Country	No. of employees	Total assets	Population for CI	Population per branch	Population per ATM	EU banking sector Population per employees
Belgium	67,080	1,298	96,564	2,400	756	158
Bulgaria	30,571	21	262,456	1,311	2,103	250
Czech Rep.	40,037	140	184,250	5,541	3,129	258
Denmark	49,644	978	28,889	2,489	1,758	110
Germany	690,900	7,562	40,603	2,068	1,528	119
Estonia	4,280	21	89,493	5,047	1,465	212
Ireland	35,658	1,337	53,613	3,750	1,287	104
Greece	61,074	383	177,329	2,902	1,654	173
Spain	243,462	2,945	125,696	986	754	163
France	435,725	6,682	78,679	1,607	1,322	133
Italy	336,661	3,332	72,252	1,785	1,349	174
Cyprus	10,480	91	3,663	855	1,474	70
Latvia	8,903	31	73,402	3,336	2,403	177
Luxembourg	22,513	915	3,079	2,044	1,086	18
Hungary	35,725	109	48,814	2,969	2,643	240
Malta	3,416	38	18,603	3,935	2,607	109
Netherlands	120,539	2,195	48,026	4,544	2,014	143
Austria	73,308	891	10,356	1,949	1,037	107
Poland	154,569	236	53,086	3,284	3,837	219
Portugal	54,350	440	60,619	1,759	721	174
Romania	46,567	72	512,201	3,393	3,575	326
Slovenia	11,816	43	75,032	2,849	1,321	168
Slovakia	19,812	50	207,560	4,616	2,702	273
Finland	26,667	288	14,689	3,228	1,606	211
Sweden	44,389	845	45,512	4,956	3,235	208
UK	487,772	10,093	155,854	4,892	1,002	134*

*2006 data.

Source: Tables 2 and 3 in ECB (2008c, pp. 38–39).

capacity indicators		Herfindahl index					Share of the 5 largest CI in total assets				
Population density	Asset per employee	2003	2004	2005	2006	2007	2003	2004	2005	2006	2007
321	19,347	2063	2102	2112	2041	2079	83.5	84.3	85.3	85.4	83.4
69	1,022	n.a	721	698	707	833	n.a	52.3	50.8	50.3	56.7
131	3,497	1187	1103	1155	1104	1100	65.8	64	65.5	64.1	65.7
127	19,700	1114	1146	1115	1071	1120	66.6	67	66.3	64.7	64.2
230	10,946	173	178	174	178	183	21.6	22.1	21.6	22	22
30	3,261	3943	3887	4039	3593	3410	99.2	98.6	98.1	97.1	95.7
62	31,945	500	500	600	600	600	44.4	43.9	45.7	44.8	46.1
85	5,923	1130	1070	1096	1101	1096	66.9	65	65.6	66.3	67.7
89	10,690	506	482	487	442	459	43.1	41.9	42	40.4	41
115	13,962	597	623	758	726	679	46.7	49.2	51.9	52.3	51.8
197	9,755	240	230	230	220	330	27.5	26.4	26.8	26.2	33.1
85	8,076	946	940	1029	1056	1082	57.2	57.3	59.8	63.9	64.8
35	2,403	1054	1021	1176	1271	1158	63.1	62.4	67.3	69.2	67.2
186	35,022	315	304	312	294	276	31.8	29.7	30.7	29.1	27
108	2,589	783	798	795	823	839	52.1	52.7	53.2	53.5	54.1
1,279	10,066	1580	1452	1330	1185	1174	77.7	78.5	75.3	71.4	70.1
401	19,183	1744	1726	1796	1822	1928	84.2	84	84.5	85.1	86.3
99	11,459	557	552	560	534	527	44.2	43.8	45	43.8	42.8
118	1,357	754	692	650	599	640	52	50	48.5	46.1	46.6
115	7,218	1043	1093	1154	1134	1097	62.7	66.5	68.8	67.9	67.8
91	1,092	1251	1111	1115	1165	1041	55.2	59.5	59.4	60.1	56.3
100	3,609	1496	1425	1369	1300	1282	66.4	64.6	63	62	59.5
110	2,544	1191	1154	1076	1131	1082	67.5	66.5	67.7	66.9	68.2
16	11,497	2420	2680	2730	2560	2540	81.2	82.7	82.9	82.3	81.2
20	19,202	760	854	945	856	934	53.8	54.4	57.3	57.8	61
248	21,783	347	376	399	394	449	32.8	34.5	36.3	35.9	40.7

total assets), Spain (8% of EU total assets) and the U.K (25% of EU total assets). The banking sector capacity seems to substantially differ across countries. Focusing on the largest six countries (accounting for 80% of the EU total assets), Spain, Italy and France display a larger branch capacity than the other countries. Spain and UK have a larger ATM capacity than other countries. Regarding the diffusion of e-banking services (Eurostat qtd. in *ECB*, 2007a, p. 43), the percentage of individuals (older than 16 years) who used internet banking at least once during the first three months of 2006 was, on average, 24% in the EU-15 and 22% in the EU-25, ranging from 1% (in Romania and Bulgaria) to 63% (in Finland). This indicator also varies significantly across the largest banking industries: 9% in Italy, 15% in Spain, 18% in France, 28% in the UK, 32% in Germany, 59% in the Netherlands.

The increasing concentration of European banking industries and the different level of concentration are not surprising since the deregulation process and the integration of the European banking sector (described in the previous section) are likely to have profound implications in the size and concentration of banking markets. The impact of an increase in market size on the growth of individual firms depends on industry products and technological characteristics. Sutton (1991) suggests that a market size expansion encourages entry and leads to de-concentration and fragmented industry structure, if products are homogenous or horizontally differentiated and sunk costs are exogenous. Differently, incumbent firms tend to increase their sunk cost expenditures on advertising, branch expansion, technology and financial innovation, leading to an increase in the minimum efficient scale, if products are vertically differentiated and sunk costs are endogenous.

In conclusion, the analysis of the structure of the EU banking system shows that there are still substantial structural differences across European countries. Despite the fact that the Financial Services Action Plan (FSAP) started many years ago to ensure the creation of a fully integrated and competitive market for financial services in Europe, there are still substantial differences in terms of number of banks (although there is a generally decreasing trend), concentration and distribution channels. Various researches (see Berger et al., 2001 and 2003; Buch and De Long, 2004) suggest that significant barriers to the integration of banking markets still exist and these may arise from national economic conditions, culture, language and differences in fiscal and legal systems. Barriers are particularly onerous in retail banking and these mainly relate to:

1. consumers doubting toward foreign banks, causing depositors to prefer local or national banks;
2. a local bank information advantage: these banks usually hold private information about a borrower's creditworthiness (see Goddard et al., 2007) unavailable to other competitors, preventing foreign banks from competing with local banks;
3. the financial services package, enabling banks to charge different prices for each component of the bundle in different markets (see Barros et al., 2005).

The extent to which European banking markets have achieved integration. in the sense of complete elimination of barriers to cross-border activity, remains an imprecise science (see Dermine 2003 and 2006). The adoption of the MiFID Directive and of the Capital Requirements Directive (CRD), respectively started in 2006 and 2007. It is likely to produce a homogenization effect over the next few years.

2.4   How banks work in the new environment

The most successful European banks responded to the changing competitive environment by expanding through internally generated growth or through M&As. Growth has enabled banks to realize scale and scope economies, reduce labour and other variable costs, and reduce or eliminate operational inefficiencies. Many banks have sought to diversify their revenue sources.

In general, these bank actions aim to create shareholder value (as any firms working in a competitive environment) and, consequently, attempt to:

1. *increase the expected cash flows to equity*; that is, the residual cash flows after meeting all expenses, tax obligations, interest and principal payments: for example, banks can achieve this target by increasing their deposits, loans, off-balance sheet activities; increasing prices (for instance, commissions, credit spreads, and so forth), reducing operating costs;

2. *reduce the hurdle rate*; that is, the cost of equity or capital: for example, managers can attempt to reduce the bank's systematic risk by
   diversifying its activities abroad;
3. match as closely as possible the bank's financing sources with
   the bank's investments. (These features are illustrated in
   Figure 2.2.)

Banks can achieve these results through endogenous channels
(that is, strategies implemented within the bank) and exogenous
channels (that is, strategies that create shareholder value by involving external parties).

Regarding the endogenous channels, all stakeholders are dependent on each other for their success in a perfect market and managing to create sustained shareholder value is not a zero-sum game.
To create a stable shareholder value requires an intense focus on
delivering benefits to customers in the most efficient way, hiring
and retaining a motivated workforce, maintaining excellent sup-
plier relationships, and being a good corporate citizen in each of the
local communities where the company is present. For this reason,
most of the endogenous channels to create a stable and sustainable
shareholder value focus on the optimal management of the bank
stakeholders (for example, customer satisfaction, human resource
motivation and management, and so forth).

Banks can also increase the expected cash flows to equity and/
or reduce the hurdle rate through "exogenous channels;" that is, all
possible strategies that create shareholder value involving external

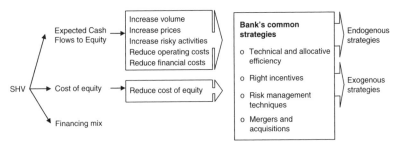

Figure 2.2   The creation of shareholder value: drivers, actions, strategies
Source: Fiordelisi and Molyneux (2006, p. 96).

parties (such as M&As, joint ventures and strategic alliance activities, and so forth). Noticeably, exogenous strategies are not alternative to endogenous channels, but complementary. All these forms of activity have been widespread in the financial sector. The analysis of the structure of the EU banking system shows that banks responded to new competitive pressures with various strategies, such as M&As, financial innovation, conglomeration and technology developments.

Looking at the profitability data of European banks between 2004 and 2007 (see Table 2.4), profits substantially increased; for instance, the Return on Equity increased from 16.8% to 20.2%. This increase is not related to more risky activities, as shown by the Return on Risk-weighted Asset increase from 1.1% to 1.9%. The higher profitability

Table 2.4 Financial conditions of large and complex banking groups in the Euro area between 2004 and the first semester of 2007 (H1_2007)

	Minimum	Median	Average	Weighted Average	Maximum
Return on equity (%)					
2004	4.30	16.35	16.78	17.22	33.20
2005	9.00	17.40	18.74	19.12	37.00
2006	7.24	18.53	18.75	18.99	37.60
H1_2007	5.11	21.00	20.19	20.21	36.00
Return on risk weighted asset (%)					
2004	0.20	1.11	1.13	1.17	2.03
2005	0.81	1.38	1.40	1.43	2.26
2006	0.77	1.42	1.48	1.51	2.66
H1_2007	0.81	1.84	1.86	1.87	3.22
Net interest income (% total assets)					
2004	0.43	0.90	1.04	0.93	1.87
2005	0.48	0.68	0.93	0.89	1.84
2006	0.24	0.69	0.95	0.87	2.03
H1_2007	0.22	0.74	0.91	0.80	1.98
Net interest income (% total income)					
2004	24.07	51.43	48.63	47.66	69.54
2005	25.53	46.95	44.57	45.39	68.70
2006	14.07	48.71	45.80	43.48	70.24
H1_2007	10.02	47.39	43.75	40.55	64.61

Continued

Table 2.4 Continued

	Minimum	Median	Average	Weighted Average	Maximum
Trading income (% total income)					
2004	2.69	9.41	11.74	12.91	28.73
2005	2.58	10.37	13.32	14.47	37.14
2006	2.45	12.95	14.80	16.97	46.83
H1_2007	7.20	19.49	21.28	23.63	53.67
Fees and commissions (% total income)					
2004	15.90	29.45	29.32	28.97	44.15
2005	17.12	29.45	28.07	28.11	40.02
2006	18.20	27.61	28.87	29.50	43.03
H1_2007	11.31	29.18	28.38	28.69	35.98
Other income (% total income)					
2004	−3.07	4.93	6.87	6.22	26.70
2005	−0.76	4.71	5.71	6.24	16.73
2006	−0.15	5.26	6.53	6.64	21.54
H1_2007	0.76	3.51	4.47	4.73	13.21
Net loan impairment changes (% total assets)					
2004	0.03	0.07	0.11	0.09	0.40
2005	−0.02	0.05	0.08	0.08	0.29
2006	0.01	0.05	0.11	0.10	0.36
HI2007	0.00	0.06	0.09	0.09	0.37
Cost-income ratio (%)					
2004	48.60	68.05	66.63	68.49	85.30
2005	43.20	63.65	63.37	63.76	89.40
2006	39.60	61.10	60.51	61.69	79.80
HI2007	38.70	58.80	58.40	59.67	77.70
Tier I ratio (%)					
2004	6.32	7.80	8.02	7.88	10.90
2005	6.70	8.15	8.45	8.25	11.60
2006	6.70	7.80	8.33	8.16	10.50
HI2007	6.09	7.90	8.21	8.00	10.80
Overall solvency ratio (%)					
2004	8.46	11.35	11.40	11.04	13.30
2005	8.50	11.55	11.70	11.42	16.30
2006	10.00	11.10	11.40	11.36	15.60
HI2007	10.20	10.70	11.20	11.13	15.10

Note: Based on figures for 17 IFRS reporting large and complex banking groups in the Euro area.

Source: *ECB (2007b)*, Financial Stability Review, December 2007, Table S5, p. 227.

seems to be due to trading income increase (from 11.8% of total income in 2004 to 21.3% in 2007) and an enhanced operating efficiency – that is, the cost-income ratio improved from 66.7% in 2004 to 58.4% in 2007. The traditional "net interest income" became less important for banks: in 2007, it accounted on average for 43.7% of total income (48, 6% in 2004) and 0.91% of bank total asset (1.04% in 2004).

2.5   The interest in Merger and Acquisition

Bank consolidation is one the main strategies adopted by banks to create shareholder value. As we have seen in Chapter 1, there has been an intense process of consolidation over the last decade. While the growth of M&A operations was primarily observed in North America and the United Kingdom over the 1980s, this phenomenon has been undertaken by all major industrialized nations from the 1990s and these deals were often made by banks from different countries – that is, cross-border M&As (see Gugler et al., 2003).

In this section, the data of the M&A phenomenon in Europe cover until the first semester 2008, since the banking crises produced a sporadic impact on the M&A trends. These data are analyzed in section 2.6. First, consolidation has contributed significantly to the reduction in the number of banks operating in the EU-15 displaying a substantial reduction of credit institutions from 2000 onwards (see *ECB*, 2008c, p. 9). According to *ECB* (2008c) recent statistics, no clear trend emerges in the latest years: the number of deals was quite stable between 2000 and 2007, while there was a rising trend of M&A value between 2002 and 2007. In the first half of 2008, the overall value of M&A deals in the EU-27 was almost 100 Euro billions.

Geographic diversification, in the form of increased cross-border activity, has also played an important role in the business and growth strategies of European banks. The importance of cross-border M&As has increased over time both within the European Union (EU) and outside the EU. *ECB* (2007c, p. 2) data show that, over the period 2000–04, domestic mergers were 63.1% of the overall value of M&A deals in European banking, cross-border M&As within the EU were 19.2% and those outside the EU were 17.7%. Between 2005 and the first half of 2007, the value of domestic transactions was 35.5% of the total M&As values, cross-border M&A within the EU were 37.7%

of the overall M&As value and cross-border M&A outside the EU accounted for 26.8%. This increase in cross-border M&As shows that the EU enlargement and the harmonization of regulations, the introduction of the Euro currency and the boosting international commerce created a demand for international financial services leading to increasing financial integration among banks in the EU. Namely, a bank may deliver its services to foreign customers either without: a) a physical presence in the foreign country (for example, directly from its home country headquarter or joining a financing syndicate of banks located in the foreign country) or b) with a physical presence in the new country (by opening branches or subsidiaries or acquiring another bank there). As noted by Berger et al., (2000, p. 29),

> establishing a physical presence in a foreign country entails a number of costs, such as the organizational diseconomies to operating or monitoring an institution from a distance. However, establishing a physical presence in the foreign country offers some potentially offsetting advantages, including (a) more effective servicing and monitoring of retail customers and (b) an opportunity to compete for retail and wholesale customers in the foreign country. Recent deregulation has reduced the costs of this delivery channel.

In the European banking, market Barros et al., (2005) observe that much of the cross-border M&A activity takes place through the creation of subsidiaries, rather than branches, which testifies to the existence of significant barriers to full market integration. Namely, some of the key procedures in the single banking market (for example, the single banking license throughout the EU, the home country control principle, the deposit insurance through a home country insurer and the single bankruptcy proceedings) do not apply, if the cross-border activity occurs through separate legal entities in the form of subsidiaries, rather than branches.

The dimension of the M&A phenomenon in the European banking has been similar to the US market in the 2000s. Figure 2.3 displays detailed data for M&A deals completed by financial institutions (as acquirers): while the number of deals in the US has been always slightly higher than in Europe, the value of these deals was higher in Europe in 2007 than in the US. Focusing on Europe (see Table 2.5),

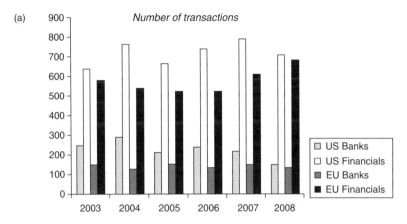

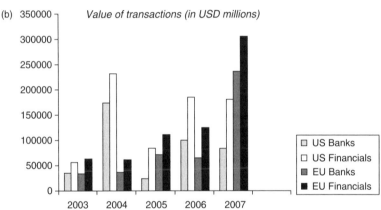

Figure 2.3 Number and value of M&A deals concluded by financial institutions (as acquirors): US versus Europe

Source: Thomson ONE Banker database.

most of the M&A transactions in the EU27 were among banks within the EU-15 (88% in terms of number and 97% in terms of value), while M&A deals from EU-15 to the new EU countries accounted for 4% in terms of number and 2% in terms of value.

As for the value of deals, most of them were domestic: 80% of all M&As value in the EU-27 were made among EU-15 banks (especially, between Italian banks) and 0.3% of all M&As value in the EU-27

Table 2.5 Number and value of M&A deals in 2007 among financial institutions (acting both as acquiror and target companies) in EU-27
Panel A) Number of transactions

	Acquiror Company's														
Target Company's Nation	BEL	DEN	FRA	GER	GRE	IRE	ITA	LUX	NET	POR	SPA	UK	EU12	AUS	FIN
BEL	14	0	2	3	0	0	0	1	3	0	0	0	23	0	0
DEN	0	15	2	1	0	0	0	1	0	1	0	3	23	0	1
FRA	4	0	106	1	0	0	2	2	0	0	0	10	125	0	0
GER	2	0	6	113	0	0	4	3	2	0	0	10	140	0	0
GRE	0	0	6	0	5	0	0	0	0	0	0	0	11	0	0
IRE	0	0	1	2	0	23	1	0	0	0	0	9	36	0	0
ITA	0	0	21	3	0	0	189	1	3	0	5	9	231	0	0
LUX	1	0	0	1	0	0	3	4	1	0	0	4	14	0	0
NET	3	0	2	1	0	0	1	0	77	0	2	2	88	2	0
POR	0	0	1	0	0	0	0	1	0	8	1	0	11	0	0
SPA	0	0	8	1	0	0	4	2	0	1	75	10	101	0	0
UK	2	0	9	7	0	0	0	1	5	2	1	496	523	0	0
EU-12	26	15	164	133	5	23	204	16	91	12	84	553	1326	2	1
AUS	1	0	1	4	0	0	2	0	0	0	1	0	9	13	0
FIN	0	2	0	1	0	0	0	0	0	0	0	2	5	0	21
SWE	0	1	0	1	0	0	0	0	0	0	0	9	11	0	0
EU-15	27	18	165	139	5	23	206	16	91	12	85	564	1351	15	22
CYP	0	0	2	0	2	0	0	0	0	0	0	0	4	0	0
CZE	1	0	0	1	0	0	2	0	0	0	0	1	5	3	0
EST	0	0	0	0	0	1	0	0	0	0	0	0	1	1	0
HUN	4	0	3	1	0	0	2	0	1	0	1	1	13	0	0
LAT	1	0	1	0	0	0	0	0	0	0	0	0	2	0	0
LIT	0	0	1	0	0	0	0	0	0	0	0	0	1	0	0
POL	3	1	1	0	0	0	2	0	3	1	0	0	11	1	0
Slk	1	0	2	0	0	0	0	0	0	0	0	0	3	0	0
SLN	0	0	0	0	0	0	1	0	0	0	0	0	1	1	0
EU-25	37	19	175	141	7	24	213	16	95	13	86	566	1392	21	22
BUL	3	0	2	1	2	1	1	0	0	0	0	0	10	3	0
ROM	1	0	2	0	3	0	0	0	1	0	0	4	11	7	0
EU-27	41	19	179	142	12	25	214	16	96	13	86	570	1413	31	22

Nation														
SWE	EU15	CYP	CZE	EST	HUN	LAT	LIT	POL	SLK	SLN	EU25	BUL	ROM	EU27
0	23	0	0	0	0	0	0	0	0	0	23	0	0	23
3	27	0	0	0	0	0	0	0	0	0	27	0	0	27
0	125	0	0	0	0	0	0	0	0	0	125	0	0	125
1	141	2	0	0	0	0	0	0	0	0	143	0	0	143
0	11	3	0	0	0	0	0	0	0	0	14	0	0	14
0	36	0	0	0	0	0	0	0	0	0	36	0	0	36
0	231	0	0	0	0	0	0	0	0	1	232	0	0	232
0	14	0	0	0	0	0	0	0	0	0	14	0	0	14
0	90	0	0	0	1	0	0	0	0	0	91	0	0	91
0	11	0	0	0	0	0	0	0	0	0	11	0	0	11
0	101	0	0	0	0	0	0	0	0	0	101	0	0	101
4	527	0	0	0	0	0	0	0	0	0	527	0	0	527
8	1337	5	0	0	1	0	0	0	0	1	1344	0	0	1344
0	22	0	0	0	0	0	0	0	0	0	22	0	0	22
0	26	0	0	1	0	0	0	0	0	0	27	0	0	27
30	41	0	0	0	0	0	0	0	0	0	41	0	0	41
38	1426	5	0	1	1	0	0	0	0	1	1434	0	0	1434
0	4	12	1	0	0	0	0	0	0	0	17	0	0	17
0	8	0	5	0	0	0	0	0	0	0	13	0	0	13
1	3	1	0	1	0	0	0	0	0	0	5	0	0	5
0	13	0	0	0	4	0	0	0	0	0	17	0	1	18
1	3	0	0	0	0	4	1	0	0	0	8	0	0	8
0	1	0	0	1	0	1	2	0	0	0	5	0	0	5
1	13	0	0	0	0	0	0	19	0	0	32	0	0	32
0	3	0	1	0	0	0	0	0	0	0	4	0	0	4
0	2	0	0	0	0	0	0	0	0	3	5	0	0	5
41	1476	18	7	3	5	5	3	19	0	4	1540	0	1	1541
0	13	0	1	0	0	0	0	0	0	0	14	10	0	24
0	18	2	0	0	4	0	0	1	0	0	25	1	1	27
41	1507	20	8	3	9	5	3	20	0	4	1579	11	2	1592

Continued

Panel B) Percentage of deals value

		BEL	DEN	FRA	GER	GRE	IRE	ITA	LUX	NET	POR	SPA	UK	EU12	AUS	FIN
														Acquiror Company's		
	BEL	0.8	0.0	0.2	0.0	0.0	0.0	0.0	0.0	0.0	0.0	0.0	0.0	1.0	0.0	0.0
	DEN	0.0	0.1	0.0	0.0	0.0	0.0	0.0	0.0	0.0	0.0	0.0	0.3	0.4	0.0	0.0
	FRA	0.0	0.0	7.7	0.0	0.0	0.0	0.0	0.0	0.0	0.0	0.0	0.0	7.8	0.0	0.0
	GER	0.0	0.0	1.7	2.7	0.0	0.0	0.8	0.0	0.1	0.0	0.0	0.8	6.1	0.0	0.0
	GRE	0.0	0.0	0.7	0.0	0.1	0.0	0.0	0.0	0.0	0.0	0.0	0.0	0.7	0.0	0.0
	IRE	0.0	0.0	0.0	1.7	0.0	0.1	0.0	0.0	0.0	0.0	0.0	0.0	1.8	0.0	0.0
	ITA	0.0	0.0	5.1	0.0	0.0	0.0	28.4	0.0	0.2	0.0	0.0	0.6	34.3	0.0	0.0
	LUX	0.0	0.0	0.0	0.0	0.0	0.0	0.1	0.0	0.0	0.0	0.0	0.4	0.5	0.0	0.0
	NET	0.0	0.0	0.0	0.0	0.0	0.0	0.0	0.0	25.5	0.0	0.1	0.0	25.6	0.0	0.0
	POR	0.0	0.0	0.0	0.0	0.0	0.0	0.0	0.0	0.0	0.5	0.0	0.0	0.6	0.0	0.0
	SPA	0.0	0.0	0.3	0.0	0.0	0.0	0.2	0.0	0.0	0.0	3.3	0.0	3.8	0.0	0.0
	U.K.	0.2	0.0	0.0	0.4	0.0	0.0	0.0	0.0	0.0	0.0	0.5	9.5	10.7	0.0	0.0
Target Company's Nation	**EU-12**	1.0	0.1	15.8	4.8	0.1	0.1	29.6	0.1	25.8	0.6	3.9	11.5	93.3	0.0	0.0
	AUS	0.0	0.0	0.0	0.5	0.0	0.0	0.3	0.0	0.0	0.0	0.2	0.0	1.0	0.5	0.0
	FIN	0.0	1.1	0.0	0.0	0.0	0.0	0.0	0.0	0.0	0.0	0.0	0.0	1.1	0.0	0.1
	SWE	0.0	0.0	0.0	0.0	0.0	0.0	0.0	0.0	0.0	0.0	0.0	0.3	0.3	0.0	0.0
	EU-15	1.0	1.2	15.8	5.3	0.1	0.1	29.9	0.1	25.8	0.6	4.1	11.8	95.7	0.5	0.1
	CYP	0.0	0.0	0.1	0.0	0.0	0.0	0.0	0.0	0.0	0.0	0.0	0.0	0.1	0.0	0.0
	CZE	0.0	0.0	0.0	0.0	0.0	0.0	1.1	0.0	0.0	0.0	0.0	0.0	1.1	0.0	0.0
	EST	0.0	0.0	0.0	0.0	0.0	0.0	0.0	0.0	0.0	0.0	0.0	0.0	0.0	0.0	0.0
	HUN	0.0	0.0	0.2	0.0	0.0	0.0	0.0	0.0	0.0	0.0	0.0	0.0	0.2	0.0	0.0
	LAT	0.0	0.0	0.0	0.0	0.0	0.0	0.0	0.0	0.0	0.0	0.0	0.0	0.0	0.0	0.0
	LIT	0.0	0.0	0.0	0.0	0.0	0.0	0.0	0.0	0.0	0.0	0.0	0.0	0.0	0.0	0.0
	POL	0.0	0.0	0.0	0.0	0.0	0.0	0.0	0.0	0.0	0.1	0.0	0.0	0.1	0.0	0.0
	Slk	0.1	0.0	0.0	0.0	0.0	0.0	0.0	0.0	0.0	0.0	0.0	0.0	0.1	0.0	0.0
	SLN	0.0	0.0	0.0	0.0	0.0	0.0	0.0	0.0	0.0	0.0	0.0	0.0	0.0	0.0	0.0
	EU-25	1.1	1.3	16.0	5.3	0.1	0.1	31.0	0.1	25.8	0.6	4.1	11.8	97.3	0.6	0.1
	BUL	0.2	0.0	0.0	0.0	0.0	0.1	0.0	0.0	0.0	0.0	0.0	0.0	0.3	0.0	0.0
	ROM	0.0	0.0	0.2	0.0	0.0	0.0	0.0	0.0	0.0	0.0	0.0	0.0	0.2	0.2	0.0
	EU-27	1.3	1.3	16.2	5.3	0.2	0.2	31.0	0.1	25.8	0.6	4.1	11.8	97.8	0.8	0.1

Source of data: Thomson ONE Banker database.

Nation

SWE	EU15	CYP	CZE	EST	HUN	LAT	LIT	POL	SLK	SLN	EU25	BUL	ROM	EU27
0.0	1.0	0.0	0.0	0.0	0.0	0.0	0.0	0.0	0.0	0.0	1.0	0.0	0.0	1.0
0.0	0.5	0.0	0.0	0.0	0.0	0.0	0.0	0.0	0.0	0.0	0.5	0.0	0.0	0.5
0.0	7.8	0.0	0.0	0.0	0.0	0.0	0.0	0.0	0.0	0.0	7.8	0.0	0.0	7.8
0.0	6.1	0.0	0.0	0.0	0.0	0.0	0.0	0.0	0.0	0.0	6.1	0.0	0.0	6.1
0.0	0.7	0.6	0.0	0.0	0.0	0.0	0.0	0.0	0.0	0.0	1.3	0.0	0.0	1.3
0.0	1.8	0.0	0.0	0.0	0.0	0.0	0.0	0.0	0.0	0.0	1.8	0.0	0.0	1.8
0.0	34.3	0.0	0.0	0.0	0.0	0.0	0.0	0.0	0.0	0.0	34.4	0.0	0.0	34.4
0.0	0.5	0.0	0.0	0.0	0.0	0.0	0.0	0.0	0.0	0.0	0.5	0.0	0.0	0.5
0.0	25.6	0.0	0.0	0.0	0.0	0.0	0.0	0.0	0.0	0.0	25.6	0.0	0.0	25.6
0.0	0.6	0.0	0.0	0.0	0.0	0.0	0.0	0.0	0.0	0.0	0.6	0.0	0.0	0.6
0.0	3.8	0.0	0.0	0.0	0.0	0.0	0.0	0.0	0.0	0.0	3.8	0.0	0.0	3.8
0.0	10.7	0.0	0.0	0.0	0.0	0.0	0.0	0.0	0.0	0.0	10.7	0.0	0.0	10.7
0.0	93.4	0.6	0.0	0.0	0.0	0.0	0.0	0.0	0.0	0.0	94.0	0.0	0.0	94.0
0.0	1.5	0.0	0.0	0.0	0.0	0.0	0.0	0.0	0.0	0.0	1.5	0.0	0.0	1.5
0.0	1.3	0.0	0.0	0.0	0.0	0.0	0.0	0.0	0.0	0.0	1.3	0.0	0.0	1.3
0.3	0.5	0.0	0.0	0.0	0.0	0.0	0.0	0.0	0.0	0.0	0.5	0.0	0.0	0.5
0.3	96.7	0.6	0.0	0.0	0.0	0.0	0.0	0.0	0.0	0.0	97.3	0.0	0.0	97.3
0.0	0.1	0.2	0.0	0.0	0.0	0.0	0.0	0.0	0.0	0.0	0.3	0.0	0.0	0.3
0.0	1.1	0.0	0.0	0.0	0.0	0.0	0.0	0.0	0.0	0.0	1.1	0.0	0.0	1.1
0.0	0.0	0.0	0.0	0.0	0.0	0.0	0.0	0.0	0.0	0.0	0.0	0.0	0.0	0.0
0.0	0.2	0.0	0.0	0.0	0.0	0.0	0.0	0.0	0.0	0.0	0.2	0.0	0.0	0.2
0.0	0.0	0.0	0.0	0.0	0.0	0.0	0.0	0.0	0.0	0.0	0.0	0.0	0.0	0.0
0.0	0.0	0.0	0.0	0.0	0.0	0.0	0.0	0.0	0.0	0.0	0.0	0.0	0.0	0.0
0.0	0.1	0.0	0.0	0.0	0.0	0.0	0.0	0.1	0.0	0.0	0.2	0.0	0.0	0.2
0.0	0.1	0.0	0.0	0.0	0.0	0.0	0.0	0.0	0.0	0.0	0.1	0.0	0.0	0.1
0.0	0.0	0.0	0.0	0.0	0.0	0.0	0.0	0.0	0.0	0.0	0.0	0.0	0.0	0.0
0.3	98.3	0.8	0.0	0.0	0.0	0.0	0.0	0.1	0.0	0.0	99.3	0.0	0.0	99.3
0.0	0.3	0.0	0.0	0.0	0.0	0.0	0.0	0.0	0.0	0.0	0.3	0.0	0.0	0.3
0.0	0.4	0.0	0.0	0.0	0.0	0.0	0.0	0.0	0.0	0.0	0.4	0.0	0.0	0.5
0.3	99.1	0.8	0.0	0.0	0.0	0.0	0.0	0.1	0.0	0.0	100.0	0.0	0.0	100.0

were made among the new EU member banks (particularly between Italian banks). Cross-border deals within the EU-15 countries (i.e. target and acquirer are from different country and both are in the EU-15) account for the 17.1% and cross-border deals from the EU-15 to the new EU member (i.e. acquirers are from the EU-15 and target banks are from new EU members). Transactions from the new EU countries to the EU-15 banks accounted for 0.4% terms of number and 0.6% in terms of value.

Looking in detail at the M&A transactions made by financial companies (see Table 2.6), the largest number (of M&As) is made by insurance companies and other financial companies (respectively, 23.8% and 23.6% of all deals), while preferred target OF financial companies are insurance companies and asset management companies (respectively, 27.1% and 23.4% of all deals). In terms of deal value, banks play a major role: banks act as acquirer in 42.4% of all deals value and as target in 70.2% of all deals value. Mergers among the same type of financial companies (likely to be horizontal mergers) account for 53%, while the case of other financial companies acquiring banks (27.7% of all deals value) is also relevant.

Regarding cross-sector M&A activities between banks and insurance, the number and value of deals (*ECB*, 2008c, p. 10) was very high between the 2000 and 2001, due to large individual transactions; namely, the acquisition of Scottish Widows by Lloyds TSB in 2000 and Dresdner Bank by Allianz in 2001 aiming to realize scope economies by means of integration with insurance companies. The number and value of deals substantially dropped in the 2002 and remained quite stable, characterized mainly by a small number of transactions (fluctuating between 19 and 40) and small overall value (especially if compared with the level of transactions in banking).

Focusing on European banks, cross-border deals, especially those involving large banks, were relatively uncommon within Europe until the early 2000s. However, recent mergers suggest an increased propensity for large cross-border mergers as shown by Table 2.7 reporting a list of the major cross-border M&A deals among banks in Europe between 2000 and 2007 showing various large deals.[6] Namely, the largest financial services M&A deal ever occurred at the end of 2007 when the Royal Bank of Scotland, working with the Belgian-Dutch bank Fortis and the Spanish Banco Santander, acquired the Dutch bank ABN AMRO; which comes down to 71 Euro billion

Table 2.6 Number and value of M&A deals between European Financial institutions (EU-27) in 2008 by type of financial institution

Panel A) Number of transactions

Target company's Industry	Acquiror company's Industry								
	AFI	AM	Banks	Brokerage	OCI	DF	Insurance	OF	Total
AFI	19	14	4	0	0	0	1	23	61
AM	28	148	63	30	4	0	33	67	373
Banks	2	17	182	6	5	0	4	31	247
Brokerage	6	17	24	47	1	0	12	32	139
OCI	4	4	21	6	24	0	3	20	82
DF	1	0	3	0	0	3	1	1	9
Insurance	13	21	25	1	1	0	317	53	431
Other Financials	27	33	22	10	2	0	8	148	250
Total	100	254	344	100	37	3	379	375	1592

Continued

Panel B) Overall value of transactions (in USD million)

Target company's Industry	Acquiror company's Industry								
	AFI	AM	Banks	Brokerage	OCI	DF	Insurance	OF	Total
AFI	39.8	440.4	0.0	0.0	0.0	0.0	0.0	258.2	738.4
AM	393.2	3834.9	3131.4	413.4	56.0	0.0	5301.0	11460.3	24590.2
Banks	0.0	3574.3	178507.6	14037.8	63.4	0.0	67.4	127519.1	323769.5
Brokerage	59.8	21.2	2393.6	4590.5	0.0	0.0	45.2	5647.3	12757.5
OCI	91.7	88.0	1855.5	1145.0	3420.7	0.0	1015.4	3153.0	10769.3
DF	0.0	0.0	640.7	0.0	0.0	0.0	7.9	144.2	792.8
Insurance	479.0	1228.1	5222.5	125.4	0.0	0.0	45801.4	6451.5	59307.8
Other Financials	5620.7	9864.5	3880.2	199.9	181.0	0.0	35.7	8583.5	28365.5
Total	6684.1	19051.4	195631.4	20511.9	3721.1	0.0	52274.0	163217.1	461091.0

Where: AFI is Alternative Financial Investments; AM is Asset Management;OCI is Other Credit Institutions; DF is Diversified Financials and OF is Other Financials.

Source: Thomson ONE Banker database.

Table 2.7 Major cross-border M&A deals in European banking market (i.e. deals above one Euro billion)

Year	Acquirer	Target	Value[*]
2007	RBS (GB), Santander (ES), Fortis (FR-BE)	ABN Ambro (NL)	71.000
2007	UniCredito Italiano SpA (IT)	Capitalia SpA (IT)	21.800
2007	Danske Bank A/S (DK)	Sampo Pankki Oyj (FI)	4.050
2007	Crédit Agricole SA (FR)	Cassa di Risparmio di Parma e Piacenza (IT)	3.800
2007	Marfin Investment Group Holdings (GR)	Marfi n Popular Bank Public Co., Ltd (CY)	2.160
2006	Banca Intesa (IT)	San Paolo IMI (IT)	55.000
2006	BNP Paribas SA (FR)	Banca Nazionale del Lavoro (IT)	10.046
2006	Crédit Agricole SA (FR)	Emporiki Bank of Greece SA (GR)	3.364
2005	UniCredito Italiano SpA (IT)	Bayerische Hypo- und Vereinsbank (DE)	13.269
2005	ABN Amro Holding NV (NL)	Banca Antoniana Popolare Veneta (IT)	6.120
2005	UniCredito Italiano SpA (IT)	Bank Austria Creditanstalt AG (AT)	2.095
2005	FöreningsSparbanken AB SE	Hansapank AS (EE)	1.808
2005	Danske Bank A/S DK	National Irish Bank Ltd – Northern Bank Ltd (IE)	1.495
2004	Banco Santander Central Hispano SA	ES Abbey National plc (GB)	12.151
2001	Bayerische Hypo- und Vereinsbank (DE)	Bank Austria Creditanstalt AG (AT)	7.807
2001	Gruppo Bipop-Carire SpA (IT)	Entrium Direct Bankers AG (DE)	2.344
2001	Société Générale (FR)	Komercni Banka AS (CZ)	1.186
2000	HSBC Holdings plc (GB)	CCF – Crédit Commercial de France SA (FR)	11.223
2000	Fortis Bank (BE)	Banque Generale du Luxembourg SA (LU)	1.620

Continued

Table 2.7 Continued

Year	Acquirer	Target	Value(*)
2000	Skandinaviska Enskilda Banken AB (SE)	BfG Bank AG (DE)	1.608
2000	Erste Bank der Österreichischen Spark. (AT)	Ceska Sporitelna AS (CZ)	1.252
2000	Banco Santander Central Hispano SA (ES)	Banco Totta & Acores SA (PT)	1.156

(*) data are in EUR billion.

Source: Adapted from *ECB* (2007c, p. 3) quoting data from Zephyr, Bureau Van Dijk, as data-source.

takeover. Over the first half of 2007, ABN AMRO was also contended by Barclays (that is, Royal Bank of Scotland's UK competitor): RBS ultimately won ABN by using a break-up strategy. In 2007, there was also a big domestic-merger between Unicredit bank and Capitalia, worth 21.8 Euro billion, that created the world's fifth largest bank by market capitalization. The combined market worth of the new UniCredit-Capitalia bank is about 100 billion Euros and the deal is expected to generate about 1.2 Euro billion by 2010 in pre-tax savings and increased revenue: around 68% of that will be related to cost savings and 32% to higher revenues.

There have been also four deals with a total value of more than 10 Euro billions: that is, Unicredito Italiano and Bayerische Hypo und Vereinsbank in 2005, Banco Santander Central Hispano and Abbey National plc in 2004, HSBC Holdings and Crédit Commercial de France in 2000 and BNP Paribas and Banca Nazionale del Lavoro in 2006.

2.6 Banking crises and the M&A phenomenon

Recent cases of bank crisis provide further evidence (if it were needed) that banking is a special business and has a higher impact on worldwide economy than any other industry. Focusing on the largest bank defaults, which are financial companies with total assets of more than 20 USD billion, the following cases of crises have been registered since September 2007 (see Masera, 2009; Webb, 2009; *Thomson Financial*, 2008):

- New Century Financial (with total assets 26 USD billion) and its related entities filed voluntary petitions for relief under Chapter 11 of the US Bankruptcy code on 2 April 2007.
- Northern Rock (with total assets 200 USD billion) asked the Bank of England for a liquidity support facility, as lender of last resort in the UK on 12 September 2007. The bank was taken into State ownership on 22 February 2008.
- IKB (with total assets 74 USD billion) announced in July 2007 to be affected by the US subprime mortgage crisis. IKB was saved by a rescue fund formed by the KfW group (along with various commercial and cooperative banks, including Deutche Banks and Commerzbank).
- Bear Stearns (with total assets 400 USD billion) was severely affected by the US subprime mortgage crisis from the beginning of 2007. The Federal Reserve Bank of New York provided an emergency loan to prevent the company's default in March 2008. However, Bear Stearns could not be saved and was sold to JP Morgan Chas for as low as 10 USD per share.
- First Integrity bank (with total assets 55 USD billion) was closed by the Office of the Comptroller of the Currency and the Federal Deposit Insurance Corporation (FDIC). It was named receiver on 30 May 2008.
- IndyMac bank (with total assets 32 USD billion) was placed by the FDIC into conservation for liquidity concerns on the 11 July 2008. A bridge bank (i.e. IndyMac Federal Bank was established to assume control of the IndyMac bank's assets and secured liabilities and this bridge bank was put into conservatorship under the FDIC's control.
- First Heritage and First National Bank (both owned by the First National Bank Holding Company and with total assets 35 USD billion) were declared insolvent by the Federal regulators and the FDIC was named receiver. The FDIC approved the assumption of more than 3 USD billion in deposits by Mutual of Omaha bank and it will retain most of its loan portfolio.
- Fanny Mae and Freddie Mac (owning or guaranteeing about 50% of the US 12 USD trillion mortgage market, with total assets

795 USD billion and 882 USD billion respectively) were placed into conservatorship by the The Federal Housing Finance Agency on 7 September 2008.

- Lehman Brothers (with total assets 691 USD billion) applied for Chapter 11 of the US Bankruptcy code on 15 September 2008; this marked the largest bankruptcy in the US history. Barclays plc announced its agreement to acquire Lehman's North American investment banking and divisions along with its New York Headquarters building. Similarly, Nomura bank announced its agreement to acquire the Lehman's Asian and European businesses.
- Merrill Lynch (with total assets 1020 USD billion) share price suffered from a 68% fall over the last year due to the US subprime mortgage crisis. Sovereign wealth funds invested into Merrill Lynch more than 10 USD billion in December 2007 and January 2008. On 15 September 2008, Bank of America announced its attempting a takeover of 100% of Merryll Lynch (that is, for 48.7 USD million): this would combine two of the largest banks in the world.
- AIG (with total assets 1050 USD billion) suffered a liquidity crisis due to its credit rating downgrading. On 16 September 2008, the Federal Reserve loaned money following the IIG's request to prevent the company's collapse.
- Bradford & Bingley (with total assets 93 USD billion) was nationalized after hammering out a deal with the Santander Spanish bank (which will buy the 21 GBP billion deposit book and branch network for about 0.6 GBP billion). On 29 September 2008, the bank was taken into public ownership since the bank retail savers withdrew tens of GDP millions as uncertainty grew.
- Fortis (with total assets 1378 USD billion):after a number of colloquia between the European Central Bank and the Netherlands, Belgium and Luxembourg Governments, on 29 September 2008 these three countries announced (effective on the 3 October 2008) that they were investing 23.1 USD billion into Fortis Bank Holding (100% acquired) to save the bank.
- Dexia (with total assets 854 USD billion): The Belgian, French and Luxembourg Governments decided to invest 6.4 Euro billion in Dexia on 30 September 2008.
- Hypo (with total assets 54 USD billion) was granted a last minute credit line of several Euro million from a consortium of German

banks to avoid its bankruptcy. On 29 September 2008, the German Government also joined the banks' consortium.

- HBOS and Lloyds Banking Group Plc.: On September 2008, the HBOS was acquired by Lloyds TSB, due to a precipitous drop in HBOS's share price connected to short selling (see BBC news, 2008a). The acquisition was agreed by Lloyds TSB shareholders on 19 November 2008 (see Lloyds TSB, 2008), and by HBOS shareholders on 12 December 2008 (see BBC news, 2008b). On 19 January 2009 (upon completion of the takeover of HBOS), Lloyds TSB changed its name into Lloyds Banking Group. On 13 October 2008, Mr. Gordon Brown (the British Prime Minister) announced a UK Government bailout of the financial system by injecting infuse 64 Euro billion of new capital into RBS Group Plc, Lloyds TSB and HBOS Plc. Namely, the British Treasury made a $22.3 billion bailout to save the Lloyds Banking Group Plc. Furthermore, on 7 March 2009 the British Treasury announced its plan to insure more than 250 GBP billion of "toxic assets" held by the Lloyds Banking Group. In return for the bail-out, the UK treasury increased its stake in the group from 43% to 65% (77% if non-voting preference shares are included). The company needed additional support due to the HBOS's 11 GBP billion losses.

- Royal Bank of Scotland (RBS): In order to offset a write-down of 5.9 GBP billion due to bad investments and to the shoring up of its reserves following the purchase of ABN AMRO, on April 22 2008 RBS announced its plan to: a) raise 12 GBP billion in new equity capital; b) divest its insurance divisions "Direct Line" and "Churchill" to raise further funds. On 19th January 2009, the British Government announced its intention to convert the RBS preference shares (acquired in October 2008) into ordinary shares: this increased the Government ownership in RBS from 58% to 70%, effectively nationalizing the group. On 13 October 2008, the British Prime Minister, Mr. Gordon Brown announced a UK Government bailout of the financial system by injecting infuse 64 Euro billion of new capital into RBS Group Plc, Lloyds TSB and HBOS Plc. This resulted in a total government ownership in RBS of 58%. Due to the RBS 2008 loss of 34.3 USD billion[7] (i.e. the largest in British history), the British Treasury further injected 36 USD billion in 2009 and is going to guarantee 325 GBP billion using their "toxic debt insurance program." Overall, the UK government now owns 95% of RBS.

Although it is probably premature to explain the causes of the banking crisis accurately, some of the potential causes can be identified focusing on banking practices.[8] First, banking crisis is related to the change of the banking business over the last decade: major international banks (especially in the US) have changed from a buy and hold business model, according to which banks grant customer loans and hold them in their balance-sheets, to an originate-to-distribute business model. On the basis of the latter model, loans are firstly originated and securitized by banks. As a result, these are often sold on to other intermediaries and the revenues used for granting new loans. The originate-to-distribute model results in a high level of leverage and in lower incentives for banks to monitor the loan portfolio quality. This was made particularly evident by the subprime crisis in the US mortgage market. In consequence, the new business model has provided banks with the opportunity to display good performance, despite the risk of operations. With this regards, J. De Larosiére (2009, p. 9) notes:

> The originate-to-distribute model as it developed, created perverse incentives. Not only did it blur the relationship between borrower and lender but also it diverted attention away from the ability of the borrower to pay towards lending – often without recourse – against collateral. A mortgage lender knowing beforehand that he would transfer (sell) his entire default risks through MBS or CDOs had no incentive to ensure high lending standards.

A second reason of banking crisis is the inadequate regulation of investment banks. The investment bank core business is to provide a wide range of services to companies and Governments in all capital market related activities. These services include the issuing of new debts and equity or or the provision of corporate advisory services in the M&A deal and/or corporate restructuring activities. Following the banking crises of the early 1900s, commercial and investment banks were separated by regulations almost in all countries: the Glass-Steagall Act in 1933 forbade commercial banks from underwriting equities and other corporate securities in the US and similar regulations were implemented in almost all European countries. As seen above, at the end of the twentieth century, almost all developed financial systems undertook a structural deregulation process: in the EU, financial conglomeration was encouraged by the Second Banking directive in 1989 and the Gramm-Leach-Bliley act in 1999 removed most of the restrictions imposed by the Glass-Steagall Act in 1933. While a prudential re-regulation process was carried out for commercial banks, all investment banks crises provided evidence that the re-regulation for these types of financial companies was inadequate.

A third reason was the risk managers' overconfidence in transferring financial risks. J. De Larosiére (2009, p. 8) notes:

> There have been quite fundamental failures in the assessment of risk, both by financial firms and by those who regulated and supervised them. [...] The cumulative effect of these failures was an overestimation of the ability of financial firms as a whole to manage their risks, and a corresponding underestimation of the capital they should hold.

For a better understanding of this point, it useful to go back to 1997 when the Harvard Business School Gazette announced that Professor Merton achieved the Nobel Price in Economics using the following words:

> Investors use derivatives to hedge their portfolios against the effects of sudden shifts in the market. Merton's work provides them with a formula for evaluating derivatives with greater precision. In fact, using Merton's formula, it is possible to construct a portfolio that is virtually risk-free. (qtd. in Gewertz, 1997, p.1)

While there is no doubt that Merton's work is a milestone in finance, banks erroneously used this framework in the 2000s by providing mortgages to bad borrowers with the illusion that the risk transferring techniques and the increasing house value would make this kind of loans safe. In addition, the originate-to-distribute business model (according to which loans are firstly originated and securitized by banks, so these are often sold on to other intermediaries and the revenues used for granting new loans) lowered the incentive for banks to monitor the loan portfolio quality. The illusion was shuttered in August 2007 as soon as the housing prices started to decline and the mortgage value was higher than the property value in most cases, so that an increasing number of borrowers stopped to repay the mortgage (labeled as "Subprime mortgage crisis.") As a result, cash flows became soon insufficient to pay coupons of financial products (labeled as "Mortgage-Backed Securities" (MBS)[9] that had been sold worldwide to financial institutions and investors in the 2000s. Immediately, these financial products lost value (and were labeled as "toxic assets,") a large number of banks incurred in high-value losses and this was the beginning of the crises (for example, the Fanny Mae and Freddie Mac above described).

A fourth reason was failures in *corporate governance practices*. As noted in J. De Larosiére (2009, p. 8),

> Failures in risk assessment and risk management were aggravated by the fact that the checks and balances of corporate governance also failed. Many boards and senior managements of financial firms neither understood the characteristics of the new, highly complex financial products they were dealing with, nor were they aware of the aggregate exposure of their companies, thus seriously underestimating the risks they were running. Many board members did not provide the necessary oversight or control of management. Nor did the owners of these companies – the shareholders.

The severe banking crisis has produced uncertainty in the economy worldwide, resulting in a drop of M&A deals. Over 2008, the volume of worldwide announced M&A was 2.9 USD trillion (–29.6% compared to 2007 totals), that is the lowest level for annual deal activity since 2005 (see Thomson Reuter, 2008). The worldwide announced M&A drop was particularly important in the 2008 fourth quarter: the total value was 555.8 USD billion (–34.6% compared to the third quarter of 2008 and –37.1% with respect to the fourth quarter of 2007) (see Thomson Reuter, 2008). The effect of the financial crisis is also evident in the number of withdrawn M&A transactions: 1,194 worldwide M&A transactions were cancelled during the year (that is, the highest level since 2000) (see Thomson Reuter, 2008). The drop of M&A activity was particularly large in Africa/Middle East (–39.6%), Japan (–37.9%), the US, (–37.2%) and Europe (–27.3%), while the M&A volume in Pacific Asia decreased by just 8.7% due to a robust deal activity in China and South East Asia (see Thomson Reuter, 2008). A similar trend has also continued in the first 2009 quarter: the value of worldwide M&A dropped to 444 USD billion, despite the two announced big deals (worth 110 USD billion) in the US drug industry (that is, Pfizer Inc's purchase of Wyeth and the Merck & Co Inc's acquisition of Schering Plough Corp) (see Webb, 2009). As reported by Webb (2009, p. 1),

> ...bankers said the tough conditions would endure until credit markets became more welcoming, shares stabilized, and the economic picture brightened, allowing acquirers to forecast earnings with more certainty. 'There's a lack of confidence in valuations, and a lack of credit' said Ian Hart at Citigroup, which advised clients, including Pfizer, Lloyds, Essent NV, and the UK Treasury on several of the year's biggest deals. 'Executives are very cautious and are focused on seeing their businesses make it through the downturn' said Hart, Citi's co-head of European M&A. 'There will come a time when people feel it's the right time to move but they don't feel any need to hurry'. David Livingstone at Credit Suisse, which ranked top for European M&A, said M&A remained highly dependent on the economic outlook. 'There's less overall confidence in making strategic moves, and continued dislocation in credit markets. We'd anticipate this situation will broadly continue through the rest of the year' he said.

Another signal of the effect of the banking crisis on M&A deals is that a substantial part of the deals was driven by Government investments. Over 2008, government entities invested 396 USD billion (that is, 13.5% of worldwide M&A) and these investments arrived with increasing frequency throughout the year, with almost 200 USD billion in the fourth 2008 quarter alone (see Thomson Reuter, 2008). Focusing on the US, government investments account for 5.5% of the all M&A deals volume in the country (that is, 0.3% in 2006). Government investment activity was driven by:

1. sovereign wealth fund investments for 20.4 USD billion, including a 6.9 USD billion investment in Citigroup by the Singapore Investment Authority's and a 2.0 USD billion investment in

Merrill Lynch by Kuwait Investment Authority and Korea Investment Corp;

2. the US Treasury's Troubled Asset Relief Program: the US Treasury has committed to purchase up to 250 USD billion in non-convertible senior preferred stock as well as receive warrants to purchase common stock with a total market value equal to 15% of each senior preferred investment for publicly traded securities and 5% for privately held securities (see Thomson Reuter, 2008).

2.7   Conclusion

This chapter has analyzed the M&A phenomenon in the European Banking. While most research undertaken to evaluate the effects produced by Merger and Acquisition (M&A) transactions focussed traditionally on the US banking, some of the most important M&A deals since the 1990s involved European banks: for example, there have been six big mergers since 2006 for an overall value of more than 170 euro billion.

M&As are certainly one of the main bank responses to higher competitive pressures in European banking. New forces of changes are mainly related to structural deregulation and prudential reregulation, competition enhancement, technology developments, globalization, etc. have occurred. Particularly, regulatory changes played a major role. Until the late 1980s, most European Banks were subject to heavy structural regulatory rules, as a response to the banking crises of the 1930s, to constrain competition so as to preserve the stability of the financial industry. Over the 1970s and 1980s, most countries went through a regulatory change moving from structural and conduct rules to a prudential regulation framework. Under this new framework, supervisors follow objective rules set in the banking system to induce banks to have cautious behaviours. Prudential regulation instruments are: bank's asset quality and monitoring effectiveness, capital adequacy requirements, large exposure portfolio restrictions. The structural deregulation and prudential reregulation processes were lead by various factors such as globalization and technological developments. In Europe, the regulatory change was also led by the integration of the various domestic banking markets in order to create a single European Banking Market.

Consolidation has contributed significantly to the reduction in the number of banks operating in the EU-15 displaying a substantial reduction of credit institutions over the 2000s. Recent statistics from *ECB* (2007a) clearly show a substantial decreasing trend of the number of credit institutions and a rising trend of M&A transactions since 2001, both in terms of number of deals and of their value. Half of the transactions took place in the domestic (involving banks in the same country) and in the Euro area, whereas the other half involved banks outside Europe. In the next chapter, the reasons of mergers are analyzed and, in particular, some big-merger deals are examined in detail to take some useful lessons.

3
Why Do Banks Merge?

3.1 Introduction

The most successful European banks responded to the changing competitive environment by expanding through internally generated growth or M&As. All largest European banks have actively taken part in the consolidation process over the last decade and the number and value of big M&A deals constantly increased. Mergers and Acquisitions (M&As) deals are usually based on the belief that gains can accrue via reduction in expenses and earning volatility and increases in market power and scale and scope of economies (Kiymaz 2004). The M&A causes have been usually classified according to various criteria.

Thu Nguyen and Yung (2007) noted that M&A deals may be justified by:

1. market timing: M&A deals occur since the acquirer bank's managers intend to take advantage of market mispricing.
2. industry-shock responding (neo-classical hypothesis): M&A transactions occur because firms are prompted to merge in order to reap the benefits of some common shocks.
3. the agency hypothesis: M&A operations would occur because they enhance the acquirer management's welfare at the expense of the acquirer shareholders.
4. the hubris hypothesis: M&A deals occur since managers make mistakes in evaluating target firms, and *engage in mergers* even when there is no synergy.

5. synergy motives: M&A deals occur because of economic gains obtained by merging the resources of the two firms.

According to this classification, some of these motives are to the benefit of shareholders, some against. A corporate decision is usually derived from more than one motive, which either add or destroy shareholder value, Berger et al., (1999a) discuss M&A motives by distinguishing between value maximization and non-value maximization motives. These classification criteria reflect our approach on the basis of which, in Chapter 2, we illustrated M&A deals as an exogenous channel of value creation. However, in Chapter 3 (see section 3.2) we prefer to discuss consolidation motives focusing on the various drivers that lead a bank to create shareholder value. Next, we will review some of the most important M&A deals in European banking (section 3.3).

3.2 Consolidation motives

M&A deals are defined as "horizontal" when the acquirer and target companies are competitors in the same industry and they offer the same product and services in terms of end-use. If the bidder and the target companies are not identical, but share some commonalities such as technology, distribution channels, customer segments, knowledge, and so forth, this is defined as a "related M&A." An M&A between two firms, which operates at successive stages of the production process chain, is defined as "vertical integration."

Most of the deals made by financial institutions worldwide are horizontal M&As. Related mergers, where the target company is classified as a different type of financial company, and other mergers in particular who target a non-financial company play a secondary role (see Table 3.1, Panel A). In terms of the value of M&As (Table 3.1, Panel B), the deals where the target company is a commercial bank have a larger role. This is expected since commercial banks usually have a larger value than other companies; therefore deals whose target is a bank have (obviously) a larger incidence.

The use of related and, particularly, horizontal M&As is often a strategy pursued by companies operating in mature industries. Where there is a low demand for the industry's product and an excess of capacity, there is a large number of competitors and substantial

Table 3.1 M&A deals in worldwide financial sectors in 2005: horizontal, related and other operations

Panel A – Number of deals

	Commercial banks		Other credit institutions		Insurance		Other financials		Real Estate; Mortgage Bankers		Savings and Loans, Mutual Savings Banks	
	No.	(%)	No.	(%)	No.	(%)	No.	(%)	No.	(%)	No.	(%)
Horizontal merger	560	55.06	115	47.52	428	69.59	27	61.36	524	54.36	30	55.56
Related merger	311	30.58	58	23.97	81	13.17	8	18.18	123	12.76	20	37.04
Other merger	146	14.36	69	28.51	106	17.24	9	20.45	317	32.88	4	7.41
Total	1017	100.00	242	100.00	615	100.00	44	100.00	964	100.00	54	100.00

Panel B – Value (in USD million) of deals

	Commercial banks		Other credit institutions		Insurance		Other financials		Real Estate; Mortgage Bankers		Savings and Loans, Mutual Savings Banks	
	Value	(%)	Value	(%)	Value	(%)	Value	(%)	Value	(%)	Value	(%)
Horizontal merger	4703897	98.96	7925	10.15	125203	48.13	2253	100.00	50171	41.55	74610	87.11
Related merger	40602	0.85	56278	72.07	123703	47.56	0	0.00	66002	54.66	11045	12.89
Other merger	8719	0.18	13887	17.78	11220	4.31	0	0.00	4579	3.79	–1	0.00
Total	4753218	100.00	78090	100.00	260126	100.00	2253	100.00	120752	100.00	85654	100.00

Horizontal M&A are deals where target and acquirer companies are classified in the same sector. Related M&A are deals where target and acquirer companies are not classified in the same sector, but both are financial companies. Other M&A are deals where the target companies are not financial institutions.

Source: Thomson ONE Banker database.

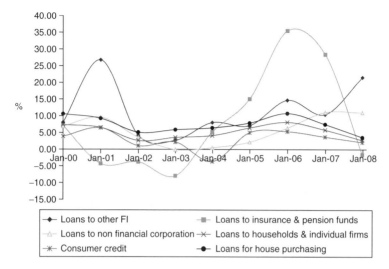

Figure 3.1 Bank loans net-growth rates in Europe during 2000–08
Source: ECB Statistical Data Warehouse.

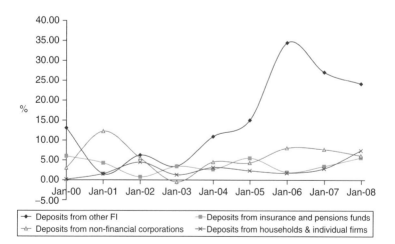

Figure 3.2 Bank deposit net-growth rates in Europe during 2000–08
Source: ECB Statistical Data Warehouse.

price pressure as well as pressure to reduce costs (see Sudarsanan, 2003). Most of these conditions seem to be met in European banking. Regarding the number of competitors, the number of MFIs between May 2000 and 2008 decreased by 5.42% in the EU-27 and by 26% in the EU-12. The drop in MFIs number was substantial in most of EU-countries (Netherlands –45%; France –35%; Germany –32%, Luxemburg –27%), while it was smaller in few countries (Italy –6.5%, Spain –6%, Ireland –1%). The industry concentration increased in most countries: on average, the concentration increased by 25% between 1999 and 2006[1] and price competition and pressures to reduce costs were very high. Looking at net growth rates of various types of deposits and loans (Figures 3.1 and 3.2), constantly increased in the 2000s and were usually lower than 10% (with a few exceptions in a few years).

Under these circumstances, horizontal and related M&A transactions usually have the following aims[2]:

1. revenue enhancement. In a horizontal merger, the two banks involved in the merger may increase their revenue. These transactions increase their market share and enhance their market power and give them the chance to fix more profitable prices on financial services provided and/or to practice successfully non-price competitive strategies. Berger et al., (1999, p.144) note that "It is difficult to determine the goals of M&A participants, but there is evidence consistent with the notion that some M&As are designed to increase market power". They also claim that "in-market M&As that substantially increase market concentration may increase market power in setting prices on retail services. Presumably, this was an expected consequence of many of these M&As and provided at least part of the motivation." There are two risks following horizontal M&As:
   a. these deals may lead the banking market to an increased concentration making the risk of diminishing competitive pressures concrete;
   b. large banks may collude and set unfavourable price to customers to increase their profits. To face these risks, the anti-trust authorities carefully monitor M&A deals among banks in order to prevent these "bad outcomes."

Revenue enhancements may be achieved by exploiting operational synergies, such as network externalities.[3] In banking, network externalities are mainly related to the distribution channels: the merger between two banks with complementary distribution channels – as for example, on-line and branch based, respectively – may increase the product/service value to individual customers. This may lead customers to intensify interactions so as to facilitate product cross-selling, to improve the bank image and also increase the number of customers. Similarly, revenue enhancements may also be achieved by leveraging marketing capabilities[4]: merging banks may be able to take advantage of each other's marketing capabilities; for example, using established distribution channels of the other bank in another country.

2. cost savings. M&A deals occur since, by combining the acquirer and target bank 's activities, there are some cost efficiency savings due to expense reduction in various business areas (e.g. marketing, sales and distribution, human resource management, etc). Cost savings may be realized by:

a. reducing excess capacity: for banks with an excess capacity, an M&A deal can help rationalize the production and take out the excess capacity by reducing fixed costs. A common case in banking concerns the branch network: in the 1990s, banks increased substantially the number of branches thus experiencing an excess of capacity over the 2000s. M&As were often used to rationalize the branch network of the two merging companies. In the European banking, these deals have been occurring in quick succession leading to an industry-wide consolidation.

b. achieving scale economies. M&A transactions can give banks the chance to change their size and reach the optimal production scale. A careful analysis of scale efficiency gains requires to account for the following factors:
  • direct associated costs (that is, all redundancy expenses, cost of branches and office closures, and so forth) and indirect associated costs (that is, cost due to the loss of skills and capabilities following workers or team's departure and, possibly, the risk that these skills will go to merging banks' competitors);
  • the risk that ineffective post-merger integration will not lead to scale efficiency gains is very relevant in banking since

companies have a complex organizational structure and their integration is complicated;

- the extent of cost savings: this can be estimated on the basis of the minimum (of the) average production cost. By analyzing a balanced panel of 130 Norwegian banks, Humphrey and Vale (2004, p. 1694) estimated that, on average, mergers are expected to lower costs since

- Overall, our *ex-ante* cost predictions for individual mergers are about as good (or poor) as those of merger participants themselves. There is greater agreement when the average of predicted ex ante cost effects (–3.09% for the spline) are compared with the average of ex post changes (–2.81%).

c. achieving scope economies. Through M&A transactions banks can reduce production costs by increasing the number of products. Formally, scope economy exists when the production cost of two or more products in a bank is lower than the sum of the separate production cost of each product in single specialized banks. In banking, scope economies exist if the production cost of a universal bank (offering services on banking, factoring, leasing, insurance, capital markets, and so forth) is lower than the sum of production cost of specialized banks in each of these financial services (that is, bank, specialized leasing company, specialized factoring firm, insurance company, investment company, and so forth). There is not clear evidence that scope economy exists in banking, although many M&As are motivated by the achievement of scope economy. This is a common motivation in Bancassurance: this term has been initially used in France, where cooperation between banks and insurance companies started earlier than in other European countries. This word was originally coined to indicate the simple distribution of insurance products by bank branches, while at present it is used to describe all kinds of relationships between banking and insurance industries (Elkington, 1993; Swiss RE, 1994; Quagliarello, 2004).

d. x-efficiency. Various studies (see Berger et al., 1999) found that larger and more efficient banks usually tend to merger with smaller and less efficient banks. This is presumably in order to spread the expertise or operating policies and procedures of the more efficient institution over additional resources. In European banking, Focarelli et al., (2002) found that large and profiTable banks tend to be acquirers, while small and unprofitable banks tend to be targets. Vander Vennet, (1996) found that large and efficient banks tend to acquire small, less efficient banks. Altunbas et al., (1995) found that similar potential for improvements existed in M&As between UK banks and building societies. In this respect, M&A aims can be viewed as an exchange of "corporate culture" as follows:

- efficient acquirer banks aim to export their "corporate culture" to inefficient target banks: in this case, the acquirer bank's culture overcomes the target bank's culture;
- inefficient acquirer banks aim to import the "corporate culture" of the efficient target banks: in this case, the target bank's culture is overcome by the acquirer bank's culture (see Ruozi 2001).

3. new growth opportunities. These arise from the creation of new technologies, products and markets. In banking, new growth opportunities are pursued through the development of new financial products (financial engineering), new delivery channels (e-banking) and new markets (cross-border). The latter's expansion was particularly relevant in the 2000s where most continental European banking entered the East-European banking markets in order to exploit new business opportunities.

All these goals aim to create shareholder value. However, M&A transactions may be motivated by other goals due to the stakeholders' influence, such as managers and Government. Managers may be able to pursue their own objectives in M&A deals when the bank's corporate control is weak. As noted by Berger et al., (1999, p. 146),

One managerial objective may be empire-building. Executive compensation tends to increase with firm size, so managers may hope to achieve personal financial gains by engaging in M&As, although at least in part the observed higher compensation of the managers of larger institutions rewards greater skill and effort ... There is evidence that banking organizations may overpay for acquisitions when corporate governance structures are not sufficiently well-designed to align managerial incentives with those of the owners.

Governments and Domestic supervisory authorities play a direct role in the consolidation decisions through the restriction of the types of M&As permitted and through approval/disapproval decisions for individual M&As. An example of supervisory authority interference was the battle for the acquisition of the Italian bank Antonveneta by the Dutch bank ABN AMRO and the Italian bank "Banca Popolare Italiana," when the Banca d'Italia Governor (Mr. Antonio Fazio) tended to favour the Italian bank bid against the negative judgement of two inspectors from Banca d'Italia in charge of the approval. At the end of the dispute, Banca d'Italia approved the Dutch bank ABN AMRO tender and rejected the one from Banca Popolare Italiana, while Mr Fazio resigned from its job.

3.3   Lessons from the past

As seen in Chapter 2, an intense process of consolidation occurred over the last decade in European banking. Half of the transactions were in the domestic (involving banks in the same country) and in the Euro area, while the other half involved banks outside Europe. Overall, the value of M&As between a EU bank and a bank outside Europe is quite small. In the 2000s, there were several big merger deals in European banking: the largest M&A deal occurred at the end of 2007 when the Royal Bank of Scotland (leading a consortium including also Fortis and Banco Santander) acquired ABN Amro bank. In 2007, there was also a big domestic merger between UniCredit bank and Capitalia that created the world's fifth largest bank for market capitalization. There have also been four deals with a total value of more than 10 Euro billions; that is, UniCredito Italiano and Bayerische Hypo und Vereinsbank in 2005, Banco Santander Central Hispano and Abbey National plc in 2004, HSBC Holdings and Crédit Commercial de France in 2000 and BNP Paribas and Banca Nazionale del Lavoro in 2006.[5] This section analyzes these M&A cases aiming to identify history and aims of the deal. Since 2007, the severe banking crisis has made various deals necessary (especially in the UK.) within the Governments' bailout of the financial system. However, these deals are not analyzed in this section since they are sporadic M&A cases with the primary aim of guaranteeing the banking system survival.

3.3.1 The Banque National de Paris and Paribas merger

The integration of Banque National de Paris (BNP) and Paribas[6] in 1999 was a key step in the consolidation process of the French banking sector which started in the late 1980s with the privatisation of some important entities such as Société Générale, Crédit Commercial de France and BNP and Paribas themselves (Table 3.2).

The BNP and Paribas merger is an interesting case of study for two reasons. Firstly, this deal was one of the largest (around 15 billion Euro) in 1999: the BNP-Paribas group is currently the largest French company, the largest bank in the Euro area and the second largest bank worldwide (in terms of total assets) (see Forbes 2008). The

Table 3.2 The history of Banque National de Paris and Paribas

Banque National de Paris (BNP)	Paribas
BNP was born in 1966 from the merger between Banque Nationale pour le Commerce et l'Industrie (BNCI) et Comptoir national d'Escompte de Paris (CNEP). The merger led to the creation of the biggest bank in France, second in Europe and seventh worldwide for total assets.	Its origins date back to 1872, when Banque de Paris et des Pays (afterwards called Banque Paribas, controlled by the holding Compagnie Financière de Paribas since 1968) was created from the merger between Banque de Paris and Banque de Crédit et de Dépòts des Pays-Bas.
In the following years, the bank went through a rapid expansion in the financial service sector: in only eight years the number of current accounts opened at BNP was more than doubled.	Since its creation, bank activities consisted mainly in the issuing of securities on the French market (mostly treasury bills and government bonds) and in the corporate finance.
The growth of the French Institute took place in France, but also in Europe and North America. Following its privatisation in 1993, BNP decided to concentrate its core business in the retail sector for the domestic market, and in the wholesale banking on the international market.	After 1997, Banque Paribas acquired several smaller banks to expand its branch network.
	In 1998, with the merger between Compagnie Financière de Paribas and Compagnie Bancaire (already under control since 1969), the Paribas group was officially born.

Source: Author's own based on information provided in http://www.bnpparibas.com.

BNP-Paribas group also operates in over 85 countries, has 162,700 employees (126,600 in Europe). Secondly, the merger was the result of a strong competition between BNP and Société Générale to acquire Paribas.

The original project included a merger of BNP with two other banks, Société Générale and Paribas, that were already negotiating a possible aggregation of a total value of approximately 15 Euro billion. As shown in Table 3.3, on February 1st 1999, Société Générale made an offer on all Paribas shares to create the first bank group in France and third in Europe for its size with an activity amounting to 679 billion euro. If the merger between the two was achieved, BNP would be isolated and weakened as the two banks in question ranked among the main private institutes in the country and would

Table 3.3 Banque National de Paris and Paribas: key dates of the transaction

1 February 1999: Société Générale and Paribas announces a friendly merger plan which created SG Paribas.

9 March 1999: BNP launches two separate public tenders on Société Générale and Paribas. The two banks speak of "hostile" offers.

6 April 1999: The Board of Directors of Société Générale and Paribas officially rejects BNP's offers and declares its intention to carry on their own merger plan.

14 June 1999: Société Générale increases the offer for Paribas, but the Governor of Bank of France withdraws his go-ahead to the new tender and invites the banks to find a friendly solution.

30 June 1999: Negotiations fail and BNP launches back public acquisition offers. The Supervisory Committee of the Credit Sector approves the new offers.

14 August 1999: The Council of financial markets releases the results: BNP has bought 65% of Paribas capital share, but stopped at 37% for Société Générale.

20 September 1999: BNP makes another offer at the Stock Exchange to take over 35% of Paribas share still on the market.

8 March 2000: The Group BNP – Paribas presents the first accounts post-merger and highlights the growth compared to the previous year.

7 May 2001 BNP – PARIBAS announces the purchase of the American Insitute Bank West Corporation, an operation which aimed to the expansion in the US (already started by BNP).

Source: Author's own.

become vulnerable to attacks from the outside. This consideration, which encouraged BNP to make two separate public acquisition offers on March 9th 1999, came from a leading banking group in Europe for total assets, capitalization and own resources:[7] one concerning Société Générale and the other on Paribas. After six months, BNP acquired Paribas, obtaining 65.1% of equity capital. BNP's public acquisition offer accepted by Paribas included an exchange ratio of 29 ordinary share of BNP for 20 Paribas shares and in addition 13 certificates of guaranteed value (CVG)[8] for Paribas's shareholders. Overall, Paribas's share price paid was 124.8 euro. This amount was 12.4% more than the original offer and 2% higher than Société Général's offer – that is, the exchange ratio of eight Paribas shares for five BNP shares. Therefore, the result of the offers made by BNP was a merger between BNP and Paribas. The consolidated group possessed total assets of approximately 700 billion euros and boasted a market capitalization of more than 41 billion, with a distribution network of more than 2000 branches.

Regarding the post merger results, BNP and Paribas achieved encouraging results after their merger: the intermediation margin was 15 billion euro, i.e. 21% higher than the two banks' combined intermediation margin over the previous year, the gross income increased by 44.7% (compared to 1998 level) and net profit also increased by 22.8%. In a longer term, BNP-Paribas's pre-tax ROE increased substantially over time after the merger: 17% in 1999, 20% in 2000, 24% in 2001, 15% in 2002, 27% in 2003, 33% in 2004, 32% in 2005, 39% in 2006 and 30% in 2007. BNP-Paribas group also increased its solvency: in 1999, its solvency ratio increased by 0.5% (that is, 7.1%).

3.3.2   The Union Bank of Switzerland and the Swiss Bank Corporation merger

On 1st July 1998, Union Bank of Switzerland (UBS) and the Swiss Bank Corporation (SBC), two of the three Swiss biggest banks, merged to form the new UBS (Table 3.4). The merger between USB – SBC has (at least) two important causes of interest.

First, although this was not a cross-border deal, it has impacted both the domestic and the international market. Secondly, UBS and SBC have traditionally been two financial conglomerates (not simply retail banks) acting in several financial areas, as for example, asset management, and private and investment banking.

Table 3.4 The history of Union Bank of Switzerland and Swiss Bank Corporation

Union Bank of Switzerland (UBS)	Swiss Bank Corporation (SBC)
UBS was born in 1912 from the merger between two regional banks: Toggenburger bank (founded in 1863) and bank Winterthur (founded in 1862).	SBC was founded in Basle in 1972 with the name of Basler Bankverein.
Contrary to what happened for Swiss Bank Corporation, the expansion of the activity took place first in the domestic market (due to various acquisitions of local institutes in the after-war period) and than on the international one. In fact, the first foreign subsidiaries were opened only after the Second World War: in London in 1967 and in New York in 1975. Similarly to SBC, UBS adopts a universal banking model and operates both on a local (in the areas of corporate retail and asset management) and global (in the commercial banking) scale.	It was the first among Swiss banks to enlarge its interests abroad. The expansion in the domestic market took place only later (starting from the early 60s).
	The opening of SBC towards the foreign market represents a stable feature in the history of the institute, as shown by some M&A deals concluded over the 1990s (such as the acquisition of O'Connor & Associates in 1992, Brinson Partners in 1995 and Warburg Dilon Read in 1997). These deals allowed SBC to have a strong market power in key sectors such as asset management and investment banking.
In 1997, UBS was the first Swiss bank for *total assets* and number of customers.	

Source: Author's own based on information provided in http://www.ubs.com/.

The agreement between UBS and SBC included an exchange of securities so that 60% of the new UBS-SBC's equity capital was controlled by the UBS' former shareholders, who received a new share for each nominal share and five for each bearer share; and the remaining 40% was controlled by the SBC's shareholders who obtained 14 shares of the new company for 13 shares owned (Table 3.5).

The business model adopted by the new bank was based on the one adopted by SBC, that is a model organized by product lines (rather than geographical areas) such as:

- private banking (with the headquarter in Basle)
- Consumer and Corporate Banking (with the headquarter in Zurich)

- Asset Management (controlled by the SBC Beinson from Chicago)
- Investment banking (controlled by the Warburg Dillon Read from London)

The integration between UBS and SBC is an example of a "reverse takeover," – that is, a transaction where the major bank – the one having the largest proportion of shares of the new bank and also giving its name – is not going to have a stronger influence on the new bank's policies. Namely, even though 60% of the equity capital was given to former UBS' shareholders, SBC took effective control of the new bank. This is confirmed by at least three factors:

- Most of the new UBS managers come from SBC and not from UBS. For example, the managing Director Ospel Marcel and three out of four Business unit directors come from USB.
- SBC's stronger position compared to UBS was also evident in the number of personnel cuts consequent to the merger.
- The new group adopted the SBC brands and organization in most strategic business areas. In the asset management, the American company SBC Brinson became the reference institute, which also took control over Phillips & Drew (one of the biggest English branches owned by UBS).

Table 3.5 Union Bank of Switzerland and Swiss Bank Corporation: key dates of the transaction

---

8 December 1997: With a joint press release, the merger between USB and SBC is announced. The deal was declared completed only after ten months of frequently stalled negotiations.

3 February 1998: USB extraordinary meeting approves the merger plan.

4 February 1998: SBC extraordinary meeting approves the merger plan.

5 March 1998: The European Commission approves the integration. The Swiss and American Competition authorities' authorization follows.

29 June 1998: The new UBS is officially born with the first day's trading of its shares on the Swiss Exchanges.

Source: Author's own.

The new group's strategy was to use the SBC model on the international market and the UBS model on the domestic market, in order to preserve the best parts of the two Institutes and guarantee a rapid growth and high profitability. Looking at the post-merger results, there was a period of initial growth, but afterwards economic results were lower than expected (with the exception of 2003, when they closed at the fixed object with 18.2% ROE). Apparently, this delay is not due either to managers' mistakes or to external events such as:

- The failure of the American long term capital management *hedge fund*, which caused heavy losses to the Warburg Dillon Read (i.e. one of the key companies in the group) and the leave of some important personalities in the bank management.[9]
- Stock Exchange Market crises over the period 2000–01: for example, the burst of the stock asset bubble, the 11/09/2001 terrorist attack, and Argentinean Government bonds default. Following these events, currency rates became also volatile and reduced considerably the UBS market performance.

Notwithstanding these exogenous adverse events, the new UBS was able to attain most of the merger aims and proved successful as a global player in almost all of its financial services. After eight years from the merger, UBS is currently one of the major banking groups for asset management in the *investment and private banking* sectors: according to Forbes (2008), UBS is the first largest company in the diversified financials with over 2000 billion euro total assets and the sixth largest bank worldwide in term of total assets.

3.3.3 The UniCredit and HypoVereinsBank merger

Announced in June 2005 and completed at the end of October the same year (but effective as of 2006), the UniCredit – HypoVereinsBank (HVB) merger in 2005 made one of the greatest banks in the Euro area: at that time, the fourth most important group in the Euro zone and the ninth in the whole European Union. This deal deserves our interest because it was one of the greatest cross-border aggregations in the Euro zone. Namely, with a total assets of 787 Euro billion, 29 million customers worldwide, 6500 branches in 19 countries, 126,000 employees and a market capitalization of 41 Euro billion, in 2005 the new UniCredit-HVB was smaller that the Spanish Santander (with a market capitalization of 59 Euro billion), Paribas (a market capitalization of 50 Euro billion) and BBVA (with a market capitalization of 43 Euro billion).

The merger ensued from three 19.2 euro billion tender offers for the Munich Group's shares: HVB, Bank Austria and the Polish PBH. The friendly bid, launched on August 25th, 2008 by UniCredit, proposed an exchange ratio of five shares to one (Table 3.6). Concerning Bank Austria, shareholders were entitled to choose between a share exchange or a cash offer (i.e. 19.92 UniCredit shares for each Bank Austria share or 69,90 euro cash); with regards the Polish BPH (controlled by HVB), UniCredit launched an offer on the whole equity capital share. UniCredit achieved the 65% threshold of HVB capital on October 15th 2005 and reached 80% of the equity capital on October 22, 2008.

Regarding the post-merger integration of the two banks' activities, the new UniCredit HVB was re-organized on a divisional and segment basis. Firstly, an "Integration Office" was introduced to support the UniCredit Managing Director in the coordination, management and monitoring of the whole integration Program between UniCredit and HVB.

Secondly, various business divisions were defined aiming essentially to optimize the long-term value creation, focusing on excellent customer management, product development/marketing and

Table 3.6 UniCredit and HypoVereinsBank: key dates of the transaction

13 June 2005: The UniCredit Board of Directors and the Supervisory Council of Hypovereinsbank approved the merger between the two groups and the creation of a new bank.

21 July 2005: Coordination of the procedure to obtain the relevant authorization needed for the transaction UniCredit/HVB.

27 August 2005: UniCredit launches its exchange offer for the aggregation with the HVB.

15 October 2005: UniCredit exceeds 65% acceptance threshold of HVB capital share, the second German bank on which Piazza Cordusio (UniCredit 's registered office) has launched a public tender.

22 October 2005: UniCredit takes control over HVB. The public offer nearly achieves 80% acceptance level. The minimum acceptance threshold for the HVB tender offer has been comfortably surpassed.

Source: Author's own.

distribution. The business division structures are therefore entitled to run business plans and actions (coherent with the whole Group strategy) by coordinating and supporting the development of the regional businesses within Italy, Germany, Austria and Central Eastern Europe (CEE) and of their global businesses. The business divisions are: Retail Division, Private Banking & Asset Management Division, Corporate/Small Medium Enterprises Division, Multinationals/Investment Banking Division, Central and Eastern Europe Division and Commercial Real Estate and Financing Division. Chairman of the new company is the German Dieter Rampl, Managing Director is the current chairman of UniCredit, Mr. Alessandro Profumo. The registered office chosen is the Milan UniCredit headquarters in Piazza Cordusio. The Board of Directors is composed of 24 advisors, 16 of which are Italian. Besides, the majority of the Group's managers are Italian.

The UniCredit-HVB merger has created one of the largest groups in Eastern Europe because of the latter's large expansion potential. UniCredit has always adopted an assertive strategy towards Eastern Europe by acquiring various local banks. UniCredit started in Poland and then went on to Slovakia, Bulgaria, Croatia, Romania, Czech Republic and Turkey. A similar strategy was followed by HVB through Bank of Austria. After the merger, UniCredit gained a dominant position in Eastern Europe market. The merger plan was also an opportunity for HVB. In spite of its importance in Germany and in the new Europe, HVB experienced substantial losses over the three years before the merger.[10] This was mainly due to the devaluation of real estates given the AS guarantee to the bank's creditors who successively proved to be insolvent. This situation caused severe cutbacks on labour costs, among other things. Thanks to the merger, HVB achieved a gradual recovery of accounts in the short term. The UniCredit-HVB merger seems to have been a win-win game: HVB activities were worth 476 billion (against UniCredit's 265 billion), while UniCredit was more profitable. (Return on Invested capital was 17.9% for UniCredit and 4.9% for HVB.) The merger aim was to bring the German bank up to the Italian standards: the forecast was to have a ROE equal to 18% in 2008 (foreseeing a saving of about one euro billion pre-tax). The results seem to have been achieved considering that the UniCredit group ROE was 17% in 2007, taking into account the combination with both HVB and Capitalia.

3.3.4 The BNP-Paribas and Banca Nazionale del Lavoro merger

The merger, which took place by means of an incorporation deal between the Italian Banca Nazionale del Lavoro (BNL)[11] and the French BNP-Paribas, was one of the biggest cross-border deals in Europe in the 2000s (Table 3.7).

The transaction took place by a merger by way of incorporation of BNL into BNP-Paribas on the basis of an exchange ratio of one BNP Paribas share for each 27 BNL shares. The transaction involved the merger of BNL into a company which had it's headquarter outside Italy. Therefore, BNL shareholders who disapproved the deal were recognized a withdraw option; that is, the chance of receiving a liquidation value. The transaction has assigned all of BNL's commercial banking activities[12] to a new company – named as "Banca Nazionale del Lavoro S.p.A." – under 100% control of BNP-Paribas. At the same time, the following BNL activities were directly absorbed into BNP-Paribas: the foreign subsidiaries of New York, London, Madrid and Tokyo and various equity participations, such as those belonging to the asset management companies, the *leasing* company (that is, Locafit) and BNL Vita. The merger simplified both the structure and activities of all banks involved in Italy and in the countries where BNL and BNP-Paribas operated (that is, the US, UK, Spain and Hong Kong), and helped to exploit cost and revenue synergies. The transaction, with the merger deal was concluded on the 25th of September 2007 and became effective from the 1st of October 2007. It has created

Table 3.7 BNP-Paribas and Banca Nazionale del Lavoro: key dates of the transaction

In 2005 the Spanish Banco de Bilbao (already a BNL shareholder) made a tender offer to obtain total BNL control. The tender offer failed.
On 03/02/2006, BNP-Paribas acquired 48% of BNL's equity capital from the Italian bancassurance group Unipol. Thereafter, BNP-Paribas made a tender offer on the whole BNL equity capital. Banco de Bilbao also accepted to sell its BNL's shares.
In 2007, the process of re-organization and integration of BNL into BNP-Paribas was completed.
On 01/10/2007 the transaction becomes effective.

Source: Author's own.

a Group with significant presence abroad but most of all in Italy, whose headquarters are, however, outside the Italian Republic.

After the merger, BNL has adopted a new organization of the General Direction which is divided into:

• Business lines: structures controlling the markets and supporting the commercial activities. They are: the Retail and Private Division, the Corporate Division, the BNPP-BNL *Corporate* and *Investment Banking* Division, the Production and Commercial Assistance Division (PAC) and AMS Italy – asset *Management* and Services.

• Business functions: these structures control the *governance* processes. They are the Legal, Financial, Human Resources, Risks, Communication, Auditing, *Compliance* and Permanent Controls, Estate and IT Divisions. The following services are also included: Institutional Relations, Media Relations and Studies. As for the distribution, the Bank has reorganized its commercial network in 5 wide Territory Directions (North–West, North–East, Centre, Lazio-Sardegna, South) in order to be even closer to the customers' needs thanks to a greater operational and management autonomy.

The new BNL therefore represents:

1. a multi-functional bank, specialized in financial services and products, with an international scope and also deeply rooted in the territory. Its *mission* is to create value in time for the customers, the shareholders, the employees and society as a whole, by pursuing such values as being customer-oriented, enterprise, expertise, ethics, transparency.

2. the new role of the main representative of BNP Paribas in Italy. Currently, BNL is a BNP-Paribas's core business resulting from the reorganization of the BNL group after its acquisition: it provides commercial banking services in Italy to individual and private banking clients, small- and medium-sized companies and territorial authorities.

At the beginning of 2008, BNL is the sixth largest bank in Italy in terms of both loans and deposits.[13] It has 16,300 employees, 703 branches, 23 Private Banking centres, 80 companies and territorial authorities centres and six Italian desks overseas. The merger with BNL has also some benefits on the corporate banking business areas: the enterprises division represents BNL' s traditional activity and leading expertise thanks to a comprehensive range of products and services, a national network of 80 specialized centres dedicated to the needs of more than 36,000 companies and 16,000 territorial authorities and non-profit organizations. Various financing products are provided including structured financing and in some cases, jointly with BNP Paribas's Corporate and Investment Banking or through Ifitalia.[14] BNL also offers companies and local authorities a broad range of products and services with a reputation for quality and excellence such as liquidity management, hedging instruments and import-export payments. Following the merger between BNP-Paribas and BNL, Italy became a "second domestic market" for the French group.

After a little more than a year from integration with BNP-Paribas, BNL strong growth potential was confirmed by the results of the second quarterly 2007. On the 30th June 2007, BNL reported a brokerage margin of 1.279 euro million (that is, 7.6% higher than the previous year), 251 euro million synergies released amounting to 52% of 480 million expected by 2009. The development plan 2007–09 includes the opening of at least 100 new branches and the employment of 900 personnel units, 500 of which already by 2007. The success of the integration can be observed both on the retail market (with the range of products being renovated and expanded) and in the corporate area (with five trade centres in the most important Italian cities and the opening of an Italian Desk in France and in some countries of the Mediterranean basin.

3.3.5 The Intesa and San Paolo merger

The merger between Banca Intesa and Sanpaolo IMI was the biggest domestic merger deal in Italy until 2007 (Table 3.8). The transaction, concluded on the 1st of January 2007, shows very interesting features in at least two respects: firstly, Intesa-San Paolo is one of the largest banks in the Euro zone and a key competitor in Italy with a strong branch network, composed of more than 5500 well-distributed branches throughout Italy, with market shares higher than 15% in most regions[15]; and secondly, it is the biggest competitor in the field of corporate and investment banking with a leadership

Table 3.8   Banca Intesa and San Paolo IMI Key dates of the transaction

---

26 August 2006: Intesa's Board of Directors met in Milan chaired by Mr. Giovanni Bazoli and approved the merger project guidelines with San Paolo IMI.

12 October 2006: Sanpaolo IMI Board of Directors met and approved with large majority the merger project by way of incorporation of San Paolo IMI into Banca Intesa.

1 December 2006: San Paolo IMI S.p.A. shareholder's meeting met on this day in its extraordinary session at its headquarters in piazza San Carlo and agreed on the proposal of a merger by way of incorporation between Banca Intesa and San Paolo IMI S.p.A.

28 December 2006: Deed of merger was stipulated.

End of December 2006: All relevant regulatory authorities approval.

1 January 2007: The merger is effective.

Source: Author's own.

in the factoring and in the Public Entities and Infrastructure sector (Table 3.9).

The transaction consisted of a merger by way of incorporation with an exchange ratio of 3.115 new ordinary shares of Banca Intesa for each ordinary and preferred San Paolo-IMI share.[16] According to the merger plan, Banca Intesa's Board of Directors approved an agreement with Crédit Agricole (concerning the disposal of Cassa di Risparmio di Parma e Piacenza and Banca Popolare FriulAdria as well as of 193 branches of Banca Intesa) and the development of a partnership in the asset management. The deal created a financial institution with a market capitalization of more than 60 Euro billion.

Similarly to the other deals analyzed, the "declared" motivation for the San Paolo and Intesa merger was to create benefits for all stakeholders: the deal was presented as a unique opportunity for shareholders to create value, for customers to access more competitive products and services and for employees to grow professionally. To achieve these results, San Paolo and Intesa aimed to successfully exploit growth opportunities in the Italian banking system in order to become a major national group and also enhance their presence on Central- Eastern Europe markets, exploiting their complementary presence in these countries. In detail, the integration plan presented attractive features both in the retail banking and the corporate

Table 3.9 History of Banca Intesa and San Paolo-IMI

Banca Intesa

Banca Intesa was originally created in 1925 as "La Centrale," with interests in the field of electricity production and distribution. In 1985, La Centrale incorporated the Nuovo Banco Ambrosiano, taking up its name and corporate subject-matter. The "Nuovo Banco Ambrosiano" had been formed in 1982 from a group of seven banks aiming to takeover the Banco Ambrosiano, following the latter's compulsory administrative winding-up.

In 1985, the Group took up a new structure with Nuovo Banco Ambrosiano at its top, controlling Banca Cattolica del Veneto and other companies operating in the para-banking business. In 1989, the parent company incorporated Banca Cattolica del Veneto and changed its brand name into Banco Ambrosiano del Veneto (Ambroveneto).

Ambroveneto acquired various minor banks over the 1990s (Banca Vallone, Ambroveneto Sud, Società Banche Siciliane, Caboto Group, Banca di Trento e Bolzano). In 1997, Ambroveneto carried out a major deal when Fondazione Cariplo privatized Cariplo bank allowing Ambroveneto to integrate the latter. The operation was completed at the beginning of 1998 based on a plan which designated as parent company of the new Group a bank entity having control over the whole Ambroveneto and Cariplo share parcel. To this aim, on January 1 1998, Ambroveneto unbundled the banking sector and transferred it into a fully controlled company. The company took the name of the purchasing company, Ambroveneto. The latter changed its name into Banca Intesa. On the following day, Intesa purchased the entire Cariplo's share parcel from Fondazione Cariplo. In order to extend the bank's presence in the economically strong parts of Italy, Intesa acquired the Banca Popolare FriulAndria and the Cassa di Risparmio di Parma e Piacenza in the late 1990s.

In 1999, Intesa made a preventive exchange tender offer on 70% of Banca Commerciale Italiana ordinary share capital and retained income: the deal was successfully carried out between September and October 1999. In 2000, Intesa also incorporated Cassa di Risparmio di Parma e Piacenza and, with this transaction, it also gained total control over the "new" Cassa di Risparmio di Parma e Piacenza." On 28 July 2000, Intesa approved the merger plan by way of incorporation of Ambroveneto, Cariplo and Mediocredito Lombardo into Intesa itself. The merger was realized on December 31, 2000. On February 28 and March 2001, Banca Commerciale Italiana and Intesa respectively approved the merger by way of incorporation of Banca Commerciale Italiana into Intesa, effective as of May 1, 2001. On 1 January, 2003, Intesa adopted the company name of "Banca Intesa S.p.A." or, in short, "Intesa S.p.A.," and consequently the Group's name was "Gruppo Banca Intesa" or "Gruppo Intesa", in short.

Continued

Table 3.9   Continued

San Paolo IMI

Sanpaolo IMI was born from the merger by way of incorporation of the Istituto Immobiliare Italiano (IMI) and the Istituto Bancario San Paolo di Torino, effective as of November 1, 1998.

The latter originates from the brotherhood "San Paolo Company," created in 1563 to help people in need (Monte di Pietà). In 1932, the bank obtained the status of Public Law Credit Institute. Between the 1960s and the 1990s the institute expanded its domestic network through successive acquisitions of local and medium- regional banks. In 1991, the Institute purchased the Cassa Depositi e Prestiti, the Crediop, and took the form of a national multifunctional group. Over the early 1990s, various banks – San Paolo, Banco Lariano, Banca Provinciale Lombarda, Banca Nazionale delle Comunicazioni – were incorporated.

The bank privatization process was achieved in 1997. On the date of the merger with IMI – Istituto Mobiliare Italiano- Sanpaolo stood out as a major national commercial bank, with wide-ranging products and a widespread and efficient distribution network.

IMI was founded in 1931 as a public entity, aiming to support the reconstruction and recapitalization of the Italian industry through the granting of loans in the medium and long term and the acquisition of shares. In the 1980s, the IMI group proceeded to a large restructuring of its operative sector and governance. Besides the existing business areas of specific credit service, it developed new activities within the investment banking and, together with Banca Fideuram, the professional management of savings and financial consulting.

In 2000, San Paolo IMI purchased Banco di Napoli, an institute deeply rooted in tradition and on the territory, which came to integrate the Group's distribution network with its capillary presence in the Centre-South. The "Banco" was incorporated in 2002 and successively the Group's operational branches located in the regions of Campania, Puglia, Calabria and Basilicata were unbundled into a new company named Sanpaolo Banco di Napoli, the only bank of the Group operating – from that time onwards – in the above mentioned territories.

In 2002, Sanpaolo IMI completed the integration with Gruppo Cardine, through the merger of Casse Venete and Casse Emiliano Romagnole. This transaction brought an extremely important market share into the Group, within territories with high economic potential.

The integration of the various banks into a group culture was executed rapidly. It also acknowledged the relevance for the Group of its numerous components as well as the importance of being rooted in the territory. The

Continued

Table 3.9 Continued

San Paolo IMI

model of "Banca Nazionale dei Territori" was introduced, which differentiates this Group from others. It guarantees the preservation and valorisation of the regional brands, the enhancement of local commercial branches and the strengthening of the relationship with families, small and medium businesses and communities. A model of "closeness" which consolidates the links with the territory and, by simplifying the chain of command, promotes immediate interaction between the general managers and the area managers.

In 2005, the Eurizon Financial Group was established (hereafter "Eurizon"), a business which concentrates the Group's insurance, professional asset management and asset gathering activities. The aim is to give value to these activities, featuring high professional expertise and high levels of value creation, through the separation of the production and distribution phases. The creation of Eurizon is expected to realize the high growth potential of such markets as integrated social security, wealth and revenue protection, long-term savings programmes.

Source: Author's own based on information provided on http://www.intesasanpaolo.com.

banking. Regarding the retail banking, the expected merger benefits are related to:

- a high complementary cooperation on the territory between these banks: the merger enables these banks to have a large branch network in Italy – about 5000 branches which is 17% market share – with complete and homogeneous geographical coverage on the whole Italian territory and capillary presence in the wealthiest regions of the country;
- becoming a leader in retail (family and small-company) and private banking and a stronger competitor in the distribution of asset management and life insurance services;
- a low execution risk in integrating bank activities since retail banking is the major component in both banking groups;
- a productive efficiency improvement due essentially to economies of scale gains;
- the similarity of their business models; that is, each bank group has a holding company managing and supervising various specialized banks;

- After the merger, the new banking group has a "European size" attaining international relevance and a solid leadership on the domestic market in the light of the experience made by various financial groups; it represents an ideal starting-point for a future development abroad. The New Group achieved a strong position in Italy.

Regarding corporate and investment banking businesses, Intesa-San Paolo became the largest bank, with 20% corporate lending market share. The new banking group is also the first in Italy for trade finance in the areas of project and acquisition finance and syndicated lending. In the public sector financing (for example, infrastructure), the bank targeted to become the first specialized operator. In the *Asset Management* and *Bancassurance* sector, Intesa-San Paolo operates through Eurizon; that is, the market leader in investment companies promotion and management with 19% market share. Moreover, the bank expects also to benefit from the Agreement between Intesa and Crédit Agricole in Asset Management.

A critical issue in this merger deal is the aggregation of the two banking groups in a new business model. Intesa-San Paolo is organized into five business units for each of the following banking areas: retail and private banking (also labelled "Banca dei territori"), corporate and investment banking, public financing, foreign activities, asset management and bancassurance. In detail:

- In retail and private banking, Intesa-San Paolo intends to increase the range of financial products for its customers to enable them to realize their respective projects. Financial product and services distribution is made by branches coupled with the highest quality remote channels such as phone banking, mobile banking and internet banking.
- *In the Corporate and Investment Banking* area, Intesa-San Paolo aims to support a balanced and sustainable development of medium-large firms and over a medium-long time period. The business unit becomes a global partner of a company, with deep understanding of its business strategies and offering wide-ranging financial service/consulting/*capital market* products to support its business. The key point of Intesa-San Paolo in the area of *Corporate & Investment Banking* is continuous enhancement of risk

management skills by combining both best methodologies/tools/
procedures and also in-depth information to customers.

- In the area of *Public and Infrastructure Financing*, the Intesa-San
Paolo is deeply involved in the financing of infrastructures and
public utilities offering product specialists and a dedicated network on the territory. Intesa-San Paolo also intends to use the
experience developed in Italy to increase new business abroad: as
for *retail* banking, the new group intends to strengthen its presence in Central-Eastern Europe and in the Mediterranean Basin.

- In the *Asset Management* and *Bancassurance* sectors, Intesa-San
Paolo intends to reinforce specialized company (Eurizon) development perspectives. Eurizon aims to have an organic growth
by exploiting the demand of innovative social security pro-
grams, medium-term saving products and innovative financial
products. At the same time, Eurizon is expected to benefit from
being a global player, while other companies tend to separate
"production" and "distribution" of financial services. For example, Banca Intesa and Sanpaolo operate through two specialized
companies in the bankassurance business; that is, Intesa Vita
and Eurizon Vita.

Over the first year after the merger, IntesaSan Paolo achieved positive results. In the first nine months of 2007, the bank registered a
consolidated post- tax revenue of 6.85 euro billion, (+79% compared
to the previous year mainly due to extra-ordinarily disposal income).
The "normalized" post-tax revenue over the same period was of
3.76 euro billion (+3.7% compared to the previous year). In a press
release[17] of the group chaired by Mr. Bazoli and Mr. Passera, Intesa-
San Paolo was reported to have a positive trend, which was obtained
against a complex market background due to the synergies deriving
from the merger and to the increased number of customers. (There
were more than 150,000 net customers in Italy over the nine months
during which the merger became effective.) Over the same period,
operational net proceeds increased by 5.5% (13.72 Euro billion), net
interests increased by 11.1% (7.27 Euro billion). Net commissions
income dropped by 2.3% (4.78 Euro billion) since Intesa-San Paolo
aimed to also create customer value after the merger deal, by reducing prices to the worth suggested by best practices, and cleaning-up
ATM/POS fees on operations made by the customers of either of the

two former-banks through the other partner's network. In details, fees on current account decreased by 11.2%, brokerage and selling commissions declined by 10.2%, while income on released guarantees and distribution of insurance products increased by 13.9% and 4.9%, respectively.

3.3.6 The UniCredit and Capitalia merger

After the Intesa and San Paolo-IMI merger (effective as of 1/1/2007), another important domestic merger in Italy was that between UniCredit and Capitalia. First announced in May 2007 and completed at the beginning of the last quarter the same year (Table 3.10), UniCredit and Capitalia merger is interesting for (at least) two reasons. Firstly, the M&A between UniCredit and Capitalia has been one of the largest domestic merger deals in the 2000s, involving two of the biggest Italian banks (Table 3.11). The merge created a banking group with over 40 million clients, total assets of 960 euro billion, 9200 branches (5000 of which are in Italy), a presence[18] in 50 countries and 170,000 employees. With regard to market capitalization, the new UniCredit – Capitalia is the second banking group in Europe (behind the British HSBC and in front of the Swiss UBS) and the world's fifth largest bank. The combined market worth of the new UniCredit-Capitalia bank is of 96.7 Euro billion. Secondly, both Capitalia and Unicredit banks were very active competitors in the retail banking business, but also in the asset management, private and investment banking businesses. The integration of the business activities of these two banking groups in a single entity provides some interesting features.

The M&A transaction was implemented via a merger by way of incorporation of Capitalia into UniCredito Italiano on the basis of an exchange ratio of 1.12 UniCredit new ordinary shares for each Capitalia ordinary share. This exchange rate implies a pre-leakage premium to Capitalia's shareholders of 23.5% on spot market price, 24.4% over the three-month average market price and 25.9% over the 12-month average market price. The implied offer price for Capitalia is of 8.46 euro per share.

As for the deal purposes, the Unicredit and Capitalia merger intended to consolidate two primary bank groups in retail banking and improve their competitiveness in other banking sectors, such as consumer credit, leasing, factoring, personal financial advisory and

Table 3.10 The history of UniCredit and Capitalia banks

UniCredit	Capitalia
UniCredito Italiano was born in 1998 from the merger between Credito Italiano banking group (composed by Credito Italiano, ROLO Banca 1473 COS'E' QUESTA DATA?) and UniCredito (composed by Cariverona, Cassa di Risparmio di Torino e Cassamarca). In 1999, Cassa di Risparmio di Trento e Rovereto (Caritro) and Cassa di Risparmio di Trieste also joined UniCredito Italia Value.	Capitalia was born in 2002 from the combination of Gruppo Bancaroma and Bipop-Carire banks.
	At that time, Gruppo Bancaroma included the holding company, the Mediocredito Centrale (MCC), Banco di Sicilia and Gruppo Mediocredito Centrale.
The above-mentioned seven banks merged into UniCredito Italiano between July and September 2002. On 1st January 2003, UniCredito Italiano adopted the Unicredit logo.	The origins of Bipop Carire Group date back to 1999, with the merger by way of incorporation between Bipop and Cassa di Risparmio di Reggio Emilia.
Three new banks were created: one for retail customers (that is, families and small business) labelled as "UniCredit Banca," one for affluent clients labelled as "UniCredit Private Banking," and a third bank for corporations, labelled and "UniCredit Banca d'Impresa."	Capitalia has a direct fundraising of 90 Euro billion (compared to 80 Euro billion at 31 December 2004), over 1900 branches in Italy, about five million customers, over 28 thousand employees and about 1700 financial promoters. As such, Capitalia imposed itself as the leader competitor in Italy for asset gathering (that is, saving collection and management), consumer finance, investment banking and in the traditional banking activity.
In 2003, Banca dell'Umbria and Cassa di Risparmio di Carpi teamed up with UniCredit.	
In 2005, the UniCredit merger with the German bank HypoVereinsbank AG (HVB-Group) led to pouring tender offers on Bank Austria Creditanstalt and BPH.	

Source: Author's own based on information provided on http://www.unicredit-capitalia.eu.

investment banking. The transaction is also expected to increase the Earnings per Share; that is, 17% over the period 2007–09 versus 14% stand-alone for both Unicredit and Capitalia and 11% for the main peer-competitors. The Unicredit and Capitalia M&A also aims to increase the normalized EPS accretion (for Unicredit shareholders

Table 3.11 UniCredit and Capitalia: key dates of the transaction

18 May 2007: Chairman of Capitalia Cesare Geronzi and Managing Director Alessandro Profumo illustrate the project of a merger by way of incorporation to the Bank of Italy, the Antitrust Authority (Italian Authority on Fair Competition), the Consob (the Italian Security and Exchange Commission), the ISVAP (Insurance Companies Supervising Authority) and to the Minister of Finance Padoa-Schioppa.
20 May 2007: UniCredit and Capitalia Boards of Directors meet in Milan and Rome respectively. Both boards approve the merger project by way of incorporation of Capitalia into UniCredito ItaliaValue. Besides, Unicredit and Capitalia Boards of Directors call an extraordinary meeting of their respective shareholders to approve the merger and the relevant changes in bylaws.
30 July 2007: UniCredit shareholders approves the merger by way of incorporation plan of Capitalia S.p.A. and UniCredito Italiano S.p.A., already co-opted in May. The exchange ratio is fixed at 1,12 UniCredit new ordinary shares for one Capitalia ordinary share.
18 September 2007: The Antitrust Authority clears the merger between UniCredit and Capitalia.
25 September 2007: The contract providing for the merger of Capitalia into UniCredit is signed.
1 October 2007: The M&A deal becomes effective while Capitalia S.p.A. ceases to exist and its shares are withdrawn from trading as of this date.

Source: Author's own.

from 2009 onwards and for Capitalia shareholders as of the first year) and Dividend Per Share (growing progressively over the coming years).

The Core Tier I ratio has been confirmed at 6,8% by 2008. Overall, the new UniCredit expects to achieve substantial pre-tax synergies: 0.3 euro billion in 2008 (100% due to cost savings), 0.8 euro billion in 2009 (3/4 due to cost savings and ¼ to revenue synergies) and around 1.2 Euro billion in 2010 (2/3 due to cost savings and 1/3 to revenue synergies).[19] The estimated net present value of all synergies is 7 euro billion, which is 39% of Capitalia' s stock market capitalization. Cost savings are expected to be generated in the IT and back – office (45% of all cost synergies), central function[20] (20%), product factories (20%) and branch network reorganization (15%). One-off restructuring charges, estimated to around 1.1 Euro billion (135% of cost synergies), will be included in the 2007 and 2008 cost-income statement.

The value creation and the EPS growth is expected to be mainly due to substantial economy of scale and scope gains. Namely, about 2/3 of pre-tax synergies will arise from cost savings and 33% from revenue enhancements.

Substantial benefits are also expected from the aggregation of the retail branch networks that are highly complementary. As reported in a joint press release of 20th May 2007, the combination of UniCredit and Capitalia retail branch networks aimed to:

1. achieve a thorough national retail network over 5000 branches and 7000 ATMs in Italy with limited expected overlap;
2. strengthen the retail penetration in underweighted business sectors, which still have high growth potential;
3. combine very well-known brands such as the "UniCredit Banca," "Banca di Roma" and "Banca di Sicilia." Cost and revenue efficiency gains should also be due to the enhancement of UniCredit's European profile since UniCredit has:[21]
   - four core markets: Italy (47% of total revenues and 46% of risk weighted assets), Germany (17% of total revenues and 28% of risk weighted assets), Austria (10% of total revenues and 11% of risk weighted assets) and Central-Eastern Europe (17% of total revenues and 13% of risk weighted assets). As such, 53% of overall revenues originate outside Italy and 54% of risk weighted assets are invested outside Italy.
   - a substantial market power in these domestic markets: the market share is of 15.8% (second largest) in Italy, 4.6% (third largest) in Germany, 18.8% (first largest) in Austria. Regarding Central-Eastern Europe, UniCredit operates in 17 countries and its total assets is twice the next competitor.

The UniCredit and Capitalia merger also aims to enhance a well–balanced business mix. Combining both banks' activities, retail banking accounts for 38% of total revenues and 24% of total risk-weighted assets. Corporate banking accounts for 20% of revenues and 39% of total risk-weighted assets. Market and investment banking activities accounts for 14% of revenues and 16% of total risk-weighted assets. Private banking and asset management cover 11% of revenues and 7% of total risk-weighted assets.

Two critical issues in this merger deal concern the corporate governance definition of the new UniCredit group and the aggregation of the two banking groups in a new business model[22]. Regarding the first point, the UniCredit Group corporate governance was worked out on account of the Italian Stock Exchange regulation and recommendations. For example, UniCredit has adopted a self-discipline code for brokers dealing with investment services in compliance with the code of conduct of the banking and financial sector set by the Italian Bankers Association (Associazione Bancaria Italiana, ABI) and the self-discipline code of listed companies, which aim at guaranteeing market transparency. UniCredit Group has also adopted a traditional management system based on two bodies[23] appointed by shareholders, and set up an internal dealing procedure to monitor the financial deals made by key people within the Group. The Board of Directors is made up of twenty-three members: one tier board with four representatives of Capitalia has been co-opted in the UniCredit board.

Regarding the second issues, the new UniCredit group has adopted a divisional business model focusing on customer segments (that is, retail, private and corporate customers) and on global financial product areas. As such, Capitalia's activities – including IT and Operations activities were integrated into the UniCredit divisions as follows:

- In Italy retail services had been offered through three separated brands – UniCredit Banca, Banca di Roma, Banco di Sicilia – with clear regional responsibilities. They had leveraged on strong local roots in order to optimize its commercial effectiveness by exploiting these strong brands. To this aim, the subsidiaries within the group were re-allocated among the three banks on the basis of their specific competence in the territory; for instance, UniCredit Banca focus on the North of Italy, Banca di Roma on the Centre-South of Italy and Banco di Sicilia in Sicily. Bipop-Carire was incorporated in UniCredit Banca.
- Specific retail business such as consumer credit, credit card and mortgage products, managed by Fineco Bank, were transferred to UniCredit's specialized factories. UniCredit was the fourth largest company in consumer credit with 8% market share and first in mortgage with 24% market share. The new value of the combined production is around 4 Euro billion in the consumer credit business and 11 Euro billion in the mortgage sectors.

- Corporate and private banking services were offered by a single bank in each sector – UniCredit Banca d'Impresa and UniCredit Private Banking, respectively. All activities from Banca di Roma, Banco di Sicilia and Bipop-Carire were transferred to the two UniCredit specialized banks. This lead to the enhancement of leasing/factoring businesses through MCC operations into Locat and UniCredit Factoring, which were the first and fourth largest companies in these segments with combined market share of 20.6% and 11.9%, respectively. Financial products are developed through global service factories with the complete integration of UniCredit and Capitalia's activities.
- Market and Investment banking services, which were offered by specialized UniCredit companies and by all Capitalia and Mediocredito Centrale (MCC) activities, were transferred to these specialized banks. MCC became the bank group reference company for public entities funding.
- Asset gathering services are offered through Fineco that became the group reference company in this segment being a leader company with over 3.000 personal financial advisors and 25.9 Euro billion managed assets. Fineco also maintains responsibility for trading on-line being one of the leading players in this business.
- All asset management activities are grouped under the Pioneer Global Asset Management (one the largest company in this business with 280 Euro billion of combined property managed, 156 Euro billion of which in Italy). This is in order to exploit scale economies and a strong global brand.
- IT & back-office operations run by "Capitalia Informatica" were transferred to UniCredit Global Information Services (UGIS) and UniCredit Processes and Administration (UPA), respectively.[24]

3.3.7 The ABN-AMRO acquisition: Barclays vs. Royal Bank of Scotland led consortium

Over 2007, ABN AMRO was contended by two British banks: Barclays and Royal Bank of Scotland (RBS), which lead a consortium composed by RBS, Santander and Fortis.

As summarized in Table 3.12, ABN AMRO and Barclays met with the regulatory authorities to discuss their merger on the 21st March 2007; two days later, the merger plan between the two banks was publicly announced. The merger between Barclays and ABN AMRO

Table 3.12   ABN-AMRO acquisition: Barclays vs. Royal Bank of Scotland: key dates of the transaction and offers

21 March 2007: The meetings between ABN AMRO and Barclays with the regulatory authorities concerning the merger were started.

23 April 2007: The merger plan between ABN AMRO and Barclays was announced. ABN AMRO Board of Directors approved the offer in shares of 67 billion Euro (that is, 36.25 euros per share). Once the transaction was concluded, ABN AMRO shareholders would obtain 3.225 Barclays's ordinary per each ABN AMRO share (controlling 48% of the "new" bank and the residual 52% of the new bank would be given to Barclays's shareholders). After a month's negotiation, the agreement was drawn up. At the same time, ABN AMRO disposed its controlled "Lasalle Bank Corporation" (that is, the American division of ABN AMRO) to Bank of America for 21 USD billion (approximately 15.4 Euro billion). On the same day, the RBS, Santander and Fortis cancelled the meeting with ABN AMRO board (scheduled in the afternoon) waiting for updates on the disposal of Lasalle bank to Bank America. In a joint press notice, RBS, Santander and Fortis stated that they "needed to know the circumstances under which the said disposal may be stopped" and enquired about ABN AMRO's intentions as this bank was ready to pay up to 40 Euro per share.

25 April 2007: The Dutch commercial court stopped the selling of Lasalle Bank to Bank of America since this deal was deemed to damage the ABN AMRO shareholders' rights. At this point, the concert party of RBS – Santander-Fortis consortium resumed their counter-offer making an offer of 39 euro per share – that is, 38,40 Euro per share to be paid 70% cash with the granting of an extra-ordinary dividend of 0.6 euro – launching a bid of 71 Euro billion for the acquisition of ABN AMRO against the Barclays's offer of 65 Euro billion.

26 April 2007: ABN AMRO announced the disclosure of its accounting books to the RBS-led consortium.

27 April 2007: One more coup de theatre, the RBS – led consortium extended its public acquisition offer to 100% ABN AMRO equity capital.

6 May 2007: The RBS-led consortium launched a 24.5 USD billion counter-offer for the Lasalle Bank Corporation, i.e. the American division of ABN AMRO.

14 May 2007: Upon request of the Dutch authorities, the RBS-led consortium produced evidence that its offer was not conditioned by any funding or grants and that ABN AMRO was worth approximately 71 billion Euro.

18 May 2007: The RBS started negotiation with Bank of America to reach an agreement on Lasalle bank.

Continued

Table 3.12 Continued

13 June 2007: Santander bank sold Spanish property assets for 4 euro billion to finance its participation in the offer.

1 July 2007: The Barclays obtained from AFM (i.e. the Dutch supervisory authority) to postpone the deadline to July 23rd to officially present the documents relating to its public acquisition offer.

23 July 1997: ABN AMRO stated that it will assess " in a fair and clear way" the two competing offers made by the RBS led consortium and Barclays, amounting to 71 and 67.5 Euro billion respectively.

6 August 2007: Final Fortis shareholders' approval of the 71 euro billion tender offer to take over ABN AMRO.

4 October 2007: Barclays launched its bid to be paid basically by its own shares. (ABN AMRO was evaluated 67 Euro billion, against 71 Euro billion cash offered by the RBS led consortium.) This offer obviously discouraged ABN AMRO's shareholders from selling their shares to Barclays.

8 October 2007: The RBS-led consortium takeover bid for the acquisition of the Dutch Bank reached 86% of consent.

10 October 2007: The RBS consortium declared its bid unconditionally.

2 November 2007: The offer received a consent for 1.826.332.482 ABN AMRO ordinary shares (98.8% of equity capital).

Source: Author's own.

would create a bank with a capital share of approximately 140 billion Euro. This is the sixth in the world and second in Europe after another British group, HSBC. The new group would have more than 47 million customers, with presence in 50 countries and 220 thousand employees, even though this figure would be reduced by employment cuts ensuing any merger operation. The new banking group would hold a key position in the consumer market activities spreading all over the world (including the US), as well as in the financial an credit card areas. (The financial are is namely ETF and investment banking.)

Stock exchange markets greeted the planned transaction positively. After the announcement, various investment banks increased ABN AMRO's target price. This is perhaps because both the Dutch and the British banks seemed to have good chances in the deal. Nevertheless, Barclays was not the only bank having moved forward to purchase ABN AMRO. Many were the claimants, including the Spanish Santander and Banco Bilbao Vizcaya Argentaria as well as the RBS, ING, Bank of America, Société Générale and BNP Paribas. The Dutch were also contended several times by private equity and hedge fund.

Among these banks, RBS, Santander and Fortis were ready to pay up to 40 Euro per ABN share on two conditions: ABN must open its accounting books to the consortium, and cancel the previously announced sale of its subsidiary LaSalle Bank to Bank of America. Indeed, RBS was particularly interested in Lasalle Bank. If this bank disappeared, the consortium would no longer make sense. Once the Dutch commercial court stopped the selling of the Lasalle Bank to Bank of America and ABN opened its accounting books to the consortium in April 2007, the RBS – Santader-Fortis consortium made a 39 euro per share offer. This figure corresponds to 38.49 euro per share, 70% of which was cash, and with additional distribution of dividends of 0.6 euro. The Barclays bid intended to pay for ABN acquisition mostly by its own shares. The estimated value of the Dutch bank was 67 Euro billion against the 71 euro billion cash offered by the rival RBS-led consortium. Obviously, ABN AMRO's shareholders found the RBS-led consortium offer more convenient, although ABN AMRO privileged Barclays's offer and attempted to protect itself from hostile RBS tender offers: ABN AMRO was therefore officially acquired on 9th October 2007, when the public offer from RBS-led consortium on the Dutch bank reached 86% of approvals, which went up to 98.8% in November.[25]

Following ABN AMRO acquisition, one of the RBS-led consortium's tasks will be to persuade the market that the acquisition of the Dutch bank has a strategic purpose and will result in substantial profit gains. The consortium has clearly pointed out its intention of dismantling ABN AMRO, which boasts 4500 branches in 53 countries and controls Antonveneta in Italy. The three banks in the consortium aimed to share the assets of ABN: RBS was especially interested in LaSalle, Santander in

ABN's business in Brazil and Italy, and Fortis wanted ABN's business in Holland. Namely, ABN AMRO's activities are unbundled between RBS, Fortis and Santader to strengthen their market position as follows:

• Santander has obtained all activities in Latin America and Italy (for example, Banco Real in Brazil and Banca Antonveneta in Italy) and some inter-banking activities. Regarding Brazil, Banco Real is the fourth largest financial institution in Brazil, a market that Santander entered in 2000 with the purchase of Banespa and the fifth largest financial institution in Brazil. By acquiring Banco Real, Santander becomes the third ranked player in Brazil, behind only Banco de Brazil and Itaú. The deal is therefore a perfect geographical fit for Santander: Brazil has strong potential for restructuring and Santander doubled its market share. The deal would increase Latin America's contribution to Santander's overall profits to 45% after the deal (37% before the deal). Regarding Italy, Santander already attempted to enter this market in the past without achieving good results, apart from the consumer loan sector.

- With this deal, Santander will come away with Antonveneta, one of the eight largest financial institutions in Italy.
- Fortis will control the Dutch activities of the global asset management and "private clients" areas.
- RBS will manage the US activities (for example, the LaSalle bank), the "global clients" and "wholesale" activities in Brazil, Asia and Europe.

The assessment of the effect of the M&A deal above is strongly influenced by the crisis in the banking industry since 2008, which has severely affected ABN AMRO, RBS and Fortis. Due to the banking crisis, RBS announced (22 April 2008) its plan to raise 12 GBP billion in new equity capital to offset a write-down of 5.9 GBP billion due to bad investments and the shoring up of its reserves following the purchase of ABN AMRO. The Dutch government nationalized the divisions owned by Fortis, while the UK government is currently in effective control of the divisions allocated to RBS due to its financial bail-out of the British bank.

3.4   Conclusion

This chapter answers a simple question: why do bank merge? While it is evident that European banks have increasingly merged in the 2000s, these operations have various motives. Our analysis focused on horizontal and related M&A deals since these are the most common and relevant in the banking industry. Generally, M&As aim to create shareholder value and this can be achieved through various drivers. Among all possible drivers, we analyzed revenue enhancement, cost reduction and new business opportunities. Indeed, we observed that there are also non-value maximization motives, essentially due to the managers and Governments' interference in the consolidation process. After discussing the M&A motives, we analyzed seven cases of big merger deals in European banking: the Royal Bank of Scotland (leading a consortium comprising also Fortis and Banco Santander) and ABN AMRO in 2007, the UniCredit bank and Capitalia in 2007, BNP Paribas and Banca Nazionale del Lavoro in 2006, the UniCredito Italiano and Bayerische Hypo und Vereinsbank in 2005, Banco Santander Central Hispano and Abbey National plc in 2004, HSBC Holdings and Crédit Commercial de France in 2000.

4
M&A of Financial Institutions: Literature Review

4.1 Introduction

There is a large number of studies dealing with M&As in the financial service industry. Despite this, it is not possible to find straightforward evidence of the M&A effects. Recently, DeYoung et al., (2009) have reviewed more than 100 studies dealing with M&As in financial sectors and note that

> there is little consensus as to the effects of this consolidation on industry performance. For example, the extant literature provides no consistent evidence regarding whether the participating financial firms benefit on average from M&As, whether the customers of these firms benefit on average from M&As, or whether societal risks have increased or decreased as a result of these M&As" (DeYoung et al., 2009, forthcoming).

With regard to the approach used to analyze the effects produced by bank consolidation, the phenomenon can be examined from either a static or a dynamic point of view (Berger et al., 1999). In the first case, the analysis intends to connect the potential consequences of consolidation with some banks' features, such as size, associated with consolidation. These studies are a useful source of relative information for the banks, but do not provide a direct evaluation of the results obtained from M&A operations. Vice versa, the dynamic approach recognizes that M&As may involve changes in organizational focus or managerial behaviour. As a consequence, these studies compare either the behaviour of banks before and after M&As or the behaviour of banks recently involved in a consolidation deal in a moment prior and successive to the operation itself.

This chapter provides an extensive review of the most recent studies applying the dynamic approach, which is preferred to the static approach because it provides analysts with a more reliable and accurate assessment of the impact produced by M&A operations. The chapter is organized as follows: first, we review studies assessing the impact of consolidation deals over a short time period (Section 4.1); next, we analyze the M&A effects on the banks' productive efficiency and operating performance over a five-year-time period (Sections 4.2 and 4.3 respectively). We also discuss which lessons may be drawn from the existing literature (Section 4.4).

4.2   The M&A effects over the short term

Dynamic studies have usually applied the event study method to investigate the M&A effect over a short period of time. The event study evaluates the benefits resulting from M&As by estimating the reaction of the market price of quoted banks involved in the operation around the time of disclosure of the operation itself (announcement date). With respect to methodologies based on the analysis of accounting data, the *event study* exploits the market data which better explain the actual economic effects produced by the operation on the announcement date of the transaction. Beitel and Schiereck (2001) suggest that the event study is the most direct methodology available to determine the impact of the M&A operation on the creation or reduction of value for the shareholders of the firms involved.

In the event study, the analysis focuses on Abnormal Returns[1] (ARs) of both the acquiring and the target firms (considered separately). The total variation of the shareholders' wealth is obtained as the weighted average of both the acquiring and acquired bank ARs: this measure can be considered as a representation of the variation in the shareholder value following the M&A operation. In other terms, this measure quantifies the creation of value estimated by the market. The event study methodology is not immune from criticism because it focuses on the analysis of the effects of an M&A operation in the short run exclusively. When considering longer periods of time, the results become less trustworthy because (it increases) there is a greater probability that market price variations are determined by factors other than the merger. Even though the literature agrees on the fact that the period analyzed (event window) must be short and near the date of disclosure of the operation, there are still a number of uncertainties on the optimal length of the time span to be considered in the event period.

Table 4.1 reports a list of the principal event studies carried out in the banking market, among which are the works of Houston and Ryngaert (1994), Madura and Wiant (1994), Zhang (1995), Cybo-Ottone and Murgia (1996), Becher (2000), Cybo-Ottone and Murgia (2000), DeLong (2001), Beitel and Schiereck (2001), Cornett et al., (2003), Beitel et al., (2004), and Kiymaz (2004), Penas and Unal (2004), Henock (2004), Lepetit et al., (2004), Olson and Pagano (2005), Campa and Hernando (2006), DeLong and DeYoung (2007), Gupta and Lalatendu (2007), Schmautzer (2008) and Ekkayokkaya et al., (2009).

Houston and Ryngaert (1994) analyze a sample of 153 M&A operations which took place between 1985 and 1991. They observe that:

1. the acquiring banks have recorded a loss of value;
2. the target firm has increased value for its shareholders;
3. at the aggregate level, a significant effect on the value of the involved banks is not observed;
4. the value created is greater when:
   a. the acquiring banks have good performance in the phase prior to the merger
   b. there is a strong territory overlap between the two firms involved in the M&A.

Madura and Wiant (1994) analyze a sample of 152 consolidation operations between banks conducted in the period 1983–87. They consider a long time span (36 months) successive to the date of the announcement. According to the authors, the acquirer's average Cumulated Abnormal Returns (CAR) are negative in the 36 months successive to the announcement date and justify such loss with an extremely high acquisition price of the target firm. Conversely, Pilloff and Santomero (1997, p. 11) believe that negative ARs are due to minor benefits than those expected or to a reorganization of the expectations formulated by the market at the time of the announcement.

Table 4.1   Studies using the event study method to analyze M&A in banking

Authors	Year	World region	Period	No. of M&A deals
Hannan, Walken	1989	US	1982–87	43
Hawawini, Swary	1990	US	1972–87	123
Baradwaj et al.,	1990	US	1980–87	53
Allen, Cebenoyan	1991	US	1979–86	138
Cornett, De	1991	US	1982–86	152
Cornett, Tehranian	1992	US	1982–87	30
Baradwaj et al.,	1992	US	1981–87	108
Houston, Ryngaert	1994	US	1985–91	153
Madura, Wiant	1994	US	1983–87	152
Palia	1994	US	1984–87	48
Seidel	1995	US	1989–91	123
Zhang	1995	US	1980–90	107
Cybo-Ottone, Murgia	1996	Europe	1988–95	26
Rudgins, Seifert	1996	US	1970–89	160
Siems	1996	US	1995	19
Pilloff	1996	US	1982–91	48
Houston, Ryngaert	1997	US	1985–92	209
Subrahmanyam et al.,	1997	US	1982–87	263
Banerjee et al.,	1998	US	1990–95	92
Toyne, Tripp	1998	US	1991–95	68
Cyree, DeGennaro	1999	US	1989–95	132
Kwan, Eisenbeis	1999	US	1989–96	3844
Tourani-Rad et al.,	1999	Europe	1989–96	56
Cornett et al.,	2000	US	1988–95	423
Cybo-Ottone et al.,	2000	Europe	1987–98	72
Becher	2000	US	1980–97	558
Brewer et al.,	2000	US	1990–98	327
Houston et al.,	2000	US	1985–96	64
Kane	2000	US	1991–98	110
Karceski et al.,	2000	Norway	1983–96	39
Zollo et al.,	2000	US	1977–98	579
De Long	2001	US	1988–95	280
Beitel, Schiereck	2001	Europe	1985–97	98
Cornett et al.	2003	US	1988–95	423
Beitel et al.,	2004	Europe	1985–2000	98
Kiymaz	2004	US	1989–99	355
Penas and Unal	2004	US	1991–98	38
Henock	2004	US	1993–99	227

Continued

Table 4.1 Continued

Authors	Year	World region	Period	No. of M&A deals
Lepetit et al.,	2004	Europe	1991–2001	180
Olson and Pagano	2005	US	1987–2000	516
Campa and Hernando	2006	Europe	1998–2002	244
DeLong and DeYoung	2007	US	1987–1999	216
Gupta and Lalatendu	2007	US	1981–2004	503
Schmautzer	2008	US-Europe	1985–2005	96
Ekkayokkaya et al.,	2009	Europe	1990–2004	993

Source: Author's own, new elaboration of Figure 1 in Beitel and Schiereck (2001, p. 4).

Zhang (1995) examines a sample of 107 M&A operations undertaken in the decade 1980–1990 in the US banking market with the following results:

1. a significant increase in share price of both firms involved in proximity of the announcement date of the operation;
2. the shareholders of the target firm obtain greater benefits than those of the acquiring firm;
3. the incremental value decreases as the dimensions of the target bank increases with respect to the acquiring bank or increases by the degree of geographic overlap between the target and acquiring firm.

Cybo-Ottone and Murgia (1996) analyze 26 mergers of financial institutions in 13 European countries between 1988 and 1995, which show a transfer of wealth from the acquiring firm to the target firm. The authors observe that, on average, acquiring firms have a negative AR while that of the target firm is close to zero.

Becher (2000) examines a sample of 558 mergers of US banks in the period 1980–97 using an *event window* of 36 days (–30, +5). The results show an increase of 22% of shareholder value of the target firm – a variation near zero for the acquiring bank. The combined calculation of the two values determine an increase of 3% (Becher, 2000, p. 199). Subsequently, Becher (2000) focuses on M&As occurred over the 1990's and finds that M&A produced positive results: target firms notably increase their market value, acquiring firms register positive ARs (obtaining results with an enhanced statistical significance compared to the results obtained when analysing M&As over the '80s). Combined entities also have positive ARs. Moreover, the author notes that the acquiring firm's ARs are substantially influenced by the event windows length. Selecting an *event window* inferior to 11 days (–5, +5), acquiring firms record a significant market value reduction, while acquiring firms and combined entities record positive ARs. As a whole, Becher (2000) shows that M&A deals produced positive effects on shareholder value, especially for deals carried out during the 1990s.

Cybo-Ottone and Murgia (2000) analyze a sample of 72 European banks with a market value greater than 100 million dollars during the period 1988–1997. The results show that the markets reaction, at the moment when the M&A transaction is announced, determines a combined performance for both the target and acquiring firm in both statistical significance and economic relevance. These results are influenced by positive ARs both for domestic bank mergers and bank and insurance mergers from the point of view of product diversification. On the other hand, according to the authors, the announcement of an M&A activity between banks from different countries does not create a positive response on the markets.

DeLong (2001) analyzes a sample of 280 mergers announced between US banks in the period 1988–95. The mergers have been classified into four types based on the activity carried out by the involved firms in the operation and by the geographic characteristics of the merger: domestic merger and *cross border*, in which the firms involved have a similar activity; domestic mergers and *cross border* in which the firms involved have different activities. The results show that the domestic mergers with similar activities lead to a significant creation of value, while for the other types of mergers the author does not find positive results.

Bietel and Schiereck (2001) analyze 98 mergers between 1985 and 2000 among European banks. They have found significant positive ARs both for the target and the combined firms. These resulted from the accounting collection of both acquiring and acquired bank, and non statistically significant ARs for shareholders of acquiring banks. Overall, M&As created shareholder value on net basis since the combined entity mean CARs are substantially positive and more than 60% of deals analyzed generated positive CARs. Following DeLong (2001), Beitel and Schiereck (2001) also examine the relevance of geographic and production diversification with the merger and find that:

1. productive diversification in European M&As has a positive impact on the creation of shareholder value;
2. the geographic diversification appears to have some positive impact on shareholder value only for acquiring banks.

Beitel et al., (2004) examine 98 mergers between European banks during the period 1985–2000. Through the use of a regression analysis, the authors identify 13 variables[2] to study the explicit factors of ARs.

According to the results, M&A operations create value for the acquiring firm when the target firm is of modest size and with an inferior level of efficiency compared to the acquiring firm. Target banks create shareholder value especially when there are substantial production and distribution synergies with the acquirer and the new bank has great potential to enhance profit efficiency.

Kiymaz (2004) proposes an event study on a sample of 227 international[3] M&As that involved US financial institutions during the period 1989–99. The results show that:

1. the US acquiring banks substantially created shareholder value around the announcement date, while acquired firms experienced irrelevant gains;
2. the localization of the foreign acquired and acquiring firms influences the value created by M&A operations;
3. macroeconomic factors are very important to explain the value creation within M&A operations.

Penas and Unal (2004) performed an event study of a sample of 38 M&A deals over the period 1991–98 to assess if acquirer banks benefit from the lower cost of funds in post-merger debt issues. The authors find evidence of bondholder gains and of a lower cost of debt post-merger.

Henock (2004) analyzes 227 US mergers between 1993 and 1999. His aim is to compare the premiums paid and the market reactions to mergers involving bidders who have been subject to takeover speculations as opposed to those involving bidders who have not been targeted. The author finds evidence of significant returns to bank shareholders in takeover speculation deals, while acquisitions designed to prevent takeover (defensive deals) are found to destroy shareholder value.

Lepetit et al., (2004) analyze a sample of 180 M&A announced deals between 1991 and 2001 in 13 European markets. By using a GARCH model to estimate abnormal returns, the authors find a positive and significant increase in value for target banks.

Olson and Pagano (2005) analyze the impact of bank mergers in the long run performance of the acquiring bank. The pay attention to the cumulative difference between the stock's return and the return on a relevant stock index benchmark during 1987–2000. They focus on the three-year cumulative buy-and-hold returns for each deal on a cross-sectional basis. By using a sample of 516 mergers of US publicly traded bank holding companies, the authors provide evidence of shareholder gains related to pre-merger growth rates.

Campa and Hernando (2006) analyze a sample of 244 M&A deals between 1998 and 2002 in European banking to investigate shareholder value effects. They find evidence of positive abnormal returns to target shareholders with no significant influence on the bidder's stock prices.

DeLong and DeYoung (2007) offer a new explanation of why academic studies typically fail to find value creation in bank mergers. The authors present four formal hypotheses: two of them concern the value creation by bank M&As and how it relates to information spill over from previous bank M&As; and the other two are about stock market valuations of bank M&As and how they relate to information spill over from previous bank M&As. By analyzing a sample of 216 M&As in US publicly listed commercial banks between 1987 and 1999, the authors find positive abnormal, yet short-lived, returns relating to bank merger announcements. They also find that the short-run market reactions as well as the long-run merger performance tend to be related to the number of mergers that took place in years prior to the deal announcement, suggesting spill over learning.

Gupta and Lalatendu (2007) examine the influence of the relative size of bidders and targets by analyzing a sample of 503 mergers between US publicly listed banks over the period 1981–2004. The authors find evidence of asymmetric effects on stockholder returns. In short, acquiring firms lose; target firms gain. The value of the acquirer-target pair increases on average.

Schmautzer (2008) analyzes 96 announced international cross-border bank mergers between 1985 and 2005. Results show that target shareholders gains outweigh bidder losses in the case of cross-border deals involving European, US and other banks – particularly when relatively cost efficient banks are acquired. Ekkayokkaya et al., (2009) use an event study approach to examine bidder returns from a sample of 993 M&A deals among European banks between 1990–2004. The authors find that bank/non-bank deals result in positive abnormal returns, especially in pre-Euro transactions.

4.3   The M&A effects over the medium-long term: the impact on banks' efficiency

Over the medium-long term, the M&A effects have been usually analyzed focusing on the banks' productive efficiency. These studies compare the efficiency levels of the banks involved in the M&A prior to and successive to the deal. Or, conversely, the efficiency levels of banks directly involved in M&As are compared to similar banks not involved in such operations. The first studies conducted go back to the early 1980's (see Frieder and Apilado, 1983; Rhoades, 1998; and Rose 1987a, 1987b). However, most recent studies are from Berger and Humphrey (1992), DeYoung (1993), Akhavein et al., (1997), Resti (1998), Rhoades (1998), Lang and Welzel (1999), Fried et al., (1999), Haynes and Thompson (1999), Hughes et al., (1999), Huizinga et al., (2001), Cuesta and Area (2002), Berger and Mester (2003), Wang (2003), Carbo-Valverde and Berger and Humphrey (2004), Humphrey and Vale (2004) and Koetter (2005), De Guevara and Maudos (2007), Ashton and Pham (2007) and Behr and Heid (2008).

Berger and Humphrey (1992) analyze large M&A deals with total assets greater than a billion dollars in the US banking system during the 1980s. Applying the Distribution-Free Approach (DFA) methodology of efficiency estimation, the authors observe that, on average, mergers do not bring about any increase of the x-efficiency. The effects produced by the merger have also been assessed in terms of Return on Assets (ROA) and ratio between total costs and total assets.

Even in this case, Berger and Humphrey (1992) do not indicate any average improvement of indices.

DeYoung (1992) uses the Thick Frontier Approach (TFA) to estimate efficiency costs on a sample of 348 US banks merging in the period 1986–87. Similarly to Berger and Humphrey (1992), DeYoung (1992) does not report substantial cost benefits, although an increase in cost efficiency is found when both the acquiring and acquired banks recorded poor performance in the period prior to the deal.

Akhavein et al., (1997) analyze the effects produced on profit efficiency (estimated by the DFA) of mergers among US banks with a value greater than one billion dollars in the period 1980–90. According to the authors, the analyzed mergers have produced a significant increase of profit efficiency on average. To check robustness, Akhavein et al., (1997) also examine the M&A effects on the profits [measured using Return on Equity (ROE) and ROA] without recording any significant increase for the banks involved in these deals. The authors explain these discrepancies in the results by the ROE and ROA inaccuracy after the M&A deals.

Resti (1998) analyzes a sample of 67 acquisitions undertaken within the Italian banking industry between 1988 and 1998 by using DEA to estimate the efficiency of both the acquiring and acquired banks. Unlike most of other studies, acquiring banks are found to be less efficient than acquired banks and the merged entity increases its efficiency after the deal. Largest efficiency improvements are found when the deal takes place between two banks, which operate in the same local market and the new bank is of small-medium dimension.

Rhoades (1998) analyzes a small sample of US banks during the 1990s, selected according to the following criteria:

1. The acquiring bank's total assets should be greater than 10 USD billion.
2. The target bank's total assets should be greater than 5 USD billion.
3. Both banks bring in a substantial territorial overlap. Rhoades (1998) uses both the event study methodology to assess short term effects and the DFA technique to estimate medium term effects. Focusing on the latter, most deals were followed by an efficiency increase.

Lang and Welzel (1999) analyze a sample of 283 mergers from Bavarian cooperative banks between 1989 and 1997. Using the SFA, the authors find that scale and scope efficiency gains arise only if the merged banks shrink the branch networks. Lang and Welzel (1999) do not find a significant increase in the x-efficiency.

Fried et al., (1999) analyze a sample of 48,000 credit unions in the US (1600 of which where involved in M&As) between 1988 and 1995 by using DEA. Results obtained show that:

1. members of the acquired credit unions have (on average) efficiency improvements lasting for at least three years;
2. half of the acquiring credit unions and 20% of the acquired credit unions record a worsening of services;
3. acquiring credit unions have a greater probability of success if they were already involved in M&As in the past and their excellent corporate organization[4] can be exported to target banks;
4. acquired credit unions have a greater probability to benefit from M&As if these introduce new business administration features from the acquiring credit unions.

Haynes and Thompson (1999) analyzed 93 M&As between British building societies over the period 1981–93 finding substantial productivity improvements.

Hughes et al., (1999) analyze a sample of 441 M&As between US banks in 1994 by assessing the effects on profit levels, profit riskiness, profit efficiency (estimated by SFA), market value and insolvency risk. The authors find that M&A have a positive influence on the performance levels and on their riskiness.

Huizinga et al., (2001) analyze 52 M&As between European banks between 1994 and 1998. The authors report large economies of scale gains and these increases are negatively related to the bank's size. Similarly, cost efficiency and profits gains are also substantial.

Cuesta and Orea (2002) examine 858 Spanish saving banks (132 of which were involved in M&As) over the period 1985–98. Their aim is to estimate differences in the cost efficiency levels (estimated using SFA) comparing banks involved in M&As with banks not engaged. The authors show that merged and non-merged banks have different patterns of change in technical efficiency. While the time-invariant technical efficiency hypothesis cannot be rejected for banks not involved in M&As, technical efficiency of merged banks initially decreased and then increased. Cuesta and Orea (2002) conclude that mergers have some impact on technical efficiency.

Berger and Mester (2003) assess the influence of technological innovation, deregulation and competition on the bank performance measured by cost and profit efficiencies. They use a sample of US banks over the period 1984–1997. On average, banks are found to increase their profit efficiency and decrease their cost efficiency. According to the authors, these trends could also have been determined by M&As since merged banks registered:

1. a decrease in cost efficiency greater than those not involved in M&As and
2. a greater improvement of profit efficiency.

According to the authors, these results can be due to the following post-merger actions:

1. new financial services offered and/or enhanced quality of existing financial services;
2. changes in their portfolio, by acquiring more risky and profitable operations.

Wang (2003) proposes a different approach with the aim of overcoming the limits resulting from the use of accounting data.[5] The author develops a new measure for the added value of bank services and analyzes a sample of 76 M&As between US banks. Wang (2003) found that:

1. banks modify their portfolio composition to benefit from a greater assets diversification after an M&A deal;
2. bank productivity increases, especially the one measured using the value added approach.

Carbo-Valverde and Humphrey (2004) analyze a sample of 20 M&As in the Spanish banking system between 1986 and 1998. They have found out that merged banks record:

1. an average increase in costs greater than the other banks;
2. an increase in profits of smaller proportions than other banks;

3. an increase in the number of ATM's similar to other banks;
4. an increase in the interest rate on deposits and a reduction on loan rates;
5. an increase in personal deposits per unit greater than other banks, but an improvement in operating efficiency lower than other banks.

Carbo-Valverde and Humphrey (2004) conclude that M&As have some positive effects both for shareholders and, particularly, for customers.

Humphrey and Vale (2004) analyze 131 Norwegian banks (26 M&A deals) by assessing the most suitable cost function. Their intention is to identify the effect of the scale efficiency produced by M&As. Using three cost functions, Humphrey and Vale (2004) find that:

1. the translog function of average cost is reduced by 0.16%, while the Fourier function is reduced by 2.06%, and the spline function is reduced by 3.09%;
2. the overall average costs reduction for the 26 M&As is equal to 2.81%.

Using the SFA methodology, Koetter (2005) analyzes the German banking sector. He has discovered that

1. M&As usually produce positive results on cost efficiency;
2. M&As between cooperative banks have a greater probability of success than those between commercial banks;
3. when acquiring banks have economic problems, M&As are usually unsuccessful; when target banks have economic problems, M&As are usually successful in the short and medium terms;
4. the spatial distance between merging banks has a negative effect on the M&A success for saving banks, while it has a positive effect in case of mergers between commercial banks.

Although De Guevara and Maudos (2007) find that the cost efficiency of Spanish banks improved between 1986 and 2002. This was a period of consolidation whose study makes evident that potential efficiency derives from the merger.

Ashton and Pham's 2007 analysis of 61 UK bank mergers between 1988 and 2004 show that these deals are on average cost efficiency improving and they appear to have little adverse pricing effects on retail deposit rates.

Behr and Heid (2008) analyze the M&A effects on banks' efficiency and performance using a sample of German banks' mergers between 1994 and 2003. Overall, the authors find evidence of cost efficiency (but not profit) improvements. They suggest that "the main motive of bank mergers is indeed to enhance the efficiency of banks, but the increase in operating profits is partly offset by revaluation effects in the course of the restructuring process" (Behr and Heid, 2008, p. 20).

4.4   The M&A effects over the medium-long term: the impact on banks' operating performance

Another part of the banking literature analyzed the M&A effects on the banks' operating performance. It compared bank performances in a time period prior and successive to M&As with the aim of assessing cost, revenue and profit changes (see Pilloff and Santomero, 1997). These studies usually use accounting data. Bank performances are measured using financial ratios (for example, ROE and ROA). The time period analyzed goes from one year before the deal to 3–5 years after the deal itself (see Beitel and Schiereck, 2001). These studies provide a direct assessment of performance changes, though the analysis of accounting data implies some problems:

1. Even though accounting data should be calculated in a way which reflects the performance, these appear inadequate under the economic profile.
2. Performance changes may not be due to M&As, but due to other events which occurred during the same period; as for example, the launching of a new product.
3. Performance improvements may be due both to a stronger market power and to an enhanced productive efficiency. However, it is impossible to distinguish between these two causes in this type of study (see Berger et al., 1999).

From the early 1980s, various studies have analyzed the M&A impact on the operating performances. These include Srinivasan and Wall (1992), Linder and Crane (1992), Rhoades (1993), Spindt and Tarhan (1993), Vander Vennet (1996), Kwan and Wilcox (2002), Focarelli et al., (2002), Díaz, et al., (2004), Knapp et al., (2006), Cornett et al., (2006), Campa and Hernando (2006), Berger and Dick (2007), Altunbas and Marques-Ibanez (2008).

Scrinivasan and Wall (1992) examine the mergers between US banks from 1982 to 1986 in order to assess the importance of expenses on commissions. The authors find that the operations analyzed have not significantly reduced the expenses on commissions.[6] Linder and Crane (1992) study the operating performance of 47 mergers of US banks over the period 1982–87. By comparing bank performances prior to the merger with the new bank performance after one or two years, the authors find that mergers do not determine a profit increase. Rhoades (1992) analyzes a sample of mergers between US banks over the period 1981–86 by regressing various performance measures (dependent variables) over various variables. According to the results obtained, cost cuts and efficiency improvements are not significantly linked to the M&A deals. Spindt and Tarhan (1993) run several non-parametric tests using a sample of 192 mergers of banks in 1996. They have found that M&As lead banks to increase their operating income due to economies of scale gains. This result is confirmed by Pilloff and Santomero (1997, p. 11), who find that scale economies exist for banks with total assets smaller than 100 USD million. In fact, the sample analyzed by Spindt and Tarhan (1993) is mainly consists of M&As between small banks. Vander Vennet (1996) analyzes a sample of 492 M&A operations in Europe over the period 1988–92 by assessing changes in bank performance (measured using ROA and ROE) and efficiency (measured by labour cost indexes, operating expense indexes and level of operating efficiency). The sample of M&As has been split in various sub-samples based on the acquiring bank's financial leverage and the degree of operating integration between merging banks. Vennet (1996) finds that:

1. in domestic deals where the majority of equity capital is transferred, target banks had poorer performance in the pre-merger period that the acquiring firm is not able to resolve;
2. in domestic deals in which the entire equity capital is transferred, target firms display similar inefficiency levels to acquirer banks in

the pre-merger period and new created banks display declining efficiency levels after the deal;

3. in *cross-border* M&As, there is an efficiency increase in the post-merger period.

Kwan and Wilcox (2002) analyze a sample of 1154 M&As between US banks during the period 1985–97 on the basis of the following criteria:

1. Both target and bidder banks should be healthy institutions at the time of the merger.
2. Both merged banks should not have engaged in other mergers two years before or after the merger date.
3. Both banks should be in operation for at least two years prior to the merger and have total assets greater than 10 USD million.
4. The accounting method for the merger transaction should be known and verified by the Wharton Research Data Service.
5. The merger should have occurred before 1996.

In order to measure the occurred changes in the bank's operating performance, the authors compare the economic results of the new born bank with those found in the previous phase of the merger operation. The results of these two phases of M&A are calculated with respect to a group of banks with similar dimensions.[7] Bank performance is measured by the following indices:

1. commission expenses over total assets;
2. labour expenses over total assets;
3. premise expenses over total assets;
4. other expenses over total assets.

Kwan and Wilcox (2002) find that M&As considerably reduce operating costs and the new bank's size does not significantly influence cost cuts.

Focarelli et al., (2002) analyze a sample of 135 mergers and 66 acquisitions between Italian banks over the period 1985–96. By distinguishing between mergers and acquisitions, the authors examine both the ex-ante phase of the deal (searching for the deal motives) and the ex-post phase (assessing the M&A effects on bank performance).

Focusing on the latter issue, the authors evaluate the existing relationship between traditional profit measures – such as ROA, ROE and profit efficiency – and various *dummy* variables representing different forms of M&As and time periods. Their results show that

1. merger operations lead banks to cost and profit efficiency decreases due to the characteristics and rigidity of the Italian labour market, poor ROA levels and ROE increases. According to the authors, these results should be interpreted as an equity capital reduction for new created banks rather than a profit increase.
2. Acquisitions lead acquired banks to revenue increases (both ROE and ROA) for the period of three years after the deal. This is due to an enhanced loan portfolio quality, as stated by the authors, while there are no gains for acquiring banks. Substantial benefits on cost efficiency and profit efficiency of the involved banks have not been found. Overall, the authors do not report substantial cost efficiency and profit efficiency increases for banks involved in M&As.

Díaz, et al., (2004) analyze the effect on banks performance of financial acquisitions (both by another bank and other non-banking financial entities) over the period 1993–2000. By using a panel data methodology and a sample of 1629 banks, the authors provide evidence of an increase in the acquirers' long-term profitability, especially in the case of bank acquisitions rather than of non-bank acquisitions.

Knapp et al., (2006) assess the occurrence of serial correlation in bank holding company profitability by using a sample of 80 US mergers each with a value in excess of $25 million between 1987 and 1998. The authors use four banks' performance indicators: ROA, cash flow ROA, ROE, and cash flow ROE. They find that bank holding company mergers generate substantial profit gains up to five years after the merger, once adjustments are made for profits reversion to the mean.

Cornett et al., (2006) analyze bank performance around mergers, focusing on changes in the long-term operating performance for both large and small banks. Operating performance changes are measured by the mean change in industry-adjusted operating pre-tax cash flow return on assets in the two years after the bank merger compared to the same value in the two years before the merger. By using a sample of 134 mergers made in the US in the period 1990–2000, the authors find evidence of revenue efficiency improvements for large mergers and for product and geographical focused mergers.

Campa and Hernando (2006) study 66 completed consolidation deals in the European banking sector between 1998 and 2002. They examine changes in banks' performance such as ROE and net financial margin; solvency (that is, capitalization ratio); efficiency which comes does not to cost to income ratio; lending intensity (that is, net loan to total assets); and risk profile which involves loan loss provisions to total loans and loan loss provisions to net interest revenue. The authors provide evidence of substantial ROE and efficiency improvements following the acquisition. They look at significant improvements in the target bank's performance, which occurred approximately two years after the transaction was completed. The target banks' ROE increased by 7% on average, and these also experienced efficiency improvements.

Berger and Dick (2007) assess the post-merger market share gains focusing on a data set covering over 10,000 bank entries in the period 1972–2002. They find that large bank holding companies entering new local markets were more successful in maintaining the target banks' market share if they were an early entrant into that market and/or had a recognized brand image.

Altunbas and Marqués-Ibáñez (2008) analyze a sample of 252 M&As (207 domestic and 55 international deals) in the European banking market between 1992 and 2000. Their aim is to assess if the compatibility of the strategic and organizational characteristics of the banks interested in M&As has an impact on their performance measured by the variation of ROE. The authors find that:

1. M&As are followed by increases in the performance;
2. the organizational and strategic similarities of the banks involved in M&A increases has a positive impact on their performance, although there are substantial differences between domestic and international M&As.

4.5 The M&A effects over the medium-long term: other issues

The dynamic approach has also been in various studies to assess the M&A effects on other corporate issues, such as in Berger et al., (1998;

2001), Focarelli and Pozzollo (2001), Amihud et al., (2002), Berger et al., (2004), Wheelock and Wilson (2004), Buch et al., (2005), Carletti et al., (2007) and Francis et al., (2008).

Berger et al., (1998) analyze the effects that concentration has on consumers and particularly on small firms financing. Using a sample of more than 6000 mergers between US banks during the period 1970–1999, the authors find that:

1. a change in the new bank's lending propensity.
2. a change in lending strategies due to the new bank size, financial soundness and competitive position;
3. differences in lending strategies for banks involved in M&As with respect to other banks (of similar size) not recently involved in M&As;
4. a reaction of bank competitors in the local market due to the M&A.

Overall, Berger et al., (1998) conclude that the first effect tends to reduce lending activities to small firms, but this reduction is offset by the other three effects. For example, the fourth effect (indicating stronger competitive pressures) leads other banks to increase their lending activity.

Berger et al., (2001) is a follow up of the 1998 study covering a time period between 1993 and 1998 and splitting the sample according to the bank total assets. The authors have found out that:

1. M&As have a minor effect on lending from both small and large banks to small companies;
2. a slight positive effect on lending from local banks due to new competitors entering the local area;
3. a negative effect on lending from large banks due to the entry of new competitors in the local area;
4. a substantial impact of firm seniority on the lending to small firms: new competitors have a greater loan request than other banks already in the market.

Focarelli and Pozzollo (2001) analyze the M&A trend by comparing banks and non-financial firms to identify which factors increase the probability that a bank expands abroad. Using a sample of nearly 2500 banks from 29 countries, the authors have discovered that

1. cross-border M&As occur less frequently in banking than in other sectors;
2. banks working in various countries have normally a larger size and greater profits than domestic banks.

Amihud et al., (2002) analyze cross-border M&A effects on the acquiring banks risk and stock returns. They use a sample of 214 mergers announced over the period 1985–98 and completed by 1999. First, the authors measure the risk change in two ways:

1. "Total relative risk –" that is, the ratio of the variance of the acquirer's daily stock returns to the variance of index return series in three banks: world, home country and host country;
2. "Systematic risk –" that is, the change in the Beta coefficient of the acquiring bank's stock return relative to the returns on three bank indexes. Risk changes following M&As are estimated by comparing the risk measures one year prior to the deal disclosure and risk measures one year after the deal itself. Results show that cross border mergers do not increase the risk of the new firm, neither on the domestic market nor on the foreign market. The regression analysis (CAR of the acquiring banks over risk change variables) does not display statistically significant results, although a small positive effect is found in the case of target firms.

According to their results, Amihud et al., (2002) conclude that the growth of cross-border banking do not present particular dangers for stability and solvency of the international banking system.

Berger et al., (2004) analyze a sample of 1849 international M&A operations between commercial banks, insurance companies and other financial companies in Europe, North America, Asia and Australia over the period 1985 to 2000. The analysis aims to identify what characteristics of a country can determine substantial advantages in M&As. Such advantages allow some countries to be important exporters of management through direct investment (M&A) in foreign countries, other countries to be importers, and others to be both. In defining this advantage, Berger et al., (2004, p. 362) base their theory on two principles: the "new theory of international trade" and the "theory of comparative advantages." According to the results, both theories can be accepted and the authors identify a series of features that can influence the financial institutions' ability to export/import management through M&A. For example, the US is found to have a substantial advantage compared to other countries taken into consideration.

Wheelock and Wilson (2004) analyze a sample of 3000 US mergers between commercial banks during the period 1987–99. They aim to identify the characteristics of a bank which influences the number and the dimensions of the acquisitions carried out in a certain time span. The authors found that:

1. the removal of new branches constraints produces in the short-term a general increase of M&As;
2. the approval process by supervisors is a true obstacle to M&As;
3. the management quality is one of the bank's internal features directly influencing M&As. In the US case, M&As increase, *ceteris paribus*, for those banks whose management is judged of primary importance by supervisors;
4. other internal factors (measured by financial indicators) are not found to be directly linked to M&As.

Buch et al., (2005) compare optimal to actual cross-border portfolios of banks in France, Germany, UK and US between 1995 and 1999. The authors conclude that banks generally over-invest domestically and they could therefore realize potential diversification gains from further international expansion.

Carletti et al., (2007) show that the regulatory process involving mergers, as shown by findings on international bank deals between 1987 and 2004, clearly demonstrates that less transparent rules on competition and supervision of bank mergers are associated with higher market returns from M&As.

Francis et al., (2008) assess the impact of tangible intensity of bank consolidation on the development of businesses in the US over the post-Riegle–Neal Interstate Banking and Branching Efficiency Act period. The authors find positive cross-border wealth effects relating to US non-bank cross border deals internationally over the 1990s to the early 2000s.

4.6 Conclusion: what does the existing literature teach us?

The previous sections reviewed a large number of dynamic studies carried out in recent years to assess the effects generated by M&As for all the banks (also non quoted ones) They focused on shareholder value, efficiency, operating performance and other features.

The US banking market has been the main object of these studies whereas there is a smaller, yet increasing, number of studies focusing on the European banking sector. Most of the findings are heterogeneous and therefore it is not possible to generalize the results outside the context considered by the analysis. On the one hand, it was possible to have a general agreement regarding event studies in the US banking in the 1980s and 1990s; that is, target shareholders earned substantial positive abnormal returns, bidder stockholders earned marginally negative returns, and the combined abnormal returns were statistically insignificant or economically trivial on average. On the other hand, studies published from 2000 have provided a varied picture so that such conclusions cannot be supported anymore.

Regarding studies investigating the M&A effect in the medium-long term in European banking, results are homogenous. They show that M&A deals lead European banks to enhance their performance and productive efficiency in contrast to US banking. However, the number of studies investigating the M&As effect on operating performance (especially in Europe) is limited. It difficult to be more conclusive.

5

Do M&As Create Value for Shareholders? The Short-term Wealth Effect

5.1 Introduction

The phenomenon of Merger and Acquisition (M&A) has been the object of many empirical studies in the past decade, especially with the United States banking sector. As shown in Chapter 2, the M&A phenomenon is very important in Europe: there has been a rising trend in M&As since 2001 both in terms of number of deals and of their value. In 2006 only, there were around 1100 M&A deals between banks in the Euro area for an overall value of more than 130 Euro billion. The impact created by M&As in the short term has been investigated by a number of studies in Europe focusing on M&A deals over the 1990s. Namely, Beitel et al., (2001; 2004) examined 98 mergers between European banks during the period 1985–2000. Cybo-Ottone and Murgia (2000) analyzed a sample of 72 European banks with a value higher than 100 million dollars during the period 1988–97.

Despite the considerable number of studies dealing with M&As, the results are mixed. DeYoung et al., (2009, forthcoming) note that

> the mixed findings could reflect the different methodologies used in previous studies; but the high incidence of contradictory findings is more likely the result of examining M&A data at the early at early stages in the industry consolidation process, mainly from the mid-1980s to the mid-1990s.

This chapter contributes to the existing literature by considering a large sample of M&A deals in the European Banking, especially in the twenty-first century. The chapter is organized as follows: firstly, we outline the methodology (Section 5.2), next, we describe the sample selected (Section 5.3) and, finally, we discuss our findings (Section 5.4).

5.2   Methods

In order to assess the impact of M&A transactions on the shareholder value over the short period, we ran a standard event study to analyze if the stock returns of banks involved in M&As have undergone an abnormal trend around the announcement date. Using the Capital Asset Pricing Model framework, we estimate the expected return as follows:

(R_{jt}) of bank *j* at time *t* as:

$$R_{jt} = \alpha_j + \beta_j R_{Mt} + \varepsilon_{jt} \tag{5.1}$$

$R_{jt} = Log[(P_t+D_t)/P_{t-1}]$, P_t and D_t are the market price and the daily flow dividend respectively. RM_t is the rate of return at time *t*, of the domestic banking sector index i.e. $RM_t = Log[(I_t/I_{t-1})]$, where I_t is the value of the market index at time; *t* and ε_{jt} is the error term.

We define the event windows (i.e. the time period of –*t* days before and +*t* days after the M&A announcement date) of different sizes: from 71 days (–50, +20) to zero.

Following the standard procedure (applied in Beitel et al., 2004; Ismail and Davidson, 2005),[1] we calculate the AR on stock *j* on day *t* ($AR_{j,t}$) and the CAR over the event window period (τ_1, τ_2) [i.e. CAR_j (τ_1, τ_2) and VAR $\lfloor CAR_j$ (τ_1, $\tau_2)\rfloor$, respectively] as follows:

$$AR_{jt} = R_{jt} - \hat{R}_{jt} = R_{jt} - \hat{\alpha}_j - \hat{\beta}_j RM_t \tag{5.2}$$

$$CAR_j(\tau_1, \tau_2) = \sum_{t=\tau_1}^{\tau_2} CAR_{j,t} \tag{5.3}$$

For a sample of *n* stocks, the mean CAR over the event window period (τ_1, τ_2) and its variance is obtained as:

$$\overline{CAR}(\tau_1, \tau_2) = \frac{1}{n} \sum_{j=1}^{n} CAR(\tau_1, \tau_2) \tag{5.4}$$

$$Var[\overline{CAR}(\tau_1, \tau_2)] = \frac{1}{n^2} \sum_{j=1}^{n} \hat{\sigma}_j^2 (\tau_1, \tau_2) \qquad (5.5)$$

Where $\hat{\sigma}_j^2(\tau_1, \tau_2) = (\tau_2 - \tau_1 + 1)\hat{\sigma}_{\varepsilon j}^2, \hat{\sigma}_{\varepsilon j}^2$ represents the variance of the estimated residuals across the regression of the market model of sock *j*.

Under the null hypothesis of no market impact, it is possible to draw inferences on $\overline{CAR}$, through the following standard Z-score statistic:

$$Z = \frac{\overline{CAR}(\tau_1, \tau_2)}{Var\left[\overline{CAR}(\tau_1, \tau_2)\right]^{1/2}} \approx N(0,1) \qquad (5.6)$$

The M&A effects are analyzed for both the shareholders of the target and the bidder banks separately and combined. The combined analysis enables us to judge on the entire transaction as a whole (Beitel, Schiereck, 2001, p. 11). Using this method, it is possible to verify if the operations of banking M&A create or destroy value or, vice versa, these deals simply imply a value transfer from bidder banks to the target banks. To calculate the ARs for the combined entity of the target and acquiring firm, we weight the AR for both the acquiring and target firm with respect to their market capitalization on the day prior to the event period.

$$AR_{i,t} = \frac{AR_{A,t} * MV_{A,t} + AR_{T,t} * MV_{T,t}}{MV_{A,t} + MV_{T,t}} \qquad (5.7)$$

$AR_{i,t}$ represents the abnormal return on day *t* of the event period for the merged entity; $AR_{A,t}$ stands for the abnormal return on day t of the event period of the acquiring firm; $AR_{T,t}$ represents the abnormal return on day t of the event period of the target firm; $MV_{A,t}$ is for the market value of the acquiring firm the day prior to the event period; $MV_{T,t}$ represents the market value of the target firm the day prior to the event period (Houston and Ryngaert, 1994, p. 1161). Once the $AR_{i,t}$ from the various M&A operations are determined, $\overline{CAR}$ is estimated using model (10). The significance test of the results obtained for the combination of the target and acquiring firm are estimated using model (13), applying an adjustment to the calculation of standard deviation as suggested in Beitel and Schiereck (2001) and Houston and Ryngaert (1994). To calculate the standard deviation, the starting point is the variance of $AR_{i,t}, (\hat{\sigma}_{i,t}^2)$:

$$\hat{\sigma}_{i,t}^2 = \left(\frac{MV_{T,t}}{MV_{T,t} + MV_{A,t}}\right)^2 * \hat{\sigma}_{T,t}^2 + \left(\frac{MV_{A,t}}{MV_{T,t} + MV_{A,t}}\right)^2 * \hat{\sigma}_{A,t}^2$$

$$+ 2\left(\frac{MV_{T,t}}{MV_{T,t} + MV_{A,t}}\right) * \left(\frac{MV_{A,t}}{MV_{T,t} + MV_{A,t}}\right) * \rho_{T,A} * \sqrt{\hat{\sigma}_{T,t}^2 * \hat{\sigma}_{A,t}^2} \qquad (5.8)$$

$MV_{T,t}$ is the market value of the target firm realized the day prior to the event period; $MV_{A,t}$ is the market value of the acquiring firm, realized the day prior to the event period; $\hat{\sigma}_{T,t}^2$ is the variance of ARs of the target firm; $\hat{\sigma}_{A,t}^2$ is the variance of ARs of the acquiring firm; $\rho_{T,A}$ is the correlation coefficient between the residuals of the Market Model of the acquiring and target firm during the estimation period. At this point, we proceed to add up the variance $\hat{\sigma}_{i,t}^2$ obtained for each t belonging to the event period:

$$\hat{\sigma}_i^2(\tau_1, \tau_2) = (\tau_1 - \tau_2 + 1)\hat{\sigma}_{i,t}^2 \qquad (5.9)$$

As such, we obtain the variance of $\overline{CAR}$, by applying model (11) to the case of the combined analysis as follows:

$$Var[\overline{CAR}_m(\tau_1, \tau_2)] = \frac{1}{m^2}\sum_{i=1}^{m}\hat{\sigma}_i^2(\tau_1, \tau_2) \qquad (5.10)$$

m represents the number of M&A operations taken into consideration. The square root of this value supplies the standard deviation that we can use to perform our hypothesis test on $\overline{CAR}$ of the combined effect.

5.3   Sample: Selected M&A deals

The M&A transactions have been selected according to the following criteria (Source of data: Thomson ONE Banker):

1. The M&A was announced between 1 January 1995 and 31 December 2006.
2. The acquiring firms are classified as banks in the EU-27.[2]
3. The target firms are classified as banks, insurances or other financial companies in the EU-27.

4. Both the acquiring and the target firms are publicly listed in European stock exchanges.
5. The value of the transaction is not inferior to 100 million Euro.
6. The M&A transaction was effectively completed and not just announced.
7. The M&A deal result in the change of control of the target bank. In other words, the acquiring bank has a complete corporate control, holding more than 50% of the target company's equity.
8. Bot the target and the acquiring banks have been publicly quoted for an entire year prior to the announcement and at least 20 days after the announcement day.

For every M&A deal analyzed, we collected the following data (by using the Datastream database):

1. Share prices for both the target and the bidder banks 273 days before the M&A announcement (t_0) and 20 days after t_0.
2. National sector equity indices 273 days before the M&A announcement (t_0) and 20 days after t_0. These indices are used as proxy for the market return (R_{Mt}). For the acquiring companies, which are always banks, we use the national banking equity index; for the target companies, we use different national banking equity indices if the target company is a bank or a retail financial company, and national insurance equity indices if the target company is an insurance company.
3. Other accounting data such as total assets, equity, and so forth are obtained by Bankscope database.

Table 5.1 displays the number of M&A deals meeting our sample selection criteria during 1991 and 2005. The number of M&A deals has increased over time, especially during 1998–2000. Moreover, the mean value of transaction completed was constantly growing. Overall, our sample comprises 297 M&A deals. The 297 target companies were acquired by 180 banks since some banks acquired more than a bank over the analyzed period. Looking at the main features of acquiring and target companies, acquiring companies have a substantially larger asset size than target banks: it is interesting

Table 5.1 The sample dimension: number of M&As in EU-27 banking

Year	Number of M&A deals	Mean of deal value (in USD million)	Target companies: mean value of total asset (in USD million)	Acquiring companies: mean value of total asset (in USD million)
1991	14	614	3,213	15,099
1992	8	869	14,480	68,057
1993	12	252	870	4,089
1994	12	553	9,538	44,828
1995	19	1,367	10,962	51,523
1996	15	446	6,905	32,452
1997	19	2,810	22,213	104,402
1998	34	2,047	10,127	47,596
1999	35	3,805	35,332	166,063
2000	32	1,564	14,741	69,284
2001	20	1,112	5,628	26,450
2002	17	2,444	28,491	133,906
2003	18	788	42,544	199,957
2004	22	1,388	17,380	81,685
2005	20	2,139	48,878	229,729
Total	297	1,735	19,511	91,704

Source: Thomson ONE Banker database.

to note that the asset size gap between acquiring and target companies increased substantially over the time period analyzed. (On average the bidder bank is five times larger than the acquired bank.) The different larger size of acquiring banks compared to target banks is also a common feature in other banking markets. For instance, Humphrey and Vale (2004, p. 1694) notes, "In the US, the average acquired bank is half the size of the acquiring institution. In Norway, the average merger is smaller: in 18 of 26 mergers the acquired bank is less than one-fifth of the size of the acquiring institution."

Most M&As are domestic transactions (i.e. both target and domestic banks are within the EU-25 area). The mean size of domestic M&A deals is substantially larger than those of cross-border deal (see Table 5.2). Despite the dominance of domestic EU deals, the quote of cross-border deals was larger than 20% from 1997 to 2005. Target companies have been usually banks, although M&A deals having insurance or other financial companies as target substantially increased in the 2000s.

Table 5.2   Sample dimension: types of M&As
in EU-27 banking
Panel A – Cross border vs. EU domestic

Year	Cross-Border	UE	(% of cross border)
1991	2	12	14
1992	–	8	0
1993	1	11	8
1994	1	11	8
1995	1	18	5
1996	5	10	33
1997	1	18	5
1998	9	25	26
1999	8	27	23
2000	8	24	25
2001	5	15	25
2002	5	12	29
2003	4	14	22
2004	6	16	27
2005	4	16	20
Total	60	237	20

Panel B – Different type of target companies

	Banks	Insurance	Other financial	% of banks
1991	11	2	1	79
1992	6	0	2	75
1993	11	0	1	92
1994	9	1	2	75
1995	15	2	2	79
1996	11	0	4	73
1997	16	2	1	84
1998	25	1	8	74
1999	30	4	1	86
2000	24	5	3	75
2001	16	0	4	80
2002	10	0	7	59
2003	14	1	3	78
2004	12	3	7	55
2005	12	3	5	60
Total	222	24	51	75

Source: Thomson ONE Banker database.

5.4   Results

In order to assess the stock price reaction to M&A announcement, we use various event period. This is because ARs may be generated before or after the M&A announcement. As a consequence, we use the following event windows (–20; +20), (–15; +15), (–10; +10), (–5; +5) and (–1; +1) to capture different reactions over different periods. We also consider a longer time period [namely, (–50; +20) and (–30; +20)][3] to establish if the M&A was anticipated by investors well in advance, and check if this produce ARs in a longer time period. In

Table 5.3 M&A in European banking: Cumulative Abnormal Return for target banks[a]

Event Window	Mean CAR[b]	Positive CAR	P-VALUE
(–50, +20) =	0.1624***	0.6900	< 0,0000
(–30, +20) =	0.1730***	0.7200	< 0,0000
(–20, +20) =	0.1630***	0.7200	< 0,0000
(–15, +15) =	0.1685***	0.6400	< 0,0000
(–10, +10) =	0.1585***	0.7200	< 0,0000
(–5, +5) =	0.1820***	0.7200	< 0,0000
(–1, +1) =	0.1319***	0.7200	< 0,0000
(0) =	0.1189***	0.4700	< 0,0000
(–1, 0) =	0.1219***	0.5500	< 0,0000
(–5, 0) =	0.1085***	0.8000	< 0,0000
(–10, 0) =	0.1458***	0.7200	< 0,0000
(–15, 0) =	0.1436***	0.6400	< 0,0000
(–20, 0) =	0.1351***	0.6400	< 0,0000
(–30, 0) =	0.1224***	0.6200	< 0,0000
(–50, 0) =	0.1151***	0.5800	< 0,0000

[a] The table presents results of the event study for a sample of 297 deals, where 180 target banks were acquired by European banks (UE-25) over the period 1991 and 2005. Abnormal returns (ARs) are computed individually for acquirers and sellers with the OLS market model using for each deal the Datastream bank sector index. Regression parameters are estimated using the Scholes and Williams (1977) procedure from t=–302 to t=–51, where t=0 is the day the deal announcement. Tests of significance are calculated from standardized AR employing the Dodd and Warner (1983) procedure.

[b] * = statistically significant at the 10% level; ** = statistically significant at the 5% level *** = statistically significant at the 1% level.

Source: Author's own.

addition, we consider various event windows ending on the M&A announcement day. As part of our examination whether investors were able to predict M&A deals, we also took into consideration various event windows ending on the announcement day: namely, (–50; 0), (–30; 0), (–20; 0), (–15; 0), (–10; 0), (–5; 0) and (–1; 0). We also consider an event window of one day, the announcement day [i.e. (0)].

Tables 5.3–5.5 report the estimated CAR for target banks, acquiring banks and the combined entity respectively. Regarding target banks, estimated mean CAR for all event windows are positive and statistically significant at 1% confidence levels. It is interesting to note that CARs are positive (between 10% and 18%) over all symmetric event periods showing that M&A deals created, on average, value for

Table 5.4 M&A in European banking: Cumulative Abnormal Return for bidder banks[a]

Event Window	Mean CAR[b]	Positive CAR	P-VALUE
(–50,+20) =	–0.0004	0.5200	0.1996
(–30,+20) =	–0.0005	0.5100	0.1655
(–20,+20) =	–0.0007	0.5100	0.1365
(–15,+15) =	–0.0011	0.5000	0.0965
(–10,+10) =	–0.0016	0.4900	0.0780
(–5,+5) =	–0.0022	0.4800	0.0577
(–1,+1) =	–0.0074	0.4300	0.0699
(0) =	–0.0143	0.4000	< 0.0000
(–1,0) =	–0.0124	0.4100	< 0.0000
(–5,0) =	–0.0106	0.4200	< 0.0000
(–10,0) =	–0.0090	0.4300	< 0.0000
(–15,0) =	–0.0075	0.4300	< 0.0000
(–20,0) =	–0.0062	0.4400	< 0.0000
(–30,0) =	–0.0050	0.4600	< 0.0000
(–50,0) =	–0.0039	0.4700	< 0.0000

[a]The table presents results of the event study for a sample of 297 deals, where 180 target banks were acquired by European banks (UE-25) over the period 1991 and 2005. Abnormal returns (ARs) are computed individually for acquirers and sellers with the OLS market model using for each deal the Datastream bank sector index. Regression parameters are estimated using the Scholes and Williams (1977) procedure from t= –302 to t=–51, where t=0 is the day the deal announcement. Tests of significance are calculated from standardized AR employing the Dodd and Warner (1983) procedure.
[b]* = statistically significant at the 10% level; ** = statistically significant at the 5% level *** = statistically significant at the 1% level.

Source: Author's own.

Table 5.5 M&A in European banking: Cumulative Abnormal Return for the combined entity[a]

Event Window	Mean CAR[b]	Positive CAR (%)	P-VALUE
(–50, +20) =	0.0406	61	0.1733
(–30, +20) =	0.0346	62	0.1563
(–20, +20) =	0.0204	62	0.1110
(–15, +15) =	0.0421*	57	0.0846
(–10, +10) =	0.0396**	61	0.0226
(–5, +5) =	0.0227**	60	0.0163
(–1, +1) =	0.0165***	58	0.0086
(0) =	0.0238***	44	< 0.0000
(–1, 0) =	0.0244**	48	0.0240
(–5, 0) =	0.0271**	61	0.0127
(–10, 0) =	0.0365***	58	0.0018
(–15, 0) =	0.0359***	54	0.0099
(–20, 0) =	0.0270***	54	< 0.0000
(–30, 0) =	0.0306***	54	< 0.0000
(–50, 0) =	0.0144***	53	< 0.0000

[a]The table presents results of the event study for a sample of 297 deals, where 180 target banks were acquired by European banks (UE-25) over the period 1991 and 2005. Abnormal returns (ARs) are computed individually for acquirers and sellers with the OLS market model using for each deal the Datastream bank sector index. Regression parameters are estimated using the Scholes and Williams (1977) procedure from $t = –302$ to $t = –51$, where $t = 0$ is the day the deal announcement. Tests of significance are calculated from standardized AR employing the Dodd and Warner (1983) procedure.
[b]* = statistically significant at the 10% level; ** = statistically significant at the 5% level *** = statistically significant at the 1% level.

Source: Author's own.

shareholders. In addition, most of the M&As analyzed generated a positive CAR.[4] It is also important to note that estimated mean CARs are also positive for all event windows before the announcement date. This provides evidence that investors were able to detect target banks. This result is not surprising since formal M&A announcements are usually anticipated by rumours/news on media. Regarding bidder companies, estimated mean CARs are constantly negative, despite the fact that the number of M&A deals with a positive CAR is higher than those with negative CAR over the longer time periods and, in general, at least 40% of the M&A deal analyzed generated a positive CAR. The estimated CARs are statistically significant at the

1% confidence levels for all event windows before the announcement date and at the 10% confidence levels for the symmetric event
windows over ten days around the announcement date. These
results provide evidence that investors were also able to detect bidder
banks – perhaps, following rumours and news on media – and penal-
ized these banks.

Our results are therefore consistent with previous studies, which
report positive wealth gains for targets and negative wealth changes
for bidders; for instance,.Hannan and Wolken, 1989; Cornett and
Tehranian, 1992; Houston and Ryngaert, 1994; Zhang, 1995; and
Kymaz, 2004; Lepetit et al., 2004; and Campa and Hernando, 2006.
To assess the whole effect on the created shareholder value, Table 5.5
reports mean CAR for the combined entity. In other words, AR for
both the acquiring and target firm are weighted with respect to their
market capitalization realized the day prior to the event period. All
mean estimated CARS are found to be positive (between 1,44% and
4,06%) and most of them are statistically significant at the 1% confidence level,More than 50% of M&A deals analyzed accomplished
positive CAR. Overall, the analyzed M&A deals appear to have created shareholder value rather than simply transfer wealth from the
bidder bank's shareholders to the target bank's shareholders.

5.5   Conclusion

This chapter analyzed the impact created by M&A on the short
term in the EU-27 focusing on M&A deals between 1991 and 2005.
While the few previous studies analyzed small samples of M&As in
the 1990s, our analysis gives a substantial contribution since it takes
into account new M&A deals and overall assessesalmost 300 M&A
deals. By applying the event study method, we found that M&A
deals created, on average, substantial shareholder value for the target
companies (between 10% and 18%) over all event periods. The estimated mean CARs are also positive for all event windows before the
announcement date showing that investors were able to detect target
banks. Instead, the estimated mean CAR for bidder companies are, on
average, negative. This result is surprising since the number of M&A
deals with a positive CAR is higher than the ones with negative CAR
over the longer time periods and, in general, at least 40% of the M&A
deal analyzed generated a positive CAR. Regarding the combined

entity of the target and acquiring firm, CARs are found to be positive. Most of them are statistically significant at 1% confidence level. More than 50% of the analyzed M&A deals accomplished a positive CAR: this provides evidence that the M&A transaction (taken as a whole) created shareholder value, rather than simply transferring wealth from the bidder banks shareholders to the shareholders of the targets.

6

Do M&As Create Value for Shareholders? The Long-Term Wealth Effect

6.1 Introduction

This chapter analyzes the effects of Merger and Acquisitions (M&As) between European banks over a five-year period by comparing shareholder value levels prior and successive to the deal itself (see Altunbus and Margques-Ibanez, 2004). Our analysis presents innovative features since, as far as we know, it is the first to analyze the effects of the shareholders' value created (measured by EVA) in the medium term for non-listed banks. Various studies analyzed the M&A effects on banks' performance, usually by focusing on traditional financial indicators. However, none used shareholder value measures to take into account for the opportunity cost of capital. In addition, we selected a large sample of banks focusing the European banking sectors – and more specifically on France, Germany, Italy, and the United Kingdom – during 1995–2002.

The chapter is organized as follows: first, we outline the methodology (Section 6.2), next, we describe the sample selected (Section 6.3), and finally we discuss our findings (Section 6.4).

6.2 Methods

The concept of shareholders' value is one of the oldest in the business field (see Hamilton 1777; Marshall 1890): in a specific time interval, an enterprise creates value for its owners when the return on invested capital is higher than its opportunity cost. In other words, the return that can be obtained by shareholders by investing in alternative assets with the same risk profile.

Focusing on the M&As undertaken between 1995 and 2002, our analysis has the following phases:

1. We estimate the Economic Value Added (EVA)[1] and the ratio between EVA and invested capital for all the banks in the sample whether or not involved in M&A operations.
2. We compare the mean EVA values created by the banks involved in M&As with those of other banks. Nevertheless, this comparison does not enable us to make an unambiguous interpretation because EVA differences could be due to factors rather to M&As.
3. As such we divide the sample in various homogeneous sub-samples. Banks are grouped on the basis of their nationality, ownership and year. We assess if merging banks display EVA changes. In the case of mergers – for example, banks A and B merged in the year *t-2* creating the bank C – we compare the bank C's EVA at time t_o with a proxy of the EVA at time *t-2*: that is, an average of the EVA created by the two banks at time *t-2*, weighted by their total assets. In the case of acquisitions – for example, bank A acquires bank B, incorporating it or not, in time *t-2* – we compare the current bank A's EVA at time t_o with its EVA at time *t-2*.

Regarding the first phase, EVA is one of the most commonly shareholder value measures and expresses the surplus of value created by a firm in a given period: EVA derives from the invested capital and from the difference between the return on invested capital and its cost – that is, excess return. EVA can also be expressed as the difference between the Net Operating Profit After Tax-NOPAT[2] and the opportunity cost of the invested capital – that is, the capital charge – (see Fiordelisi and Molyneux, 2006),[3] as follows:

$$EVA = CI * (ROIC - CC) = (CI* ROIC) - (CI* CC) = NOPAT - (CI* CC) \quad (6.1)$$

Where CI is the Invested Capital in the bank, ROIC is the Return rate On Invested Capital, CC is the invested Capital Charge, and

NOPAT is Net Operating Profit After Tax. The EVA calculation requires three elements: the NOPAT; the invested capital and the invested capital charge. With regards to NOPAT and invested capital, it is necessary to face distortions contained in accounting data to mirror the economic reality of the bank. Various accounting adjustments are used to:[4]

1. avoid to confuse operating and financial choices;
2. give a long term perspective;
3. avoid confusion between flow and stock data;
4. face the distortions introduced in the accounting practice (especially on the future and expected cost).

Even if the meaning of EVA is the same for any type of firm, its calculation procedure needs to be taken into account for the firm core business. In case of banks, we follow the procedure suggested by Fiordelisi and Molyneux (2006) and Fiordelisi (2007). On this basis, invested capital is measured by focusing on the total equity and, as a consequence, its cost is measured as cost of equity (see Maccario et al., 2002; Di Antonio, 2002, p. 103). Regarding the adjustments to face accounting data distortions (see Fiordelisi and Molyneux, 2006), the adjustments made concern:

1. loan loss provisions and loan loss reserves;
2. restructuring charges;
3. security accounting;
4. general risk reserves;
5. R&D expenses and
6. operating lease expenses.

Figure 6.1 summarizes the EVA calculation procedure specific for banks.

6.3   Analyzed M&A deals

Given the high number of the EU members, our study has been restricted to the countries most involved in the M&A phenomenon; therefore our focus is on France, Germany, Italy, and the UK

$\psi_{t-1,t} = \pi_{t-1,t} - k \cdot K_{t-1}$ [1]

where:

$\pi_{t-1,t} = \pi_{acc}$ + R&D Expenses + Training expenses + Operating Lease Expenses + Loan loss provisions − Net charge-off + General risk provisions − Net charge-off

K_{t-1} = Book value of equity + Capitalized R&D expenses [2] + Capitalized training expenses [2] − Proxy for amortized R&D expenses [3] − Proxy for amortized training expenses [3] + Proxy for the present value of expected lease commitments over time [4] − Proxy for amortized operating lease commitments [4] + Net

Loan loss reserve + General Risk Reserve

Figure 6.1   EVA calculation tailored for banking

Legend: ψ is the EVA; π is the "economic measure" of the bank net operating profits; πacc is the "accounting" net operating profits; K is the capital invested; k is the estimated cost of capital invested; R&D is "Research and Development"; i and t subscripts denote the cross-section and the time dimensions, respectively.

Notes: (1) The capital invested cannot be simply measured using total assets and the cost of invested capital is not estimated as the Weighted Average Cost of Capital (WACC). Since financial intermediation is the core business for banks, debts should be considered as a productive input in banking rather than a financing source (as for other companies). As such, interest expenses represent the cost for acquiring this input and, consequently, should be considered as an operating cost rather than a financial cost (as for other companies). As a consequence, if the capital charge is calculated following a standard procedure (that is,. applying WACC on total assets), EVA will be biased since it will double count the charge on debt. As such, the charge on debt should be firstly subtracted from NOPAT (the capital charge is calculated on the overall capital – i.e. equity and debt – invested in the bank and, consequently, it includes the charge on debt) and, secondly, it would be subtracted from operating proceeds in calculating NOPAT: interest expenses (that is, the charge on debt capital) are in fact subtracted from operating revenues. In the case of banks, it seems reasonable to calculate the capital invested (and, consequently, the capital charge) focusing on equity capital (among others, Di Antonio, 2002; Resti and Sironi, 2007): as such, we measure the capital invested in the bank as the book value of total equity and the cost of capital as the cost of equity. The cost of equity is estimated by the following procedure: 1) for quoted banks, we use a standard procedure applying a two-factor model using both market and interest rate risk factors (following Unal and Kane 1988); and 2) for non-quoted banks, we apply the mean of the cost of equity capital for comparable domestic quoted banks (in terms of total assets).

(2) Capitalized R&D expenses and capitalized training expenses are obtained by summing annual R&E expenses and training expenses, respectively, over a period of five years (e.g. Stewart, 1991 suggests that five years is the average useful life of R&D expenses).

(3) The proxies for amortized R&D expenses and amortized training expenses are obtained as the mean of the R&D expenses over the 1996–2005 period.

(4) Since data availability does not allow us to evaluate the present value of expected lease commitments over time, the present value of expected future lease commitments capitalized is assumed to be equal to the overall amount of operating leases expenses over a five – year period. The amount annually amortized is close to the amount of R&D expenses divided by 3 years (assuming a straight-line amortization process).

Source: Adjusted by Fiordelisi (2007, p. 2169).

(see Table 6.1): 72.25% of the M&As realized among firms in Europe has interested firms in one of these four countries, and 68.4% of the Gross Domestic Product (GDP) of the European Union is produced in one of these countries.

The overall sample is of 10,049 observations comprising commercial, cooperative and savings banks between 1995 and 2002.[5] Table 6.2 presents the main descriptive statistics relative to the total sample (data source: Bankscope database). Information on M&A comes from the Zephyr database.[6] Accounting data are obtained from Bankscope and market information is obtained from Datastream. We analyze 141 M&As (both domestic and cross-border) over the

Table 6.1   M&A deals across countries in the European Union

Country	1990–93		2000–03	
	Share in terms of number of M&A operations (%)	Share in terms of value of M&A operations (%)	Share in terms of number of M&A operations (%)	Share in terms of value of M&A operations (%)
United Kingdom	34.5	13.8	33.4	17.1
France	18.6	17.2	15.0	15.9
Germany	11.1	24.7	14.6	22.2
Italy	8.6	15.3	9.2	13.2
Netherlands	6.6	4.3	6.6	4.6
Sweden	6.3	3.2	6.0	7.2
Spain	5.6	7.3	3.4	2.7
Belgium	2.3	2.9	2.2	2.7
Finland	1.2	1.5	2.1	1.5
Ireland	1.0	0.7	1.6	1.9
Portugal	0.9	1.1	1.2	1.3
Denmark	0.8	1.9	1.0	1.3
Austria	0.7	2.4	0.9	0.2
Other old EU members	1.8	1.6	1.1	5.7
Total old EU members	99.2	97.9	98.3	96.2
New EU members	0.8	2.1	1.7	3.8

Source: European Commission (2004, p. 4) based on the source SDC M&A, Ameco.

Table 6.2 Descriptive statistics of the overall bank sample

	Loans	Deposits	Total assets	Total equity	Net income	EVA	ROE	ROA	EVA over invested capital
FRANCE									
No. of observations	1623.0	1623.0	1623.0	1623.0	1623.0	1623.0	1623.0	1623.0	1623.0
Minimum	0.1*	0.5*	10.4*	2.7*	-2134.3*	-4810.0*	-158.3%	-8.04%	-89.19%
Median	953.8*	1266.3*	1813.7*	133.3*	7.0*	0.5*	7.1%	0.4%	0.6%
Maximum	273212.0*	379858.0*	682139.0*	44545.0*	3925.0*	4260.1*	270.7%	19.5%	215.2%
Standard deviation	19887.1*	35347.6*	55516.8*	3284.4*	245.4*	375.6*	23.1%	1.3%	15.1%
GERMANY									
No. of observations	9301	9301	9301	9301	9301	9301	9301	9301	9301
Minimum	0.1*	6.5	10.8*	0.7*	-2901.0*	-4022.3*	-340.00%	-13.81%	-241.02%
Median	253.1*	366.9*	418.5*	24.5*	1.0*	-0.2*	4.32%	0.24%	-0.99%
Maximum	217673.4*	437571.0*	566509.0*	29450.0*	3360.2*	2673.5*	57.49%	8.25%	179.74%
Standard deviation	7799.5*	12110.9*	16722.7*	989.5*	59.7*	72.8*	6.37%	0.40%	6.84%
ITALY									
No. of observations	2317	2318	2318	2318	2318	2318	2318	2318	2318

Minimum	0.3*	5.2	11.6*	1.6*	−1504.7*	−2437.1*	−165.38%	−7.21%	−66.31%
Median	181.3*	208.9*	367.6*	45.5*	2.3*	−0.2v	5.95%	0.67%	−1.14%
Maximum	797.9*	984.8*	1635.7*	154.4*	7.6*	1.0*	8.22%	0.99%	2.15%
Standard deviation	8789.8*	10373.9*	16575.1*	1362.4*	95.2*	112.1*	8.82%	0.79%	7.37%
UNITED KINGDOM									
No. of observations	391	391	391	391	391	391	391	391	391
Minimum	0.1*	2.0*	18.6*	4.0	−109.9*	−1400.6*	−44.20%	−5.87%	−53.36%
Median	554.3*	759.8*	1072.9*	115.4*	8.5*	−1.1*	11.13%	0.82%	−3.59%
Maximum	96790.0*	114173.0*	163139.0*	12397.0*	2172.0*	721.6*	66.67%	48.92%	57.49%
Standard deviation	2709665*	3225697*	5002626*	267945*	41230*	−7045*	47	6	−10

*Data are in Euro millions.

Source: Bankscope database.

period 1995–2002, which are selected on the basis of the following criteria:

1. The bank headquarter should be in France, Germany, Italy and United Kingdom.
2. The transaction was effectively completed and there was in effect a change of control of the target bank.
3. The banks involved in the merger should not be affiliated.
4. Data relative to both acquiring and acquired banks should e available at least one year before and one after the transaction. Table 6.3 shows some descriptive statistics of our sample.

Table 6.3   Number of M&A operations analyzed between 1997 and 2002

Year	Bank	Country				Total
		France	Germany	Italy	UK	
1995	Bidder	0	1	1	0	2
1995	Target	0	0	0	0	0
1996	Bidder	1	2	1	1	5
1996	Target	0	0	1	0	1
1997	Bidder	0	2	2	2	6
1997	Target	0	0	1	0	1
1998	Bidder	1	5	10	0	16
1998	Target	2	4	7	0	13
1999	Bidder	3	5	6	1	15
1999	Target	1	4	5	0	10
2000	Bidder	4	8	13	3	28
2000	Target	2	2	12	1	17
2001	Bidder	3	4	7	2	16
2001	Target	2	2	7	1	12
2002	Bidder	4	11	10	3	28
2002	Target	0	9	7	1	17
Total	Bidder	16	38	50	12	116
Total	Target	7	21	40	3	71

Source: Zephyr database.

6.4 Results

First, Table 6.4 reports EVA mean values for the whole sample – that is, both banks involved and not involved in M&As – differentiated by country? Almost 95% of the banks in the sample obtained profits and the mean net income amounts to €11.62 millions. Nevertheless, the analysis of the shareholder value does not show similar positive results since the opportunity cost of the invested capital is often higher than bank profits. Namely, less than 40% of the banks created shareholder and, on average, banks destroyed shareholder value by 4.5 Euro million. Even if there are differences from country to country, we observe that only part of the profitable banks create value for shareholders (see Fiordelisi and Molyneux, 2006).

To evaluate the M&As impact on EVA, we first compare the mean shareholder value created by banks involved in M&As and those not involved. Shareholders' value is measured both in absolute and relative values; that is, the EVA created in the period in Euro and the ratio between EVA and capital invested respectively.[7] French and German acquiring banks are able to generate, on average, an EVA slightly higher than the EVA created by target banks (see Table 6.5). The opposite occurs in Italy: the banks with higher capacity of creating value seem to export this capacity through the acquisition of banks less oriented to the shareholder value creation in France and Germany; whereas in Italy, bidder banks are less able to create value (but of larger size[8]) than target banks. The analysis of the mean EVA created in a given period is, of course, influenced by the bank size.[9] We also use a relative value indicator such as the ratio between EVA and invested capital. Our findings confirm what was previously observed for France and Italy: in the first case, acquiring banks has a better capacity in creating value than acquired banks while, in Italy, acquired banks display a better capacity in creating value compared to the acquiring ones. As for the other two countries, negative mean values of the ratio between EVA and invested capital have been registered for the acquired banks, consistently with the poor banks ability to create shareholder value previously discussed. Similarly to Italy, acquiring banks show a worse relative capacity in creating value than acquired banks.

In order to verify if M&As increased the shareholder value, we also compare over time – that is, before and after the operation – both

Table 6.4 Mean bank performance indicators in banking

		1995		1996			1997			1998		
		Mean	St. dev	% Positive	Mean	St. dev	% Positive	Mean	St. dev	% Positive	Mean	St. dev	% Positive
France	Published Net income*	17.61	76.61	80.13	20.91	93.86	86.00	17.26	168.02	84.42	26.86	157.32	87.72
	EVA$_{bkg}$*	-14.43	100.66	39.36	-13.43	91.67	43.72	-11.47	154.41	49.27	-7.44	120.66	46.95
	EVA$_{bkg}$/Inv. Capital+	-0.68%	11.26%	39.36	-1.40%	12.62%	43.72	0.82%	11.76%	49.27	-0.69%	9.93%	46.95
Germany	Published Net income*	4.31	12.33	97.88	4.13	13.05	97.36	4.24	14.23	97.62	5.20	21.60	97.16
	EVA$_{bkg}$*	-1.00	11.00	32.45	-0.58	5.60	57.12	-0.45	7.43	57.92	-0.58	20.28	38.21
	EVA$_{bkg}$/Inv. Capital+	-0.64%	4.42%	32.45	0.74%	4.10%	57.12	0.76%	3.34%	57.92	-0.17%	5.02%	38.21
Italy	Published Net income*	7.26	43.64	91.77	4.89	74.88	95.20	3.02	90.61	95.70	14.45	39.14	94.84
	EVA$_{bkg}$*	-34.89	89.88	12.12	-26.39	71.73	13.28	-18.58	81.58	37.42	-6.03	54.21	42.58
	EVA$_{bkg}$/Inv. Capital+	-7.25%	6.17%	12.12	-4.87%	5.94%	13.28	-1.47%	5.90%	37.42	-0.13%	6.12%	42.58
United Kingdom	Published Net income*	58.41	139.31	95.00	63.81	176.68	97.06	65.50	163.78	96.21	60.70	150.73	90.00
	EVA$_{bkg}$*	5.88	112.47	35.00	8.17	95.29	50.00	5.81	66.54	39.88	-14.31	105.12	31.11
	EVA$_{bkg}$/Inv. Capital+	-2.26%	9.82%	35.00	-0.89%	8.52%	50.00	-1.38%	12.95%	39.88	-4.86%	18.69%	31.11
Total	Published Net income*	8.52	30.40	94.29	8.65	38.40	95.42	8.03	51.34	95.45	11.60	46.82	95.27
	EVA$_{bkg}$*	-7.17	38.20	30.98	-5.57	29.82	49.14	-4.21	40.17	53.34	-2.93	42.33	39.88
	EVA$_{bkg}$/Inv. Capital+	-1.55%	5.87%	30.98	-0.37%	5.73%	49.14	0.40%	5.20%	53.34	-0.39%	6.33%	39.88

* + Values are in Euro millions and percentage respectively.

Table 6.4 Continued

		1999			2000			2001			2002	
		Mean	St. dev	% Positive	Mean	St. dev	% Positive	Mean	St. dev	% Positive	Mean	St. dev	% Positive
France	Published Net income*	29.25	166.47	79.61	41.69	236.06	85.07	53.22	249.72	86.89	53.86	329.04	86.60
	EVA_{bkg}*	−1.23	83.04	47.94	−30.96	292.61	54.16	−26.98	351.08	57.57	−22.78	488.34	63.39
	EVA_{bkg}/Inv. Capital+ Published	0.12%	14.94%	47.94	0.36%	14.94%	54.16	0.85%	17.72%	57.57	1.85%	14.25%	63.39
Germany	Net income*	4.29	25.80	95.92	3.21	23.05	96.65	0.13	83.84	93.74	−0.01	38.42	94.14
	EVA_{bkg}*	−0.84	22.59	33.05	−2.40	45.42	29.13	−2.43	41.06	20.47	−4.27	54.30	39.57
	EVA_{bkg}/Inv. Capital+ Published	−0.66%	4.26%	33.05	−0.97%	4.21%	29.13	−2.13%	5.55%	20.47	−0.26%	6.19%	39.57
Italy	Net income*	13.52	38.38	95.51	16.67	51.94	93.51	19.08	57.29	94.06	18.09	60.63	93.27
	EVA_{bkg}*	3.21	44.35	63.06	7.39	43.41	46.03	−2.98	63.81	31.78	−0.01	65.16	39.34
	EVA_{bkg}/Inv. Capital+ Published	2.05%	5.89%	63.06	0.21%	7.13%	46.03	−1.77%	6.76%	31.78	−0.93%	8.43%	39.34
United Kingdom	Net income*	94.10	233.35	89.60	91.22	259.68	94.17	108.64	295.95	91.59	100.03	273.60	83.96
	EVA_{bkg}*	9.53	123.81	30.98	−33.34	139.71	25.24	−29.40	176.70	28.97	−39.22	192.68	29.25
	EVA_{bkg}/Inv. Capital+ Published	−1.57%	11.15%	30.98	−3.83%	11.26%	25.24	−2.90%	9.89%	28.97	−3.20%	10.75%	29.25
Total	Net income*	12.82	53.41	93.67	13.30	60.88	94.59	13.57	103.45	92.97	12.82	81.81	92.83
	EVA_{bkg}*	0.37	38.28	40.80	−4.48	75.78	35.49	−6.16	85.17	27.36	−6.40	107.69	41.77
	EVA_{bkg}/Inv. Capital+	−0.06%	6.12%	40.80	−0.66%	6.28%	35.49	−1.74%	7.32%	27.36	−0.27%	7.69%	41.77

*+ Values are in Euro millions and percentage respectively.
Source: Author's own.

Table 6.5 Mean EVA levels for banks in the sample

Country		Bidder Banks		Target Banks		Banks not-involved in M&A	
		EVA	EVA over invested capital (%)	EVA	EVA over invested capital (%)	EVA	EVA over invested capital (%)
France	Min.	−1269.66	−4.75	−392.72	−10.56	−6135.58	−97.93
	Max	4260.12	11.71	19.47	11.00	1868.83	89.23
	Mean	299.69	1.03	−56.79	0.96	−46.80	1.45
	St. Dev	1468.82	4.99	141.40	6.72	519.34	12.83
Germany	Min.	−1223.12	−34.10	−4022.32	−21.26	−2465.37	−58.51
	Max	2177.00	13.04	9.64	15.70	2673.47	75.03
	Mean	−14.24	−1.37	−149.16	−0.96	−2.06	−1.20
	St. Dev	350.53	5.17	718.74	5.37	71.73	5.19
Italy	Min.	−1037.38	−39.53	−322.47	−21.65	−816.35	−61.11
	Max	429.13	18.90	848.53	40.70	1612.23	80.29
	Mean	−19.11	0.13	47.21	1.03	8.02	0.29
	St. Dev	178.89	7.60	192.55	10.83	106.08	8.00
UK	Min.	−267.48	−20.62	−46.15	−8.91	−793.14	−97.44
	Max	7.41	13.66	−6.88	−1.94	427.82	143.87
	Mean	−53.59	−4.44	−26.52	−5.43	−32.13	−3.84
	St. Dev	79.66	8.52	27.77	4.93	129.66	29.17

Source: Author's own.

the absolute and relative EVA values of banks involved in M&As.[10] According to our results (see Table 6.6),[11] M&As have been followed, on average, by an EVA increase of 83.74 Euro million in case of mergers and of 49.03 Euro million in case of mergers. Distinguishing among countries, EVA of the banks involved in M&As increase (on average) in Germany and Italy; in France, banks' EVA increases in case of mergers, but not in case of acquisitions. Similarly to what has been previously pointed out, EVA mean values are influenced by the bank size so that we also consider the ratio between EVA and invested capital. Despite the positive picture shown by overall results. M&As have been followed, on average, by an enhanced relative capacity of creating a shareholder value of 0.23% in the case of acquisitions and of 0.41% in the case of mergers. At a single country level, results offer a different picture from what has been previously drawn. The ratio between EVA and the invested capital of the banks involved in M&As improves for both mergers and acquisitions only in Germany. It gets worse for both operations in Italy. In the United Kingdom, mergers are followed by a substantial worsening of the bank ability to create shareholder value and by a substantial improvement in the case of acquisitions.

Finally, we compare shareholder value indicator changes for banks not involved in M&A with those of non-involved banks. According to our results, it is not possible to reject the null hypothesis of Mannp-Whitney Wilcoxon test according to which both the banks involved and uninvolved in M&As come from the same. However, it is possible to reject the Kolmogorov-Smirnov test null hypothesis, which is based on the assumption that the two sub-samples have the same distribution.

6.5 Conclusion

This chapter contributes to the debate on the effects of M&As on shareholders' value. Our analysis presents innovative features since it uses EVA to assess banks' performance. It changes and analyzes both listed and not-listed banks over five-year period. In addition, the sample is one of the largest ever used and includes banks from European countries mostly interested by the M&A phenomenon: that is, France, Germany, Italy and the United Kingdom.

Our results provide evidence that M&A produce positive effects for shareholders: the relative ability of the bank to create value

Table 6.6 Value creation after M&A deals

Panel A) mean EVA levels (data are Euro millions)

	T_{-1} Acquisitions (bidder)	T_{-1} Mergers	T_{-2} Acquisitions (bidder)	T_{-2} Mergers	T_{-3} Acquisitions (bidder)	T_{-3} Mergers	T_{4} Acquisitions (bidder)	T_{4} Mergers	T_{5} Acquisitions (bidder)	T_{5} Mergers	T_{0-5} Acquisitions (bidder)	T_{0-5} Mergers
France	-383.79	-27.45	43.46	77.36	-4.79	176.09	N/A	224.48	N/A	N/A	-203.31	171.51
Germany	-0.22	657.69	202.32	10.76	360.04	0.19	876.90	1.52	1957.97	N/A	122.06	141.74
Italy	51.51	51.89	136.70	54.69	156.57	-34.82	86.25	-33.38	40.91	N/A	52.45	26.78
U.K.	0.45	-15.53	-74.24	-45.16	4.58	N/A	N/A	N/A	-13.91	N/A	-45.38	-30.35
Total	-32.26	150.54	133.38	41.38	228.29	27.16	411.81	29.36	661.66	N/A	49.03	83.74

Source: Author's own.

Panel B) EVA over invested capital (data are Euro millions)

	T_{-1} Acquisitions (bidder) (%)	T_{-1} Mergers (%)	T_{-2} Acquisitions (bidder) (%)	T_{-2} Mergers (%)	T_{-3} Acquisitions (bidder) (%)	T_{-3} Mergers (%)	T_{4} Acquisitions (bidder) (%)	T_{4} Mergers (%)	T_{5} Acquisitions (bidder) (%)	T_{5} Mergers (%)	T_{0-5} Acquisitions (bidder) (%)	T_{0-5} Mergers (%)
France	-0.79	3.25	-1.71	-1.67	-5.91	-1.81	N/A	-4.75	N/A	N/A	-1.49	0.32
Germany	0.32	3.44	0.47	8.42	0.03	0.33	5.88	3.98	10.73	N/A	0.09	4.81
Italy	-1.16	0.26	-0.93	2.65	-0.22	-8.57	-1.52	-6.55	-3.43	N/A	-0.97	-1.62
UK	2.58	-18.58	2.21	0.72	10.87	N/A	N/A	N/A	21.73	N/A	9.07	-8.93
Total	-0.48	0.72	-0.19	3.72	0.11	-3.84	1.53	-3.91	9.67	N/A	0.23	0.41

Source: Author's own.

(measured by the ratio between EVA and invested capital) increases by 0.23% in case of acquisitions and 0.41% in case of mergers. This is consistent with previous studies dealing with the European banking sector. For example, in their review of studies on banks' consolidation, DeYoung et al., (2009) note that studies on European bank mergers provide evidence of performance improvements. In any case, our results vary with respect to the country considered: M&As have been followed (on average) by improvements in shareholder value (both in case of mergers and acquisitions) in Germany, while the opposite is observed in Italy.

7
Do M&As Create Value for Shareholders? The Effect on Bank Efficiency

7.1 Introduction

Similarly to Chapter 6, this chapter provides a dynamic study et al., to assess the Merger and Acquisition effects on cost efficiency in European banking over a five-year period. By using a large sample from the countries mainly involved in the M&A phenomenon – that is, France, Germany, Italy, and the United Kingdom – our analysis compares cost efficiency levels in a moment prior and successive to the deal itself (Altunbus and Margques-Ibanez, 2004).

Since the 1990s, various studies have assessed merger-induced improvements in productive efficiency by directly comparing pre- and post-merger levels; as for example, Berger and Humphrey (1992), De Young (1993), Akhavein (1997), Resti (1998), Rhoades (1998), Lang and Welzel (1999), Fried et al., (1999), Haynes and Thompson (1999), Hughes et al., (1999), Huizinga et al., (2001), Cuesta and Area (2002), Berger and Mester (2003), Wang (2003), Carbo-Valverde and Humphrey (2004), Humphrey and Vale (2004), Koetter (2005), De Guevara and Maudos (2007), Ashton and Pham (2007), and Behr and Heid (2008) (for further details, see Chapter 4). The consensus view on mergers of financial institutions (mostly commercial bank mergers) during the 1980s and the early 1990s is that accounting ratio, cost efficiency, and profit efficiency improvements, though less studied, were elusive.

When considering M&A performance studies published from 2000 onwards, DeYoung et al., (2009, forthcoming) note that "the recent literature suggests that North American bank mergers are (or can be) efficiency improving" and that "European bank deals have resulted in both efficiency gains and stockholder value enhancement".

This chapter contributes to the existing literature by considering a large sample of M&A deals in the European Banking, especially in the 2000s. Moreover, we use the same dataset used to analyze the M&A effect on shareholder value in order to assess if efficiency improvements effectively result in shareholder value gains.

The chapter is organized as follows: firstly, we outline the methodology (Section 7.2), next, we describe the sample selected (Section 7.3) and discuss our findings (Section 7.4). In Section 7.5, we discuss the contribution of our study to the existing literature by comparing the M&A effects on banks' shareholder value and cost efficiency.

7.2 Methods

The first step of the analysis is to assess the effects produced by M&As on the cost efficiency (*x-efficiency*) of the banks involved.[1] Our approach is based on the assumption that bank cost efficiency is influenced by quantities, prices of the inputs and outputs used in the production process (as it is traditionally considered in the cost function), and the organizational and managerial bank structure. The latter factors are usually taken into account by including dummy variables in the cost function to isolate the effect generated by the factors themselves. The cost function is estimated using the Battese and Coelli (1995) model:

$$ln\ TC_{it} = x_{it}\ \beta + (V_{it} + U_{it}) \tag{7.1}$$

ln TC$_i$ is the natural logarithm of the total of the production costs for *i-th* bank of the sample; x_i is a vector of dimension *kx1* of the standardized prices of inputs and outputs for the *i-th* bank; and β is a vector of unknown parameters. V_i is a random variable assumed to be i.i.d $N(0,\ \sigma^2_v)$ and independent from the variable U_i. U_i is a non-negative random variable that represents the cost inefficiency of the bank *i* and which is assumed to be i.i.d $N(m_{it}\ \sigma^2 u)$, where $m_{it} = z_{it}$, δ, in which z_{it} is a vector of dimension *px1* representing the variables that may influence the bank's efficiency, δ is a vector of dimension *px1* embodying the parameters subject to the estimation.

Our sample, which covers the period 1995–2002, encompasses different typologies of banks ranging from commercial and cooperative to saving banks. It is located in different countries such as France, Germany, Italy, and the United Kingdom. The model of Battese and Coelli (1995) allows us to control these factors when estimating x-efficiency. As such, we use the following translog function commonly used in the literature:[2]

$$
\begin{aligned}
\ln TC = {} & \alpha_0 + \sum_{i=1}^{3} \alpha_i \ln y_i + \sum_{j=1}^{3} \beta_j \ln w_j \\
& + \frac{1}{2}\left[\sum_{i=1}^{3}\sum_{j=1}^{3} \delta_{ij} \ln y_i \ln y_j + \sum_{i=1}^{3}\sum_{j=1}^{3} \gamma_{ij} \ln w_i \ln w_j \right] \\
& + \sum_{i=1}^{3}\sum_{j=1}^{3} \rho_{ij} \ln y_i \ln w_j + \sum_{i=1}^{2} Z_i + \sum_{i=1}^{3} C_i + \sum_{i=1}^{6} T_i + \ln u_c + \ln \varepsilon_c
\end{aligned}
\tag{7.2}
$$

ln TC is the natural logarithm of the total of the production costs, α_o is the constant term; y_i is the output quantity for *i-th* output used by the bank; w_i quantity is the price of the *i-th* input used by the bank; Z_i (i = 1,2) are the control variables for the influence of the bank type; C_i (i = 1,2,3) are the control variables for the influence of the bank nationality; and T_i (i = 1,...,6) are the control variables for the influence of the different years. The standard symmetry conditions have to be imposed on the translog function: $\delta_{ij} = \delta_{ji}$ and $\gamma_{ij} = \gamma_{ji}$ (where i = 1,2,3 and j = 1,2,3). The following linear restrictions on model (2) are necessary and sufficient for linear homogeneity in factor prices: $\sum_{j=1}^{3} \beta_j = 1; \sum_{i=1}^{3} \gamma_{ij} = 0$ and $\sum_{j=1}^{3} \rho_{ij} = 0$.

In order to assess the impact of M&As on x-efficiency, we compare the mean x-efficiency levels of banks involved in M&As with those of other banks. Nevertheless, the comparison does not enable us to give an unambiguous interpretation because those differences could be due to factors other than M&As. For this purpose, we divide banks into various sub-samples on the basis of their nationality, ownership and year, and we assess if merging banks display efficiency changes. In the case of mergers – for example, banks A and B merged in the year *t-2* creating the bank C –, we compare the bank C's x-efficiency at time t_o with a proxy of the x-efficiency at time *t-2* [that is, obtained by repeating the cost function estimation (in model 1) by summing up the data on inputs and outputs of banks A and B]. In the case of acquisitions – for example, bank A acquires bank B, incorporating it or not, in time t-2 –, we compare the current bank A's x-efficiency at time t_0 with its x-efficiency at time *t-2*. According to Huizinga et al., (2001), efficiency changes should be measured in terms of ranking in the sub-sample itself rather than in terms of the absolute value of efficiency. It is because this value depends on other factors such as the number of banks analyzed and other environmental factors.

Finally, following Haynes and Thompson (1999), the M&As impact on x-efficiency is analyzed by adding a set of variables (M_i) useful to evaluate the influence of M&A operations on the cost function occurred in the analyzed period:[3]

$$
\begin{aligned}
\ln TC = {} & \alpha_0 + \sum_{i=1}^{3} \alpha_i \ln y_i + \sum_{j=1}^{3} \beta_j \ln w_j \\
& + \frac{1}{2}\left[\sum_{i=1}^{3}\sum_{j=1}^{3} \delta_{ij} \ln y_i \ln y_j + \sum_{i=1}^{3}\sum_{j=1}^{3} \gamma_{ij} \ln w_i \ln w_j \right] \\
& + \sum_{i=1}^{3}\sum_{j=1}^{3} \rho_{ij} \ln y_i \ln w_j + \sum_{i=1}^{2} Z_i + \sum_{i=1}^{3} C_i + \sum_{i=1}^{6} T_i + \sum_{i=1}^{i} M_i + \ln u_c + \ln \varepsilon_c
\end{aligned}
$$

$$(7.3)$$

TC_i is the natural logarithm of the total of the production costs borne by the bank; α_0 is the constant term; y_i is the quantity of the *i-th* output used by the bank; w_i quantity is the price of the *i-th* input used by the bank; Z_i (i = 1,2) are the control variables for the influence of the bank type; C_i (i = 1,2,3) are the control variables for the influence of the bank nationality; T_i (i = 1,...,6) are the control variables for the influence of the different years; and M_i are dummy variables controlling the influence of M&A deals. As for the specification of these variables (M_i), an unambiguous indication on the length of the period needed for the M&A to be effective does not exist. Haynes and Thompson (1999) analyze bank data in the five years following the M&A operation. Rhoades (1993) considers a period of four years. Fixler and Zienschang (1993) focus on the data that immediately follow the operation. Given the uncertainty existing in previous studies, we adopt different solutions, consistently with what Haynes and Thompson (1999) propose. First, we consider a period of five years[4] after the M&A, using a dummy variable for each year: for example, M_1 is 1 if the bank *i* was interested by a M&A in the previous period and 0 otherwise; M_2 is 1 if the bank *i* was involved in a M&A two years before and 0 otherwise and so on. This solution enables us to assess multiple acquisitions made by the same bank in different moments within the time interval considered (5 years), although we have to impose a predefined structure to time lags. Secondly, we consider a single dummy variable expressing that if the bank has been involved in the M&As over the period of five years (M_{any5}).

Since the distribution of x-efficiency estimates of each sample is not normal, the comparison is conducted through the non-parametric Mann-Whitney-Wilcoxon and Kolmogorov-Smirnov tests. The first test is based on the x-efficiency ranking; it tests the null hypothesis that the banks in the two groups (banks involved in M&As vs. not involved banks) – come out from the same population. Through the Kolmogorov-Smirnov test, the presence of differences in the locations and in the form of the distribution can be identified.

In the cost efficiency measurement, the choice of inputs and outputs is a fundamental moment. Distortions in efficiency estimates could be derived from an imperfect choice of the variables and the constraints of the selected model or from an inaccurate definition of the orientation of the production efficiency measures adopted (input- vs. output-orientation). Various approaches have been proposed in the economic literature, including the production and the intermediation approaches (see Altunbas et al., 1996). According to the production approach, a bank is a firm which uses capital and labour to produce deposits and loans. In regards to the intermediation approach, a bank is a financial intermediary that uses labour, capital and deposits to produce loans. In our study, bank inputs and outputs are selected according to the value-added approach in which inputs and outputs are defined on the basis of the contributions given by the various items of the asset side and of the liability side in terms of value creation.

As shown in Table 7.1, we posit that bank inputs are labour factors (measured by the ratio between personnel expenses and total assets), financial capital (measured by the ratio between interest costs and total amount of available funds for loans), and physical or non-financial capital (measured by the ratio between total equipment capital expenses and total fixed-tangible assets). We also claim that outputs are total demand deposits,[5] total loans and other earning assets (for example, bonds and shares). Differently from previous studies (see Altumbas et al., (2000) and Carbo-Valverbe et al., (2000)),

Table 7.1 Inputs and outputs used in estimating cost efficiency[26]

Total Costs (TC)	Total production costs (including operating costs and interest paid on deposits);
Input 1 (w_1):	Average cost of labour (i.e. personnel expenses/total assets);
Input 2 (w_2):	Average cost of physical capital (i.e. total equipment capital expenses/total fixed-tangible assets);
Input 3 (w_3):	Average cost of financial capital deposits (i.e. interest costs on borrowed funds on the average amount of borrowed funds);
Output 1 (Y_1):	Demand deposits;
Output 2 (Y_2)	Total loans;
Output 3 (Y_3)	Other earning assets.

Source: Author's own.

we do not consider off-balance sheet items even if they contribute to the creation of value. This is because our sample comprises a large number of small banks[6] (especially, cooperative and saving banks) to whom the off-balance sheet items have a marginal relevance and whose data are often not available.

7.3   Analyzed M&A deals

Given the high number of EU members, our study has been restricted to the countries most involved in the M&A phenomenon (see Table 6.1). Consequently, our focus is on France, Germany, Italy, and the UK for two reasons: first, 72.25% of the M&As in European bankinghas involved banks of (at least) one of these four countries; and second, 68.4% of the Gross Domestic Product (GDP) of the European Union is produced by these countries.

Various samples have been used according to the type of analysis carried out. In order to estimate cost efficiency, the sample is of 10049 observations comprising commercial, cooperative and savings banks between 1995 and 2002.[7] Table 7.2 presents the main descriptive statistics relative to the total sample (datasource: Bankscope). Information on M&A comes from the Zephyr database, accounting data are obtained from Bankscope and market information are obtained from Datastream. In order to make our results comparable

Table 7.2 Descriptive statistics of the overall bank sample in the period 1995–2002

	Loans	Deposits	Total assets	Total equity	X-efficiency
FRANCE					
No. of observations	1623.0	1623.0	1623.0	1623.0	1623.0
Minimum	0.1*	0.5*	10.4*	2.7*	22.4%
Median	953.8*	1266.3*	1813.7*	133.3*	73.9%
Maximum	273212.0*	379858.0*	682139.0*	44545.0*	100.0%
Standard deviation	19887.1*	35347.6*	55516.8*	3284.4*	13.0%
GERMANY					
No. of observations	9301	9301	9301	9301	9301
Minimum	0.1*	6.5	10.8*	0.7*	12.72%
Median	253.1*	366.9*	418.5*	24.5*	80.08%
Maximum	217673.4*	437571.0*	566509.0*	29450.0*	100.00%
Standard deviation	7799.5*	12110.9*	16722.7*	989.5*	9.46%
ITALY					
No. of observations	2317	2318	2318	2318	2318
Minimum	0.3*	5.2	11.6*	1.6*	1.60%
Median	181.3*	208.9*	367.6*	45.5*	81.97%
Maximum	797.9*	984.8*	1635.7*	154.4*	87.64%
Standard deviation	8789.8*	10373.9*	16575.1*	1362.4*	14.80%
UNITED KINGDOM					
No. of observations	391	391	391	391	391
Minimum	0.1*	2.0*	18.6*	4.0	32.53%
Median	554.3*	759.8*	1072.9*	115.4*	83.80%
Maximum	96790.0*	114173.0*	163139.0*	12397.0*	100.00%
Standard deviation	2709665*	3225697*	5002626*	267945*	306

* Data are in Euro millions.

Source: Bankscope database.

with those obtained in Chapter 6, we use the same sample used to assess the M&A effects on banks' EVA (see Table 6.3).[8]

The choice of estimating a single "common" frontier for banks working in different countries, having a different nature and over a period longer than one year (even if there are control variables for each of these aspects) may be criticized. Efficiency measures have in fact a relative nature (i.e. these are obtained by comparing banks with the best-practice firms in the sample) and it is explicitly assumed that all banks in the sample:

1. compete among themselves even if only potentially;
2. are homogeneous in terms of input and output used in the production process;
3. are subject to the same set of environmental factors (such as economic, regulation demographic and market conditions) that can4. not be controlled by the banks themselves.[9]

Dietsch and Lozano-Vivas (2000) note, for example, that the efficiency estimates obtained using a "common" frontier tend to be lower for firms working in countries with worse environmental conditions.[10] In order to increase the soundness of our results, the cost efficiency estimation has been repeated using cross-section samples (divided by country and year) repeating the procedure described in Section 3.1 of this chapter.[11]

7.4   Results

Before discussing our results, it is useful to recall that efficiency estimates are obtained by using the whole sample (that is, all banks are aggregated) and various sub-samples (that is, banks are grouped in homogeneous clusters according to their nationality and ownership). Even if more computationally expensive, this enable us to:

1. have different sets of efficiency estimates so as to verify their consistency[12] and increase their robustness;
2. restrict the comparison of the efficiency level to most accurate set of efficiency estimates according to the purposes of the analysis. For instance, the comparison of efficiency along time (that is, the comparison of the efficiency estimates for the same bank in different time periods) and space (that is, the comparison of mean efficiency levels of different countries in the same time period) can be accurately carried out using efficiency estimates obtained from the whole sample (that is, estimating a "common" single efficiency frontier). Vice versa, the comparison between the

efficiency estimates of the banks involved in M&As and that of banks not involved requires maximum homogeneity in the sample to minimize the influence of other determinants such as nationality and type of bank.

Table 7.3 shows the mean cost efficiency levels for the whole sample, divided by the country of origin, obtained through the estimation

Table 7.3   Mean cost efficiency levels in European banking
Panel A) Homogeneous sub-samples according to country and year

Country	Year	Min.	Max	Mean	St. Dev
France	2002	0.294	0.939	0.769	0.089
France	2001	0.335	0.898	0.652	0.083
France	2000	0.289	0.985	0.576	0.106
Germany	2002	0.230	0.922	0.705	0.103
Germany	2001	0.290	0.972	0.697	0.111
Germany	2000	0.301	0.919	0.767	0.078
Italy	2002	0.265	0.921	0.670	0.045
Italy	2001	0.322	0.946	0.523	0.151
Italy	2000	0.297	0.924	0.564	0.135
U.K.	2002	0.311	0.952	0.611	0.302
U.K.	2001	0.255	0.964	0.489	0.229
U.K.	2000	0.385	0.975	0.409	0.213

Panel B) Overall sample

Country	Year	Min.	Max	Mean	St. Dev
France	2002	0.239	0.883	0.723	0.133
France	2001	0.261	0.896	0.714	0.141
France	2000	0.232	0.899	0.704	0.149
Germany	2002	0.209	0.890	0.619	0.158
Germany	2001	0.202	0.889	0.618	0.160
Germany	2000	0.212	0.893	0.620	0.161
Italy	2002	0.205	0.885	0.670	0.157
Italy	2001	0.224	0.890	0.671	0.153
Italy	2000	0.231	0.896	0.664	0.160
U.K.	2002	0.275	0.903	0.741	0.142
U.K.	2001	0.222	0.890	0.757	0.125
U.K.	2000	0.363	0.903	0.751	0.117

Source: Author's own.

of model (1). Results obtained analyzing sub-samples underline that the cost efficiency levels range from 40.9% for British banks in 2000 to 76.9% for French banks in 2002. The mean cost efficiency levels obtained from the whole sample seems to be more homogeneous, ranging from 61.8 % for German banks in 2000 to 74.1% for British banks in 2002. Focusing on the efficiency estimates from the whole sample,[13] British banks show a mean cost efficiency (75%) higher than other countries, followed by French banks (71%), Italian banks and finally German ones (62%).

Since this is a dynamic study on efficiency, M&As impact is firstly analyzed by comparing the efficiency level of banks involved in M&A with those of not involved banks.[14] According to our results (Table 7.4), banks not involved in M&As show, on average, substantially higher cost efficiency levels than those of banks involved in M&A operations, mainly in France, Germany and the United Kingdom. Acquiring banks seem to be, on average, more efficient in France and the United Kingdom, whereas there are not substantial

Table 7.4 Mean cost efficiency levels in banking

Country	Position	Homogenous sub-samples				Overall sample			
		Min.	Max	Mean	St. dev	Min.	Max	Mean	St. dev
France	Bidder	0.376	0.903	0.638	0.144	0.414	0.869	0.767	0.098
France	Target	0.387	0.777	0.597	0.130	0.498	0.856	0.725	0.134
France	Not involved M&A	0.201	0.962	0.667	0.121	0.232	0.899	0.713	0.142
Germany	Bidder	0.185	0.952	0.690	0.155	0.304	0.856	0.618	0.160
Germany	Target	0.212	0.950	0.703	0.146	0.315	0.863	0.619	0.156
Germany	Not involved M&A	0.121	0.963	0.722	0.103	0.202	0.893	0.619	0.159
Italy	Bidder	0.013	0.726	0.637	0.246	0.326	0.876	0.658	0.151
Italy	Target	0.028	0.739	0.639	0.248	0.301	0.888	0.638	0.149
Italy	Not involved M&A	0.005	0.794	0.643	0.236	0.205	0.896	0.670	0.157
UK	Bidder	0.071	1.000	0.595	0.236	0.448	0.895	0.724	0.150
UK	Target	0.200	0.524	0.436	0.168	0.541	0.858	0.724	0.164
UK	Not involved M&A	0.002	0.999	0.604	0.265	0.222	0.903	0.751	0.127

Source: Author's own.

differences in the other cases. These results seem to suggest that M&As are used in France and the UK by less efficient banks as a way to regain efficiency, particularly through the acquisition of those banks that turn out to be even less efficient.

In order to verify if M&As determine cost efficiency gains, we also compare over time the cost efficiency of banks involved in M&As.[15] By dividing banks in various sub-samples according to the country, ownership and year, x-efficiency changes are measured in terms of ranking[16] within the sub-samples. The bank ranking is measured in percentage[17] so that a positive change over time[18] expresses the percentage improvement of the firm's ranking. Table 7.5 reports only results obtained by the sub-samples' investigation since these are the

Table 7.5　Cost efficiency changes after M&A deals[(*)]

		France (%)	Germany	Italy (%)	U.K.	Total (%)
T_{-1}	Acquisitions (bidder)	6.54	–1.78	–0.20	–5.69	0.79
T_{-1}	Mergers	0.00	15.93	–6.45	28.82	4.10
T_{-2}	Acquisitions (bidder)	1.94	1.92	3.21	12.11	3.76
T_{-2}	Mergers	15.03	–24.04	–1.09	–8.25	–1.76
T_{-3}	Acquisitions (bidder)	–6.63	14.39	–13.15	18.16	–0.62
T_{-3}	Mergers	3.59	19.58	–9.61	20.52	–0.54
T_{-4}	Acquisitions (bidder)	–6.45	–13.99	9.02	6.32	–0.68
T_{-4}	Mergers	–2.00	5.45	1.73	N/A	2.57
T_{-5}	Acquisitions (bidder)	–27.46	–1.05	–17.76	–17.51	–12.72
T_{-5}	Mergers	–7.96	10.86	–9.66	N/A	–3.43
T_{-6}	Acquisitions (bidder)	N/A	0.04	–3.63	27.35	12.78
T_{-6}	Mergers	N/A	N/A	–30.16	N/A	–30.16
All $T_{-0}.T_{-5}$	Acquisitions (bidder)	0.37	4.25	–5.15	5.30	0.67
All $T_{-0}.T_{-5}$	Mergers	2.07	9.19	–6.96	3.27	–0.54

(*) Cost efficiency changes are estimated using homogeneous sub-samples.

Source: Author's own.

most relevant for the purpose of our analysis.[19] Our results show that M&As were not followed by substantial efficiency improvements: the mean efficiency change is 0.67% for the acquiring banks and –0.54% for the new created bank. Nevertheless, the situation varies from country to country. in Italy, x-efficiency declined by 5.15% in the case of acquisitions and by 6.96% in the case of mergers, whereas the other three countries – especially Germany and the UK – registered (on average) efficiency improvements.[20] In the United Kingdom and France, M&As seem to be used as a way to regain efficiency by less efficient banks through the acquisition of even less efficient banks. Vice versa, German acquiring banks are, on average, less efficient than the acquired ones. Banks are able to regain efficiency by importing new managerial skills from acquired banks; as for example, the ability to control costs and manage financial risks.

Next, we compare our efficiency estimates (obtained by estimating model 1) with those obtained following the approach suggested by Heines and Thompson (1999); that is, adding a series of variables necessary to control the M&As influence on the cost function (model 2). Since efficiency estimates do not show to have a normal distribution, the three sets of efficiency estimates are compared through the non-parametric tests of Mann-Whitney-Wilcoxon and Kolmogorov-Smirnov. According to our results, it is possible to reject the hypotheses that banks involved in M&As and banks not involved come from the same population (that is, the null hypothesis of Mann-Whitney-Wilcoxon test) and that the two sub-samples have the same distribution (that is, the Kolmogorov-Smirnov test null hypothesis). These results are consistent for each of the three samples of efficiency estimates.

7.5   Contributing to the existing literature

By using the same dataset (that is, 141 M&As in France, Germany, Italy and UK between 1995 and 2002), we have assessed the M&A effects on banks' cost efficiency and shareholder value (see Chapters 6 and 7 respectively).

This section establishes a connection between these results and highlights our contribution to previous studies. First, the M&As analyzed do not seem to have caused substantial effects on bank x-efficiency: in a five-year period, the acquiring bank improves, on average, its own cost efficiency by 0.67%, while the new bank resulting from the merger has, on average, a worsening of 0.54%. In terms of shareholder value, the M&A effect seem to be a more positive one: the relative bank ability of creating value (measured by the ratio between EVA and invested capital) increases by 0.23% in the case of acquisitions and by 0.41% in the case of mergers. Nonetheless, results vary according to the country analyzed. In Germany, M&As have been followed, on average, by an improvement in efficiency and the bank relative ability of creating value in the cases of both acquisitions and mergers. Even if the efficiency increase is common to the other countries, German banks seem the be the only ones where cost efficiency is followed by a shareholders' value increase. These results seem to underline that efficiency improvements are obtained by importing new managerial skills – as for example, the ability to control costs and manage risks – from acquired banks that are, on average, more efficient: the new managerial skills of the acquired companies are not rejected by the acquiring ones, which integrate them by achieving a consequent improvement of their competitive capacity to create shareholder value.

A totally opposite situation is observed in Italy, where M&As are followed by a reduction in cost efficiency and in value creation. Italian banks show a reduction in efficiency in the five years following the M&A deal. They are not able to avoid – for example by improving product quality, customer satisfaction or by other business actions – the lower cost efficiency that is followed by the destruction of shareholder value.

A microeconomic analysis of the M&A operations studied enable us to observe that:

1. these results are given on average and do not concern all banks; this is evident from some successful cases in the Italian banking system;
2. negative M&A effects seem to be mainly related to the wrong choice of the target bank, which that has an efficiency level similar to that of the acquiring bank;
3. the Italian labour market rigidity does not make the firm reorganization easy in the phase following the merger and this makes it difficult to achieve economies of scale gains. As such, the post-merger phase – that is, the integration of the two organizational structures – is more difficult in Italy than in other countries. It

determines first a cost efficiency decline and, secondly, the unsuccessful development of productive and distributive synergies able to create value for shareholders.

In the United Kingdom and France, M&As seem to be one of the ways to regain efficiency by less efficient banks in the market through the acquisition of even less efficient bank. Efficiency improvement, for instance, are obtained through the improvement of the company's image (for example, as a consequence of the larger size and/or territorial presence), product and/or distributive synergies, a reorganization of the bank itself, and so forth. Moreover, in these two countries, the M&A form seems to influence the results obtained by shareholders. In the United Kingdom, there is a substantial improvement in cost efficiency to which corresponds an increase in the relative average capacity of creating value for shareholders, but only when the aggregation takes place through acquisition (and not merger) of the company. Conversely, there is a slight growth of the value created in the case of mergers (but not acquisitions) in France. Similarly to what happens in Italy, our results for the M&A effects refer to mean values so that the situation above described does not refer to all the operators, as there are some successful cases of acquisitions both in France and in the United Kingdom.

According to the sources of data available, it is not possible to give precise explanations of the reasons behind those results.,[21] However, it is possible to describe a series of potential relevant determinants. One of these determinants are the features of the labour market, whose flexibility/rigidity can surely influence the ability to manage the post-merger phase. Some other determinants are the achievement of productive and distributive synergies, and the reorganization of the loans portfolio of the banks involved. These results can be compared with the (rare) contributions focused on the estimate of the efficiency changes of the banks involved in M&As, while there are not previous studies analyzing the M&A effects on shareholders' value over a long period. Focusing on cost efficiency, our results are consistent with those obtained in the previous studies for Germany and the United Kingdom (see Lang and Welzel (1999); Haynes and Thompson (1999)), whereas some differences can be observed with respect to the results obtained in Italy by Resti (1998) and some analogies with the results of Focarelli et al., (2002). In the first case, the variations observed are due to the radical differences in the period analyzed (1988–98 in Resti (1998) and 1995–2002 in our study) and to the methodology of the efficiency estimation used (DEA in Resti (1998) and SFA in our study). In the second case, our results obtained present some analogies with Focarelli et al., (2002): the negative effects on shareholders' value and cost efficiency both for mergers and acquisitions in our study are consistent with the profitability improvements (but not with cost and profit efficiency) just for the acquired banks showed by Focarelli et al., (2002). Once again, it is necessary to underline that both samples and methodologies are substantially different so that it is not accurate to directly compare our results with other studies. According to our results, the following statement by *Amel* et al., (2004, p. 2504) can be accepted only for some European countries (for example, Italy) and for some specific forms of business organization (for example, acquisitions in the UK): "The empirical evidence suggests that commercial bank M&As do not significantly improve cost and profit efficiency and, on average, do not generate significant shareholder value." In conclusion, the fragmentation and complexity of the European banking industry need specific analysis and make it extremely difficult to draw conclusions that can be generalized.

7.6   Conclusion

This chapter gives a contribution to the debate on the effects of M&As on cost efficiency and shareholders' value. Previous dynamic studies evaluated the M&As effects on shareholders value over the short term through an event study, efficiency and operating performance. Our analysis presents innovative features since it focuses on not-listed banks and on a medium-time period (no more than five years). As far as we are aware, the sample is one of the largest ever used and includes banks from European countries mostly interested by the M&A phenomenon; that is, France, Germany, Italy and United Kingdom.

Regarding the methodology, cost efficiency has been estimated through the SFA, while the shareholders' value has been determined with EVA. According to our results, M&As do not seem to have had substantial results on cost efficiency: the acquiring bank improves its efficiency of 0.67% on average, while the bank resulting from the merger seems to face an average worsening of 0.54%. Focusing on shareholders' value, M&A effects seem to be more valuable: the relative ability of the bank to create value (measured by the ratio between EVA and invested capital) increases by 0.23% in the case of acquisitions and 0.41% in the case of mergers.

In any case, the results vary with respect to the country considered: M&As have been followed, on average, by improvements in efficiency and shareholder value (both in the case of mergers and acquisitions) in Germany, while the opposite is observed in Italy. In the United Kingdom, cost efficiency improvements are substantial: this leads banks to create value for shareholders in the case of acquisitions but not mergers. Our results are consistent with those reported in the previous literature for Germany and the United Kingdom, while there are some differences for Italy. Our analysis gives a useful contribution to the literature, where the M&A effects on cost efficiency were often accompanied by the analysis of profitability. Our study takes into consideration the inadequacy of focusing on the analysis of profits; for example when banks are profitable after M&As without creating value because the operation involved high risks. It points out that the efficiency change finds its crosscheck in the bank ability to create shareholders' value.

Annex 7.1 Efficiency estimation methods

The methodological development in frontier production estimation has been rapid and a multitude of approaches are currently available. This literature may be roughly divided into two groups, according to the method chosen to estimate the frontier production function. These two methodologies are: the deterministic approach (being also referred to as non-parametric or mathematical programming) and the stochastic approach (or parametric or econometric). The main difference between these two approaches is that, whilst parametric approaches identify a specific form for the production function, non-parametric approaches do not specify any functional forms except for the linear interpolation among data points. These two branches of literature have grown lively, but separately, by producing at least five different methodologies: Data Envelopment Analysis (DEA), Free Disposal Hull (FDH), Distribution-Free Approach (DFA), Stochastic Frontier Approach (SFA), and Thick Frontier Approach (TFA).

As noted by Berger and Humphrey (1997), these methodologies differ in the assumption they make with regards to the shape of the efficient frontier, the existence of random error and (if random error is allowed) the distribution assumption imposed on inefficiencies and random errors in order to disentangle one from the other.

In addition, the underlying concept of efficiency is often different: whilst non parametric methods usually measure technological efficiency, parametric techniques tend to measure economic efficiency.[22.]

Parametric approaches[23]

Parametric approaches identify a specific form for the production function while non-parametric techniques do not specify any functional forms. Parametric approaches have the disadvantage of imposing a structured shape of the frontier by specifying a pre-determined functional form. However, these models have the advantage of allowing for errors, so they are less likely to misidentify measurement errors and transitory differences in costs, as inefficiency.[24]

There are three main parametric frontier approaches which differ according to the distribution assumption imposed. The first methodology is the "Stochastic Frontier Approach" (SFA) which "specifies a functional form for the cost, profit or production relationship among inputs, outputs and environmental factors and allows for random error" (Berger and Humphrey, 1997). In this approach, given a sample of size n of decision making units (DMU), the relation between the level of input x and the technically efficient level of output y^* is parameterised as $y^* = f(x_i, \beta)$ where $f(\ )$ is a suitable functional form such as the Cobb-Douglas or translog. Unfortunately, the y^* are not observable. To avoid this problem, error variable terms are included, assuming the relation between the observed y and the unobservable y^* can be expressed as $y^* = y_{i} + v_{i} - u_{i}$. This method adopts a composed error model in which distance between the observed value and the value on the frontier depends on two terms: (v_i) is a symmetric random error that is assumed to account for measurement error and (u_i) is an asymmetric non-negative error assumed to account for technical inefficiency. The two components of disturbance are assumed to be independent. Moreover, the inefficiency terms are assumed to have an asymmetric distribution (usually half-normal) and random errors are assumed to have a symmetric distribution (usually standard normal). These assumptions are based on the observation that inefficiencies cannot be subtracted from costs. In effect, they must be drawn from a truncated distribution, while random errors can both add and subtract costs, and so they may be drawn from a symmetric distribution. The efficiency of each firm is based on the conditional mean of the inefficiency term, given the residual which is an estimate of the composed error.

The second methodology is known as "Thick Frontier Approach" (TFA). This technique specifies a functional form for the cost function, but it does not impose any distributional assumptions on inefficiency estimates and random error terms. This methodology uses only the ostensibly best performers in the data set. Data are stratified into size classes and their average cost over the entire period is calculated, then the highest and the lowest quartile of the observations represents a random error, whilst predicted performance between the highest and lowest class sizes represents inefficiencies. In general, TFA does not provide point estimates of efficiency for all individual firms.[25]

The third methodology is the Distribution-Free Approach (DFA). Similarly to SFA and TFA, this methodology specifies a functional form for the cost function, but it adopts a different system to distinguish between inefficiency and random error. DFA assumes that there is "core" efficiency for each firm which is constant over time, whereas random terms tend to average out to zero over time.

Non-parametric approaches

Non-parametric approaches do not require the specification of a functional form because the efficient frontier is determined by enveloping a data set as tightly as possible. There are currently two main techniques: Data Envelopment Analysis (DEA) and the Free Disposal Hull (FDH).

The prevailing technique is Data Envelope Analysis (DEA), which involves the use of linear programming methods to construct a nonparametric piece-wise surface (or frontier) over the data (Coelli et al., 1997). DEA determines an envelopment surface and the frontier is derived by joining points in the input-output space in such a way that there is no method to increase outputs with the same inputs or reduce the inputs with the same outputs. In other words, DEA derives a frontier for each organization in the sample based on the output and input utilization of all institutions in the sample and identifies the best-practice subset of institutions: firms outside the frontier are relatively inefficient compared with the best-practice organizations. This is the methodological approach applied in this study.

The Free Disposal Hull approach (FDH) is a special case of DEA. It differs mainly because "the points on lines connecting the DEA vertices are not included in the frontier. Instead, the FDH production possibilities set is composed only of the DEA vertices and the FDH points interior to these vertices. Because the FDH frontier is either congruent with or interior to the DEA frontier, FDH will typically generate larger estimates of average efficiency than DEA" (Berger and Humphrey, 1997).

8
Post-acquisition Integration

8.1   Introduction

The M&A deals in European banking produced, on average, a fairly small positive impact on banks' ability to create shareholder value and they do not have caused substantial improvements in banks' cost efficiency. In order to create shareholder value, an M&A operation has to achieve some or all of the following benefits (KPMG, 2000, p. 7):

- Added growth prospects;
- Acquisition of strategic asset(s) such as technology or R&D;
- Reduced SG&A costs (combined basis);
- Reduced capital expenditures in the future (combined basis);
- Enhanced gross margins (for example, better market pricing power or greater purchasing power from suppliers);
- More efficient use of working capital;
- Better perception by the investment community (for example, the company appears to be more focused, or committed to market leadership, or less likely to be "steamrolled" by competitors, or has more broadly traded shares);
- One-time cash "creation" (for example, by selling idle assets or non-core divisions):
- More immediate (or likely) future "exit" / "liquidity" event (that is, IPO or sale of company, thanks to better size/scale, after the deal is done);
- Lower (combined) borrowing costs;
- Tax-related savings or efficiencies.

Banks may fail to achieve these benefits for a variety of reasons. These reasons vary from the the wrong choice of the target bank to the bad management of the post-acquisition phase; that is, the integration of the two organizational structures. The post-merger phase is when expectations are fulfilled or broken and excellent management is crucial to achieve the expected gains from the deal, as shown in Chapter 3, which reviews some M&A recent cases. Similarly, Cummins and Weiss (2004, p. 15) note,

> M&As also may reduce value to the extent that firms are not very successful in conducting post-merger integration. Post-merger integration is likely to be particularly difficult for cross-country and cross-industry mergers due to larger national and corporate cultural differences than must be overcome.

This chapter explores different ways of conducting the post-integration phase and achieve the M&A deal goals. The chapter is organized as follows: firstly, we present some critical issues in the post merger phase (Section 8.2); secondly, we outline some principles to define an integrated strategy (Section 8.3) and then we discuss how to implement an integration strategy (Section 8.4). Section 8.5 presents some conclusions.

8.2   Critical issues in the post-merger integration

Every M&A deal has unique benefits such as. operating scale economies, geographical coverage, access to technology, and management talent. Each of these is likely to be differently valued by the various stakeholders. In the post-acquisition integration, the frictional effect generated by latent conflicts among stakeholders needs to be understood and addressed. As such, the integration of two merging banks is not a matter of simply changing their organization structure and establishing a new hierarchical authority. It involves the integration of the banks' systems, processes, procedures as well as strategy, reporting system, incentives and, in particular, people. On the whole, integration deals often require that the banks involved in the deal change their corporate culture: the workforce may have to change their mindset, cultures and behaviour. In addition, M&A deals involve transformation in the organization structure and, consequently, power redistribution among the managers of the two banks: the conflict of interest and loyalty may deter the success of the M&A deal.

This section analyzes some common issues that have to be addressed to successfully manage the integration phase. First, it is necessary to ask: When will the post-acquisition phase start? While it is obvious that this phase starts when the acquisition deal has been closed, failing to recognize integration issues in the transaction planning phase – as for example, the bargain table – cn generate problems and prevent the achievement of strategic and value-creation objectives. As Lewis Carroll put it: "If you don't know where you are going, any road will get you there." The post-acquisition process might not have been accurately planned from its beginning since it includes a number of valuation inaccurateness or is unrealistic. This may happen since:

1. Managers did not account for environmental conditions or were not able to accurately forecast macroeconomic scenario changes.
2. The initial planning understimates the "true" economic investment necessary to successfully complete the post-acquisition phase. For instance, bank managers plan to make only some organizational change and information system integration, while it is customary to plan a radical re-engineering of operating practices, information systems, incentive plans and corporate cultural developments. Adequate integration would require the rationalization of both the workforce and the existing information systems of the two merging banks to reduce costs and minimize wastes (as in the case of managers) and, particularly, change the bank corporate culture, business model and new information systems.
3. The integration project may have been worked out using the assessment of the target bank's financial, strategic and organizational strengths and weaknesses known around the deal signature. Later, this information may not correspond to the reality.

In all these cases, the post-acquisition integration should be sufficiently flexible to achieve the M&A aims by adjusting to unexpected circumstances. Of course, unexpected circumstances may be also so strong as to prevent the achievement of the original M&A objectives.

Second, the post-acquisition integration has been accurately planned but the people entrusted to carry out the process are unable to complete their tasks for the following reasons:

1. The M&A deal was decided by people different from those entrusted to manage the post-merger phase and create shareholder value: as such, the M&A goals may have changed from the pre- to the post-acquisition phases. For example, banking supervisors have often practised moral suasion to ensure the system stability. Various M&As have been decided to solve bank crises (for example, Governments' bailout of the financial system in 2008): in the post-acquisition phase. The deal objectives usually become the shareholder value creation or productive efficiency improvements. Under these circumstances, the final integration process differs from the ideal-projected one since the determinants of the integration have been (at least, partially) out of the bank managers' control.

2. People entrusted with the post-acquisition phase are unable to change the corporate culture of the two merging banks. The corporate culture is embodied in its collective value systems, thinking, attitudes, rules, behaviours and ideologies which influence the workforce motivation and ability to perform.[1] Cartwright and Cooper (1993) suggest that the merger outcome is influenced by two factors. The first is the cultural affinity of the two combining organizations: as the cultural fit decreases, it is possible to expect an increasing fragmentation, uncertainty and cultural ambiguity, which are usually experienced as stressful by individuals. The second factor is the degree and scale of stress generated by the merger process and its duration. A stressful experience usually results in lower workforce confidence and commitment and higher confusion and hopelessness: overall, this has a dysfunctional impact on corporate performance. Figure 8.1 reports the cases proposed by Cartwright and Cooper (1993) for good, problematic and disastrous mergers.

3. `Managers entrusted with the post-acquisition phase are unable to successfully manage human resource issues. A key reason for the M&A failure is the bad understanding of its reasons and goals by all stakeholders. Every change in a complex organization system is likely to generate some resistance from stakeholders, especially if stakeholders are not informed and/or involved in the integration process.

The most sensitive stakeholder to M&A announcement is the work-force: *Nohria* et al., (2008, p. 81) note that

> The drive to defend tells us a lot about people's resistance to change; it's one reason employees can be devastated by the prospect of a merger or acquisition – an especially significant change – even if the deal represents the only hope for an organization's survival.

Davy et al., (1988) note that problems with employees have been estimated to be responsible for one-third to one-half of all merger failures.

Culture of acquirer	Culture of potential partner in marriage type…		
	Good	**Problematic**	**Disastrous**
Power	–	Power	Role, task, person/support
Role	Power, Role	Task	Person/Support
Task/ Achievement	Power, Role, Task	Person/Support	–
Person/support	All types		

Where the main characteristics of the corporate cultures are:

Power	• Centralization of power – swift to react
	• Emphasis on individual rather than group decision making
	• Essentially autocratic and suppressive of challenge
	• Tend to function on implicit rather than explicit rules
	• Quality of customer service often tiered to reflect the status and prestige of the customer
	• Individual members motivated to act by a sense of personal loyalty to the "boss" (patriarchal power) or fear of punishment (autocratic power)
Role	• Bureaucratic and hierarchical
	• Emphasis on formal procedures, written rules and regulations concerning the way in which work is to be conducted
	• Role requirements and boundaries of authority clearly defined

Continued

Continued

	• Impersonal and highly predictable • Values fast, efficient, and standardized customer service • Individuals frequently feel that as individuals they are easily dispensable in that the role a person serves in the organization is more important than the individual/personality who occupies that role
Task/ Achievement	• Emphasis on team commitment and a zealous belief in the organization's mission • The way in which work is organized is determined by the task requirements • Tend to offer their customers tailored products • Flexibility and high levels of worker autonomy • Potential extremely satisfying and creative environments in which to work but also often exhausting
Person/Support	• Emphasis on egalitarianism • Exists and functions solely to nurture the personal growth and development of its individual members • More often found in communities or co-operative than commercial profit-making organizations

Source: Adapted from Cartwright and Cooper (1993).

Figure 8.1 Good and bad corporate integration based on cultural compatibility

In general, the integration phase usually fails to achieve the planned goals for the lack of:

1. Vision: the new bank's goals, strategy and organization are not made crystal clear to all stakeholders in the M&A planning immediately and, in any case, well before the deal is signed.
2. Social and economic legitimating: a careful, social, responsible management is not undertaken to lessen stakeholders (for example, employees, customers, authorities) resistance from the beginning.
3. Managerial excellence: the most excellent managerial resources are not devoted to the post-acquisition phase. As the bank size increases, the integration complexity increases too and top managers' turnaround may be appropriate if the new bank is a substantially different bank: banks' owners have the responsibility to

make this type of decision, but they usually tend to avoid it to preserve the pre-deal equilibrium conditions.

4. Organizational analytic and planning ability: people entrusted with the integration rely on the managerial skill available in the two merging banks, while it is often necessary to acquire this knowledge outside the consulting companies. The integration complications increase as merging banks are less similar and the desired degree of integration is deep. In this case, new organizational, analytic and planning abilities are necessary.

5. Speed of the integration process. Delays in the integration process (especially, if due to uncertainty and misunderstanding) may create conflict of interest and reduce the operational efficiency. Of course, the duration of the post-acquisition phase is related to corporate similarity of the two merging banks and the desired degree of integration.

6. Constant monitoring and reinforcement: there is no constant monitoring and support on the levels of organization (for example, employees, mid-managers and managers) and corporation (for example,. information systems, incentive plans, branch network definition, new business organization, and so forth). Constant monitoring is a continuous and progressive process towards the desired organizational and cultural changes; it is based on the direct top-managers involvement and an appropriate capital allocation related to the complexity of the integration phase.

7. Internal communication: without providing information to all stakeholders regarding the aims, process steps and times, waste gains, and so forth, it is impossible to legitimate the M&A deal by showing the rationale of the desired changes and their compliance with the regulation, and ensure consensus, enthusiasm and involvement of all shareholders.

8. Customer orientation. The integration between two banks may produce anxiety among customers due to brand change, workforce rotation, branch network rationalization, change in financial products and services. To face customer resistance, it is necessary to develop a specific external communication for customers (e.g. one for private banking customers, one for retail customers, one for corporate customers, and so forth) and monitor their satisfaction over the whole process. Customers should be

able to perceive these changes as positive, otherwise they will be discouraged by the M&A deal and decide to change bank.

8.3   The post-acquisition strategy

The post-acquisition aim is to create an organization capable of achieving strategic M&A motives. While the two banks need to share these goals, they also have to agree on how to achieve these goals by aligning the banks' structures and strategies. The actual plan of the integration phase depends on several factors, such as bank strategy, environmental conditions and the M&A deal's rationale and structure. Haspeslagh and Jemison (1991) identify two dimensions in the integration strategy (that is, autonomy and interdependence) and Bruner (2001) adds an extra one (that is, control).

The first factor is the "autonomy" of the target bank. This refers to various aspects such as the brand name continuation, the corporate culture, leadership and the decision-making process. The brand name continuation is more apparent than the others, the preservation of culture, leadership and decision making are crucial to achieve the M&A strategic aims: for instance, a higher degree of autonomy would be appropriate if the target bank has excellent skills (such as the workforce ability to minimize wastes and/or customer-orientation) that are important to preserve. Vestring et al., (2003) analyze 125 M&A public deals from 1996 to 2000 to assess the effect of proactive strategies on corporate cultural integration and find evidence that companies following proactive integration strategies outperformed sector indexes and the do-nothing strategies. By grouping the deals according to objectives, whether they were made to grow scale or to build scope, Vestring et al., (2003, p. 3) find that

1. in Scale-driven deals, companies which take a proactive approach to cultural integration outperformed their relevant sector indices by 5.1%, while those ignoring culture underperformed by 7.9%;
2. in scope-driven deals, companies which take a proactive approach outperformed their relevant sector indices by 6.4%, while those ignoring culture underperformed by 0.5%. Namely,

best-performing acquirers in scope-driven deals achieved this result by intentionally keeping the merged companies' cultures separate (in the case of a very limited customer segments overlap) or by creating an altogether new culture (in the case of significant customer segments overlap).

The second aspect of the integration strategy is the "strategic interdependence" between the two merging banks. Its role depends on the synergies obtained through the acquisition. If M&A synergies are achieved by know-how transferring, there may be also low interdependence; if synergies are achieved by operating resource sharing (for example, brand names, distribution channels, and so forth), a high interdependence is appropriate.

By joining the "autonomy" and "interdependence" dimensions, Haspeslagh and Jemison (1991) identify four integration strategies through which the acquiring bank managers select an appropriate approach to achieve a sustainable competitive advantage, as follows:

1. Absorption; that is, low need for organizational autonomy, high need for strategic interdependence: This is the most straightforward integration strategy. Company A acquires company B, and Company B essentially disappears. The absorption strategy is appropriate if the two banks have a strong need to work together. Consolidation gains are achieved through a complete integration of the two banks' activities, organization and culture. The absorption strategy implies therefore that operational resources are pooled to eliminate duplication; this has inevitably a direct effect on the workforce by increasing their anxiety. While legal regulations usually guarantee a minimal decency level of treatment to employees, best-practice banks manage the workforce reduction following a transparent genuine concern for the redundant employees' welfare rather than legal minimalism.

2. Preservation; that is, high need of organizational autonomy, low need for strategic interdependence: in this situation it is necessary to preserve the culture and manage the acquisition differently from the absorption. Consolidation gains are achieved through the target bank's autonomy in order to preserve, develop and exploit its functional skills to the full. The acquirer banks plan a series of

interactions with the acquired banks to import positive practices in the acquired bank's management; as for example, functional abilities, general management, and corporate culture.

3. Symbiosis; that is, high need for organizational autonomy, high need for strategic interdependence: this situation implies that the two banks initially coexist without sharing the operational resources. But there may be a gradual transfer of functional skills, which makes the two banks interdependent so as to achieve the expected consolidation gains. For instance, a commercial bank acquiring an IT company to provide online banking services needs to preserve the boundary of each company and to allow interaction across that boundary.

4. Holding company; that is, low need of organizational autonomy, low need for strategic interdependence: the acquired bank's investment is passive and has the nature of a financial portfolio diversification. As such, consolidation gains are achieved by guaranteeing simultaneous protection and permeability of the boundary between the two banks.

Finally, the third dimension of the integration strategy is "control." As noted by Bruner (2001, p. 895),

> Control deserves special recognition apart from autonomy and interdependence. It captures a dimension of merger integration strategy that is not easily grasped by the other two dimensions. A merging target firm could be granted a high autonomy and either high or low control. Control could either worsen the sense of autonomy (because of the intrusiveness of these systems) or enhance it (if control systems works they may encourage the buyer to leave the target alone). Similarly, the target could be tightly controlled without strong links of interdependence.

The "control" dimension plays a fundamental role in M&As among banks since risk management is a key issue in the banking business. An acquired bank needs to identify the acquired bank's risks in order to assess the adequacy of its risk control system. Secondly, the merging banks need to align their risk management systems to control the overall bank risk-taking. While large banks in Europe hold effective risk management units, most medium and small banks do not often have the same accurate risk management systems. An accurate integration among the information systems used in risk management is also important for the supervisory authorities: e.g. the new advanced capital adequacy framework, proposed by the Basel Committee on Banking Supervision (Basel II)[2] imposes minimum capital levels to banks in connection with their risk-taking, and outlines a supervisory review process. Supervisory authorities are consequently interested that the risk-taking control system complies with the banking regulation.

8.4 Implementation of the integration strategy

The integration strategy (for example, the absorption or symbiosis) is usually selected before the public announcement of the deal. However, its implementation, which comes down to the the process through which the integration strategy is realized, formally starts after the shareholders have voted, and the merger agreement has received the regulatory approval, as required by the antitrust regulation in several countries. The integration strategy has two steps: the planning and the execution.

The integration strategy of "planning"

There is no single way to design a successful integration strategy as noted by David Jemison:[3]

> Each deal creates value in a different way, so it makes sense that each deal will be implemented or integrated in a different way. For example, one way you create value through a merger is by sharing resources. You may decide to lay people off to help get the economies of scale and scope that come with sharing resources. On the other hand, if you've bought the company for its human assets– its intellectual capital–then layoffs defeat the purpose. In fact, in that case you want to be sure your integration efforts encourage people to stay. That sounds obvious, but employees of acquired firms tend to assume they'll be laid off or that the new organization will change so much they won't want to work there. You need to anticipate those reactions, and act accordingly–before the opportunity to create value is lost. (KPMG, 2000, p. 8)

According to the best-practitioners' experience, the following actions seem to be necessary to successfully plan the integration strategy:

- The appointment of an integration leader and team: This is the first and probably the most critical step of the integration strategy implementation: the process leader and its working team have to be completely aligned to the goals attained in the M&A deal. The "integration team" member should be selected from both merging banks and has the core objective of extending the attention to the integration process through the bank organization. The "integration leader" is a high-profile and skilled person, and is selected within one of the two banks or externally: its appointment may be either temporary or permanent; for example, in the case that the acquirer bank is a very active acquirer.

- The development of a cultural integration strategy: The integration team should firstly profile the corporate culture of two merging banks. Next, it is necessary to assess the compatibility of these cultures and identify the potential conflict areas. Finally, the integration team should develop a cultural awareness programme: education, training and working together are useful tools to achieve this goal.

- Planning an integrated and continuous communication process with employees in order to convey a vision of the deal, progress reports, their role in the integration success, and future milestones: Overall, CEOs should communicate with all bank stakeholders to persuade them that the right deal has been made and that it will create value for all of them (or, at least, that it will be minimally disruptive to stakeholder support).

- Adopting a project management approach to define and communicate deadlines and a list of tasks to be completed. Namely, a project management approach involves:
  1. setting up clear goals;
  2. announcing a stimulating argument for change and its meaning;
  3. defining the M&A outcomes; that is, "where and what we will be at the end of the deal;"
  4. appointing an integration leader to supervise the transition and accept overall responsibility;

5. appointing an integration team to plan all necessary activities and various specialized task forces to undertake them;

6. carefully defining lines of authority, reporting, accountability between integration leader, team and specialized task forces;

7. accurately resourcing all actors – that is, integration leader, team and specialized task forces – in terms of people with relevant background, experience, commitment to change, taken from both banks;

8. outlining feedback and mid-course correction procedures;

9. setting up milestones and realistic deadlines to achieve them;

10. arrange rewarding for milestone achievements and penalization for project impassiveness;

11. discuss these items (especially, tasks and deadlines) with managers and employees.

- Arranging a detailed plan for talent retention. Integration teams often focus on workforce redundancies to achieve scale economies, but it is also necessary to consider the other side of the coin, i.e. the retention of key employees and managers (labelled as "talent") so to prevent the loss of knowledge they carry with them. Senior managers may decide to leave the company if they feel uncertain or are afraid of the new culture and the compensation system of the business model. The integration team should also be aware that bank's competitors tend to exploit the uncertainty surrounding the M&A deal to appeal to key managers. The first tool to retain the "stars" in the banks is compensation: special bonuses of stock options (golden hand-cuffs). However, titles and work assignment are also useful tools to achieve talent retention: most talents are likely to be already wealthy and may be tempted to stay for position of power (reflecting their merit) rather than for more wealth.

- Setting up a new supply chain management: Most M&A deals aim to reduce bank production expenses through scale and scope economies. The integration leader and its team have to carefully design the supply-chain management: e.g. various banks have established specialized financial products factories and redesigned their distribution channels.

1. Managing the intangible capital to maximize the bank market value: Invisible assets such as brand names, corporate names

and images are critical in M&As. This is because they are a source of considerable market value.

2. Planning work-space integration: The integration of offices and work spaces (for example, branches) sends signals that may assist or vanquish integration. Consequently, the integration team should carefully plan their size, location and facilities.

3. Management of information systems. Information systems play a key role in banking in the management of financial risks, the provision of accurate customer reports and the development of the marketing policy of the bank's services. The achievement of M&A aims requires the integration of a company's information on customers, markets and process with that of the other company. Consequently, compatibility between the information systems (as for example, risk management systems, customer information data warehouse, and so forth) adopted by the two merging banks has to be:

   a) seriously considered even at the pre-deal or due diligence stage;

   b) cautiously carried out BY implementing the most efficient and effective solution for the new bank aims. The information systems integration depends on a mix of technical and organizational factors. As such, new system designers have to account for the corporate culture, human resources. A detailed communication and training program should be achieved for the work force to share the benefits of the new information systems.

The integration strategy of "implementation"

The implementation of the integration strategy starts shortly after the planning. In this phase, actions go into effect and expectations will result to be either fulfilled or broken. Of course, the implementation phase directly follows the planning phases. But it should be also sufficienty flexible to eventually accommodate unexpected events. There is not one and only best way to do it.

As for the best-practitioners experience, Bruner (2001) identifies the following issues in successful implementations: speed (that is, the rapidity of execution), determination (that is, the adherence to the integration planning and the avoidance of unexpected problems), and communication (that is, the flow of information about the post-merger implementation). Regarding the integration speed and decisiveness, Feldman and Spratt (1999) argue that these are illustrated by seven common errors:

1. *obsessive list-marking*: the simple identification of tasks does not help decision making processes.
2. *content-free communications*: for example, vivacious catchphrases usually do not smooth away the stakeholders apprehension and doubts.
3. *creating a planning circus*: for example, unnecessary accounting and monitoring are time consuming and delay decision making.
4. *respecting barnyard behaviour*: for example, the existing hierarchies in the two banks may not be ease for the integration success.
5. *preaching vision and values*: for example, permanent and overstated attention to very high issues is likely to delay the implementation of the integration strategy.
6. *putting the turtles on fence posts*: in all integration deals, there will be rival claims for senior executive positions (for example, CEO, head of divisions, and so forth) if both merging banks had these position prior to the merger. The choice of the right person for the job is critical to achieve M&A goals and it should be based on meritocracy: the criteria adopted for the selection signal the style, culture and intent of the new management. Of course, meritocracy criteria are difficult to apply and it is common practice to assign a pro-quota assignment to the two banks' management: this may be a soft option, but it is frustrating for the workforce, and for talents in particular. Conflict of interest and loyalty may also arise and hinder an effective integration process.
7. *Rewarding wrong behaviours*: incentive systems should motivate the workforce to achieve the M&A objectives, while an inappropriate incentive plan will result in delays in the integration phase and employees resistance.

8.4   Conclusion

Banks often fail to achieve the expected M&A benefits because of the bad management of the post-acquisition phase. This is a particularly complex process since it is necessary to understand and address the frictional effect generated by latent conflicts inherent in stakeholders.

Every acquisition target has unique benefits (for example, operating scale economies, geographical coverage, access to technology, management of talents), each of which might be valued differently by separate stakeholders. As such, the integration of two merging banks is not a matter of simply changing their organization structure and establishing a new hierarchy authority. It involves the integration of the banks' systems, processes, procedures, strategy, reporting system, incentives and, especially, of people.

There are various reasons why the integration process may not achieve the expected results. First, the integration process may have been planned with some valuation inaccurateness. Second, managers entrusted to carry out the post-merger phase are not able to complete their tasks. For example, the assessment of the target bank's financial, strategic and organizational strengths and weaknesses made around the deal signature is found not to correspond to the reality over the integration process. In order to avoid this situation, the post-acquisition phase needs to focus on the following deal items: vision, social and economic legitimating, managerial excellence, organizational analytic and planning ability, speed, monitoring and reinforcement, internal communication, customer orientation. Of course, there is no single way to design a successful integration strategy. The actual design of the post-acquisition phase depends on several factors, such as the bank strategy, environmental conditions, and the rationale and structure of the M&A deal. Three dimensions of the integration strategy are particularly important: the autonomy of the target bank, the strategic interdependence between the two merging banks and the control. Focusing on the "autonomy" and "interdependence" dimensions, Haspeslagh and Jemison (1991) identify four integration strategies through which the acquiring bank managers select an appropriate approach to achieve a sustainable competitive advantage: Absorption, Preservation, Symbiosis and Holding company.

While the integration strategy is usually selected before the M&A deal public announcement, the strategy implementation is the process aiming to realize the integration strategy. The implementation process consists of two steps: planning and execution. In the planning phase, banks should:

1. plan the appointment of an integration leader and team;
2. develop a strategy for cultural integration;

3. plan an integrated and continuous communication process;
4. develop a project management approach to define and communicate deadlines and list of tasks to be completed;
5. arrange a detailed plan for talent retention;
6. set up a new supply chain management;
7. manage the intangible capital to maximize the bank market value;
8. plan the work space integration;
9. manage the information systems integration.

In the execution phase, the following issues are particularly important: speed (that is, the rapidity of execution), determination (that is, the adherence to the integration planning and the avoidance of unexpected problems), and communication (that is, the information diffusion about the post-merger implementation).

9
Conclusion

The aim of this book is to provide a substantial contribution to previous economic literature. Previous books deeply analyzed the M&A phenomenon, especially in the US market, with regards to various aspects such as management, organizational structure, corporate finance, and taxation issues. However, this book proposed an independent assessment of the effect produced by M&A transactions on bank efficiency and shareholders' value. M&A deals have usually been justified to increase the company efficiency and, finally, create shareholders' value, but few studies have analyzed the overall result of M&A deals to support these motivations, especially in European banking. We firstly substantiated that our research aims were worthy by showing that:

1. M&A is an important phenomenon worldwide; for example, the volume of worldwide M&A announced during 2007 reached US$4.5 trillion in announced deals and US$3.8 trillion in completed deals. M&As concern all countries; for instance, in 2007, M&A deals increased by 21% in the US, 18% in Europe, and 61% in the Asian-Pacific;

2. M&A is particularly important in banking: most deals are in the financial industry and, especially in banking. For example, in 2007, M&As between financial institutions worldwide were more than 7000 for an overall value of more than USD 700 billion;

3. the M&A phenomenon is particularly exciting in European banking: in terms of number of transactions completed in 2005, the European financial institutions were involved as targets for 32%

of transactions (EU-15 banks account for 27%) and as acquires for 31% of transactions (EU-15 banks account for 28%). In terms of value of the deals completed in 2005, the European financial institutions were involved as targets for 40% of transactions (EU-15 banks account for 36%) and as acquirers for 36% of transactions (EU-15 banks account for 32%).

In Chapter 2, we provide a framework for analyzing the M&A phenomenon by discussing some peculiar features of the European banking industry and analyzing recent trends of the consolidation process. Some of most important M&A deals worldwide from the 1990s onwards involved European banks. For example, there have been six big mergers from 2006 onwards for an overall value of more than 170 euro billion. M&A is certainly one of the main bank responses to higher competitive pressures in European banking. New forces of changes are mainly related to structural deregulation and prudential reregulation, competition enhancement, technology developments, globalization, etc. Especially, regulatory changes played a major role; that is, the structural de-regulation and prudential reregulation processes.

In Chapter 3, we answer a question: *why do banks merge?* Focused on horizontal and related M&A deals, which are the the most common and relevant in banking, M&As generally are carried out to create shareholders' value through various drivers, such as revenue enhancement, cost reduction and new business opportunities. We also analyzed non-value maximization motives for the M&A, essentially due to the managers and Governments' interference in the consolidation process. After discussing M&A motives, we critically analyzed seven of the largest merger deals in European banking: the Royal Bank of Scotland (leading a consortium comprising also Fortis and Banco Santander) and ABN AMRO in 2007, the Unicredit bank and Capitalia in 2007, BNP Paribas and Banca Nazionale del Lavoro in 2006, the Unicredito Italiano and Bayerische Hypo und Vereinsbank in 2005, Banco Santander Central Hispano and Abbey National plc in 2004, HSBC Holdings and Crédit Commercial de France in 2000.

In Chapter 4, we review literature dealing with M&As in the financial services industry. Despite the large number of studies, there is mixed evidence about M&A effects on the participating financial firms, bank customers and societal risks. We have focused on studies carried out over the last decade that compared either the behaviour of banks before and after M&As or the behaviour of banks recently involved in a consolidation deal in a moment prior and successive to the operation itself (labelled as dynamic studies). First, we reconsider studies assessing the impact of consolidation deals over a short period: see Houston and Ryngaert (1994), Madura and Wiant (1994), Zhang (1995), Cybo-Ottone and Murgia (1996; 2000), Becher (2000), De Long (2001), Beitel and Schiereck (2001), Cornett et al., (2003), Beitel et al., (2004), Kiymaz (2004), Penas and Unal (2004), Henock (2004), Lepetit et al., (2004), Olson and Pagano (2005), Campa and Hernando (2006), DeLong and DeYoung (2007), Gupta and Lalatendu (2007), Schmautzer (2008), and Ekkayokkaya et al., (2009). These studies usually applied the event study method to assess benefits resulting from M&As by estimating the reaction of the market price of quoted banks involved in the operation around the time of disclosure of the operation itself (announcement date). There was general agreement on event studies in US banking in the 1980s and 1990s; that is, target shareholders earned substantial positive abnormal returns, bidder stockholders earned marginally negative returns, and the combined abnormal returns were statistically insignificant or economically trivial on average. However, the studies published from 2000 onwards have provided a varied picture so that such earlier conclusions are no longer valid.

Second, we review studies which assess M&A effects on banks' productive efficiency: Akhavein et al., (1997), Resti (1998), Rhoades (1998), Lang and Welzel (1999), Fried et al., (1999), Haynes and Thompson (1999), Hughes et al., (1999), Huizinga et al., (2001), Cuesta and Area (2002), Berger and Mester (2003), Wang (2003), Carbo-Valverde and Humphrey (2004), Humphrey and Vale (2004), Koetter (2005), De Guevara and Maudos (2007), Ashton and Pham (2007), and Behr and Heid (2008). Namely, they compare the efficiency levels of the banks involved in M&A prior to and successive to the deal or, conversely, the efficiency levels of banks directly involved in M&As are compared to those of similar banks not involved in such operations.

Third, we summarize studies which assess M&A effects on banks' operating performance (measured through financial ratios) by comparing bank performances in a time period prior and successive to M&As: Srinivasan and Wall (1992), Linder and Crane (1992), Rhoades (1993), Spindt and Tarhan (1993), Vander Vennet (1996), Kwan and

Wilcox (2002), Focarelli et al., (2002), Díaz, et al., (2004), Knapp et al., (2006), Cornett et al., (2006), Campa and Hernando (2006), Berger and Dick (2007), and Altunbas and Marques-Ibanez (2008).

Overall, papers investigating the M&A effect over the medium-long term in European banking are more homogenous than in US banking. They show that European banks enhance their performance and productive efficiency through M&A deals. However, the number of studies investigating M&As effect on operating performance (especially in Europe) is limited and it is difficult to draw unambiguous conclusions.

In Chapter 5, we answer the question: *do M&A's create value for shareholders in the short term?* By selecting a large sample of M&As between 1991 and 2005 within the EU-27 (almost 300 deals), we applied the event study method and found that M&A deals created, on average, substantial shareholder value for the target companies (between 10% and 18%) over all event periods. Instead, acquiring banks achieved, on average, negative CAR, although the number of M&A deals with a positive CAR is higher than those with negative CAR over longer periods. In general, at least 40% of the M&A deals we analyzed generated a positive CAR. Regarding the combined entity of the target and acquiring firm, CARs are found to be positive providing evidence that the M&A transaction (taken as a whole) created shareholders' value rather than having simply transferred wealth from the bidder banks' shareholders to the shareholders of the target banks.

In Chapters 6 and 7, the questions are: *do M&A's create value for shareholders in a medium time period?* and *do M&A's improve banks cost efficiency in a medium time period?* We compare the efficiency levels and EVA of banks recently involved in a consolidation deal in a moment prior and successive to the operation itself. Our sample includes both listed and non listed banks from France, Germany, Italy and the United Kingdom. Our results show that the M&A operations we analyzed do not have significant results on efficiency. The effect produced on the value created for shareholders is more valuable. In any case, the results of the analysis vary with respect to the country considered. Our findings are consistent with those reported in the previous literature for Germany and the United Kingdom, while for Italy some differences have been observed due to the differences in the time interval analyzed and to the methodology used to estimate efficiency. These analyses give a useful contribution to the literature in which the effect produced by M&A operations on efficiency levels was often accompanied by the analysis of profitability levels. The present study acknowledges the existing inadequacy in focusing the analysis on profits. For example, a bank could be profitable after an M&A operation without, however, creating any value because of a high level of risk. It shows that the variation in efficiency following M&A operations finds its crosscheck in the variation of the capacity of the bank in creating value for shareholders. Overall, M&A deals seem to have a positive impact on shareholders' value, but the impact is stronger in the short term and weaker in the medium term (up to five years after the merger). This difference may be interpreted as a sign that capital markets perceive the M&A announcement positively; for example, investors optimistically judge the business plan of the new created bank. But, as the time passes, the new created bank fails (at least partially) to achieve the expected benefits (that is, higher efficiency, lower risks and enhanced cost and scale efficiency) due to problems in the post-merger phase (for example, setting up a new bank organization structure). Finally, we believe that the fragmentation and the complexity of the European market need specific analyses and make it extremely difficult to arrive to a conclusion that can be generalized on the basis of the sample considered in each study. Further contributions to the analysis on this theme may focus on the analysis of possible benefits in terms of the opportunity cost of the capital invested by banks in consequence of M&A operations that may determine, *ceteris paribus*, a higher capacity of creating value.

Finally, we analyze the post-acquisition integration phase in Chapter 8. Banks often fail to achieve the expected M&A benefits because of the bad management of the post-acquisition phase. This is an extremely complex process since it is necessary to understand and address the frictional effect generated by latent conflicts inherent in stakeholders. Every acquisition target has unique benefits, as for example, operating scale economies, geographical coverage, access to technology, and management talent. Each of them may be valued differently by individual stakeholders. As such, the integration of two merging banks is not a matter of simply changing their organization structure and establishing a new hierarchical authority. It involves the integration of their respective banks' systems, processes, procedures, strategy, reporting system, incentives and, especially, of people. In Chapter 8, we discuss some critical issues in the post-merger phase, outline some principles to define an integrated strategy and, finally, suggest how to implement an integration strategy.

Notes

1 Why Study M&A in Banking?

1. The number and the value of M&A transactions are substantial in all sectors. For example, the retail sector – that is, the industry less concerned by the M&A phenomenon – registered more than a thousand deals for an overall value of USD 4.5 billion (see *Thomson Financial*, 2007).

2 Merger and Acquisition Trends in European Banking

1. The process was completed with the Directive 2006/48/EC (relating to the taking up and pursuit of the business of credit institutions) and the Directive 2006/49/EC on the capital adequacy of investment firms and credit institutions.
2. A Monetary Financial Institution is defined as One of a number of financial institutions which together form the money-issuing sector of the euro area. These include the Eurosystem, resident credit institutions (as defined in Community law) and all other resident financial institutions whose business is to receive deposits and/or close substitutes for deposits from entities other than MFIs and, for their own account (at least in economic terms), to grant credit and/or invest in securities. The latter group consists predominantly of money market Funds. *(http://www.ecb.int/stats/money/mfi/general/html/index.en.html).*
3. *A Credit institution is defined as* "any institution falling under the definition contained in the Banking Coordination Directive 2000/12/EC of 20 March 2000, as amended by Directive 2000/28/EC of 18 September 2000 (including the exempt credit institutions), namely "(a) an undertaking whose business is to receive deposits or other repayable funds from the public and to grant credits for its own account; or (b) an electronic money institution within the meaning of Directive 2000/46/EC of the European Parliament and of the Council of 18 September 2000 on the taking up, pursuit and prudential supervision of the business of electronic money institutions" (*www.ecb.int*).
4. A Money market fund is defined as "A collective investment undertaking, the issued units of which are close substitutes, in terms of liquidity, for deposits and which primarily invests in money market instruments and/or in other transferable debt instruments with a residual maturity of up to and including one year, and/or in bank deposits, and/or which pursues a rate of return that approaches the interest rates on money market instruments. For non-euro area Member States, it should be noted

that the applicable national legislation may differ from the provisions of ECB Regulation ECB/1998/16" (*www.ecb.int*).

5. If we exclude France, these countries account (overall) for 20% of EU total assets and 17% of total EU number of employees.

6. Deals in the Government bailout of the financial system over the 2008 are analyzed in section 2.6.

7. Most of RBS' losses are due to the purchase of ABN AMRO (i.e. the Dutch bank it bought in 2007).

8. For a comprehensive analysis of the banking crisis causes, see De Larosiére J. (2009).

9. These financial products derive their value from mortgage payments and housing prices.

3   Why Do Banks Merge?

1. Own calculation on data reported in Table 8.8 (*ECB*, 2008a, p. 31).

2. The list of M&A motives is not intended to be exhaustive and all-embracing. For example, we omit to consider vertical M&A motives (i.e. M&A to combine various successive activities in a production chain in the same company) such as enhance technical efficiency and coordination efficiency.

3. Formally, network externalities exist whenever the value of a product/service depends on the number of other users of the products. Network externalities do not exist for traditional banking services, that may be rather found in distribution channels of banking services.

4. Formally, network externalities exist whenever the value of a product/service depends on the number of other users of the products. Network externalities do not exist for traditional banking services, but may be rather in the distribution channels of banking services.

5. For a review of older M&A deals (for example, Allianz-Dresdner in 2002, Citicorp-Travelers in 1998, Lloyds Bank-TSB in 1995), see Resti (2006).

6. The original name was "Compagnie Financière de Paribas, Banque Paribas": "Paribas" had been its well known telegraph address since the beginning of the century.

7. The estimated total value of the whole deal was around 30 Euro billion.

8. Options were put on these certificates to guarantee over the following three years a minimum 100 Euro share price.

9. The new UBS experienced heavy losses over the third quarter. Consequently, the chairman and three members of the Board resigned on 02/10/1998. On 13/12/1998, Moody's reduced UBS rating down from Aaa to Aa1. From 17/02/2000, UBS adopted a new organizational structure divided into UBS Switzerland (including the Private banking and Consumer & Corporate banking divisions), UBS Asset management and UBS Warburg. On 12 July 2000, the US announced the acquisition of Paine Webber (11.8 billion dollar). The latter was incorporated in the UBS Wartburg Division (investment banking) in November.

10. HVB lost 5 Euro billion over the period 2002–04 as a consequence of the real estate rating crash in Germany.
11. BNL was established in 1913 and is one of the main Italian banking groups.
12. Including bonds issues.
13. Namely, BNL has more than 2.5 million retail banking clients: 13,000 private banking clients and 112,000 small businesses clients.
14. Ifitalia is a BNL's subsidiary specialized in factoring services.
15. Intesa-San Paolo market power is also strengthened by the Banca Nazionale dei Territori model.
16. Source: Intesa and San Paolo-Imi (2006), Notice pursuant to art. 84 of consob regulation no. 11971/99, and subsequent amendments and integrations, http://www.group.intesasanpaolo.com
17. Published on the Italian financial newspaper "Il Sole 24 ore" on 14/11/2007.
18. Including branches, representative offices and small banking subsidiaries.
19. Estimated net synergies are 0.2, 0.5 and 0.8 Euro million in 2008, 2009 and 2010, respectively.
20. For example, light regional headquarters and no duplicated functions.
21. All data refers to the combination of Unicredit and Capitalia data at the end of 2006.
22. Corporate Governance refers to the system of rules and procedures to which companies refer to inspire their actions and meet their various responsibilities towards all *stakeholders.*
23. These are the Board of Directors and Advisory Council.
24. UPA's headquarters moved to Rome to ease the integration of domestic activities by exploiting UPA's resources in Lombardy to expand the branch network in this area. In order to achieve its objective, the re-structuring activities started immediately after the completion of the merger to optimize the Group's economic result in the shortest time possible.
25. The three banks are not new to similar transactions. For example, RBS acquired the British Natwest, which was initially bigger than RBS but was later completely absorbed and disappeared from the banking market. Fortis closed about 40 acquisitions and Santander about ten, in addition to the acquisition of the British Abbey National.

4   M&A of Financial Institutions: Literature Review

1. An *Abno*rmal Return (AR) is the difference between the expected *return* of a security and the actual return.
2. Some of the 13 independent variables are the interest income divided by the total operating income of the target firm; a dummy variable specifies the geographic diversification of the merger, with value 1 for domestic M&A and value 0 for cross border M&A; the log of the total assets of the

target firm divided by the log of the total assets of the acquirer; percentage growth of total assets of the target firm registered the year prior the announcement date; earning per share of the target firm; relationship between ROE of the firms (Beitel et al., 2004, p. 122).
3. In detail, there are 207 M&As in which the acquiring firm is American and 70 of which the acquired firm is American.
4. A high ROA is used as signal an excellent organization.
5. Accounting data have often considered to be responsible of paradoxical results such as, for example, the contextual increase of profit efficiency and the reduction of cost efficiency.
6. Because this study omits to analyze the effect on the other components of bank costs, the conducted analysis draws an incomplete picture of the relative benefits to the reduction of costs associated with the merger. Piloff and Santomero (1997, p. 10) observe that, since we cannot attribute an increase in efficiency, a change in the method of collocation or a different choice of investment is necessary to estimate the total bank costs.
7. The benchmark to measure the performance of the banks involved in the M&A consist of a sample of banks, which were not involved in merger operations from 1985 to 1997.

5   Do M&As Create Value for Shareholders? The Short-term Wealth Effect

1. This procedure was originally developed by Scholes and Williams (1977), Dodd and Warner (1983) and Brown and Warner (1980; 1985).
2. Namely, EU 12: Belgium, Denmark, Germany, France, Greece, Ireland, Italy, Luxemburg, the Netherlands, Portugal, Spain, and UK; EU 15: Austria, Finland, and Sweden; EU-25: Czech Republic, Cyprus, Estonia, Hungary, Lithuania, Latvia, Malta, Poland, Slovenia, and Slovakia; and EU-27: Bulgaria and Romania.
3. While an event window up to 20 days before the announcement date (that is, -20) is usually selected, we chose a longer time period (that is, –50). This is because Duso et al., (2007) note that the forecasting power of post-merger performance of CAR increases if these are measured over longer periods before the announcement date.
4. Only around the announcement date, the number of deals with a negative CAR is slightly higher than the one with positive CAR.

6   Do M&As Create Value for Shareholders? The Long-Term Wealth Effect

1. EVA is a registered mark of the consulting society Stern Stewart.
2. The NOPAT is obtained through the following formula: NOPAT=Operating Profit (1- tax incidence). The operating profits are obtained by adding the

financial charges to net profits. The tax rate has been approximated by the ratio (tax/gross profits).

3. For further insights, see Fiordelisi and Molyneux (2006)

   In order to pass from an accounting perspective to an economic one, Stern Stewart has pointed out more than 160 potential changes to add to the computation of EVA. In this respect, Al Ehrbar (1998) recognizes the difficulty in the realization of most of these corrections and identifies different configurations of the EVA according to the number of corrections made. For instance, the "basic EVA" is obtained by computing the EVA on non corrected accounting data. The "disclosed EVA", instead, considers the application of some standard adjustments by using publicly-known information. Finally, the "true EVA" is the correct measure obtained by making all the possible corrections on the basis of the internal accounting data of the enterprise. The EVA configuration used in this study is the disclosed one.

4. In order to pass from an accounting perspective to an economic one, Stern Stewart has pointed out more than 160 potential changes to add to the computation of EVA. In this respect, Al Ehrbar (1998) recognizes the difficulty in the realization of most of these corrections and identifies different configurations of the EVA according to the number of corrections made. For instance, the "basic EVA" is obtained by computing the EVA on non corrected accounting data. The "disclosed EVA", instead, considers the application of some standard adjustments by using publicly-known information. Finally, the "true EVA" is the correct measure obtained by making all the possible corrections on the basis of the internal accounting data of the enterprise. The EVA configuration used in this study is the disclosed one.

5. The choice of limiting the sample until 2002 is motivated by the following elements: (1) The moment of the analyses, since 2004 data are not available in the dataset used; (2) The number of M&A operations has registered a substantial slow down in 2003: the operations conducted in this year may present different features compared to the ones conducted in the period considered in the sample.

6. The data relative to M&A operations have been collected through the database ZEPHIR (Bureau Van Dick).

7. For this kind of comparison, it is advisable to focus the analysis on the data obtained from the analysis of the homogeneous sub-samples.

8. Fiordelisi and Molyneux, 2006.

9. For instance, when in a certain country in a given year there have been four M&A operations involving a large bank, with a negative EVA, and four small banks, with a positive EVA, the average amount of EVA for banks involved in these operations would probably be negative even if the bank with a negative EVA is only one.

10. Different from the approach used in evaluating the variations produced by M&A operations in terms of cost efficiency, a division in clusters for the banks included in the sample and an evaluation of the variation in terms of percentage ranking do not seem to be necessary. This is because

EVA does not derive from a comparative evaluation with other banks as in the case of the estimations of cost efficiency. Therefore the sample does not need to be homogeneous.

11. Data on the variations of value created, intervened over time for each single country, should be interpreted with caution. This is because of the small sample analyzed. In some cases, the variations reported are the result of a single M&A operation. They are not representative of the entire sample.

7   Do M&As Create Value for Shareholders? The Effect on Bank Efficiency

1. It is a methodology used in previous studies as, for instance, Defouney et al.,1985, Cable and Wilson 1989, Wadhwani and Wall 1990, Kruse 1992, Jones and Kato 1995, Haynes and Thompson 1999.

2. The choice of the translog function is essentially due to two reasons: first, Altunbas and Chakraty (2001) identify some problems, which are associated with the functional flexible form of Fourier (largely used in the literature as the translog one), especially when used to analyze a sample made up of heterogeneous data. Secondly, Bergar and Master (1997) observe that translog functions and the Fourier flexible form are substantially equivalent from an economic point of view. Both determine more or less the same efficiency ranking among banks.

3. In order to guarantee the linear homogeneity in the price factors

$$\left(\sum_{j=1}^{3} \beta_j = 1; \sum_{i=1}^{3} \gamma_{ij} = 0 \ and \ \sum_{j=1}^{3} \rho_{ij} = 0 \right),$$

it is necessary (and sufficient) to impose the following conditions: (1) the "standard symmetry" assuming that $\delta_{ij} = \delta_{ji}$ and $\gamma_{ij} = \gamma_{ji}$; (2) the linearity of the cost function as underlined in the model 1.

4. A period of five years seems to be in line (and sufficient) with the assumption that the M&A operation can produce its effects in the long term.

5. Since the linear homogeneity of the process is assumed, TC, π, w1 and w2 are standardized with respect to the price of physical capital (w2).

6. Deposits are considered as an output since banks charge commissions to depositors.

7. Numerous studies ranging from Dietsch and Lozano-Vivas (2000) to Sathye (2001) do not consider the off balance sheet items as output using the value added approach.

8. The choice of limiting the sample until 2002 is motivated by the following: (1) The moment of the analyses, since 2004 data are not available in the dataset used; (2) The number of M&A operations has registered a substantial slow down in 2003. The operations conducted in this year may present different features compared to the ones conducted in the period considered in the sample.

9. We analyze 141 M&As (both domestic and cross-border) over the period 1995–2002 selected according to the following criteria: (1) The bank headquarter should be in France, Germany, Italy and the United Kingdom; (2) The transaction should be effectively completed and there was in effect a change of control of the target bank; (3) The banks involved in the merger should not be affiliated; (4) Data relative to both acquiring and acquired banks are available at least one year before and one after the transaction. Data were collected through the Zephyr database.

10. Furthermore, the parametric methodologies of estimation assume that the production function has the same functional form for all the firms considered in the sample.

11. For further insights on the distortions coming from the use of a common frontier, see Bos and Schmiedel (2003).

12. The only difference is that the estimated cost function and the estimated profit function do not contain the control variable for time, nation, and bank.

13. For a summary of the consistency conditions of the estimates of efficiency, see Bauer et al., (1997).

14. For this kind of comparison, it is necessary for the analysis to be focused on the estimates obtained from the analysis of the overall sample.

15. For this kind of comparison, it is advisable to focus the analysis on the data obtained from the analysis of homogeneous sub-samples.

16. For this kind of comparison, it is advisable to focus the analysis on the data obtained from the analysis of homogeneous sub-samples.

17. Banks have been ranked from the lowest score (rank = 1) to those with the better judgement of efficiency; for instance, in case of a cluster of 200 banks, the bank with the highest cost efficiency score has a rank equal to 200.

18. Given the different dimensions of the clusters, the ranking has to be expressed in percentage so as to compare the variation occurred in cost efficiency over time. For instance, in case of a cluster composed by 200 banks, the bank with the better cost efficiency score has a rank equal to 200 that, in percentage, is equal to 1 (200/200).

19. The variation is measured comparing the efficiency at time t-1 with the one at time t ($EFF_{t-1} - EFF_t$). For instance, if the bank with the best efficiency score in the year t-1 (so with at percentage ranking equal to 1) obtains in year t an efficiency score that places it at the half of the cluster distribution (therefore with a percentage role equal to 0.5), a worsening of the efficiency ranking is estimated to be equal to 50%.

20. In reality, the measurement of the variation of the efficiency ranking of banks estimated on the basis of the efficiency obtained from the entire sample does not seem to be correct. This is because the banks in the sample are very heterogeneous. The analysis of the ranking variation is based on the assumption that the banks considered compete in the same market and that it is then possible to make a classification on the basis of their efficiency.

21. Data on the efficiency variations occurred for the single country over time have to be interpreted carefully. This is because the sample is small and these variations might be the result of a single M&A operation and are not therefore representative of the entire cluster. Conversely, the aggregate data of the four countries seem to be more reliable and show that the effects of the operations of acquisition on the efficiency of the acquiring banks are irrelevant in the first year and more significant in the fourth and fifth year. It is necessary to observe that the average result related to the effect created by merger operations after the sixth year derives from a single operation conducted by a small Italian bank and it definitely does not mirror a significant result in the entire European banking system.
22. Focarelli et al., (2002) illustrate the micro-economic reasons behind the results obtained by M&A operations using both data from public sources and data related to supervisory activity.
23. This is due to data required to apply these two approaches. Parametric approaches usually require input, output, and price data, whilst non-parametric techniques need input and output data but not price. Non-parametric techniques were in fact specifically developed for measuring technical efficiency in public and non-profit sectors (where prices may not be available or reliable and behavioural assumptions may not be appropriately made). However, if price data are available and behavioural assumptions are appropriate, non parametric techniques can estimate Allocative Efficiencies and Economic Efficiency.
24. This paragraph does not aim to deeply analyze stochastic methodologies, but it aims to review the main assumption on which these techniques rely. For further details, see: Fried et al., (1993), Humphrey and Berger (1997), Hjalmarsson et al., (1997), Coelli et al., (1997).
25. Comprehensive reviews of literature on the econometric estimation of stochastic frontiers are provided by Bauer (1990) and Greene (1993).
26. Thick Frontier Approach (TFA) and Distribution Free Approach (DFA) were developed by Berger. For further details on these two methodologies, see Berger (1993), DeYoung (1997), Berger and Mester (1997) and Berger and Humphrey (1997).

8 Post-acquisition Integration

1. There is no generally accepted definition of corporate culture. Most definitions include shared basic assumptions and meanings; as for example, Smircich (1983), Ashforth (1985); Reichers and Schneider (1990), Rentsch (1990), Langan et al., (1997).
2. In the European Union, Basel II has been implemented by the EU Capital Requirements Directives. In the US, the Office of the Comptroller of the Currency approved a final rule implementing the advanced approaches of the Basel II Capital Accord on 1 November 2007. The federal banking and thrift agencies (i.e. The Board of Governors of the Federal Reserve System; the Federal Deposit Insurance Corporation; the Office of the Comptroller of the Currency, and; the Office of Thrift Supervision)

issued on 16 July 2008 a final guidance, outlining the supervisory review process for the banking institutions that are implementing the new advanced capital adequacy framework. Regarding other banking systems, 95 national regulators indicated they were to implement Basel II by 2015 in some form or another (FIS 2006).

3. David Jemison is the Foster Parker Centennial Professor of Management and Finance at the University of Texas at Austin, US.

References

Akhavein, J.D., Berger, A.N. and Humphrey, D., (1997). The Effects of Megamergers on Efficiency and Prices: Evidence from a Bank Profit Function', *Review of Industrial organization*, 12, 95–139

Al Ehrbar, E., (1998). *EVA – The real key to creating wealth*. John Wiley & Sons, Inc, New York, U.S.

Altunbas, Y. and Chakravarty, S. (2001). Frontier cost functions and bank efficiency. Economic letters 72, 233–40

Altunbas, Y. and Marqués-Ibáñez, M., (2008). 'Mergers and acquisitions and bank performance in Europe. The role of strategic similarities', *Journal of Economic and Business*, 60, 204–22

Altunbas, Y., Evans, L. and Molyneux, P., (2000). 'Bank ownership and efficiency', *Journal of Money, Credit and Banking*, 33, 926–54

Altunbas, Y., Molineux, P. and Gardener, E.P.M. (1996*). Efficiency in banking*. John Wiley and Sons, London

Amel, D., Barnes, C., Panetta, F. and Salleo, C., (2004).'Consolidation and efficiency in the financial sector: a review of the international evidence', *Journal of banking and finance* 28, 2493–519

Amihud, Y., DeLong, G.L. and Saunders, A., (2002). 'The effects of cross-border bank mergers on bank risk and value', *Journal of International Money and Finance* 21, 857–77

Ashforth, B.E., (1985). 'Climate formation: Issues and extensions' *Academy of Management Review*, 10, 837–47

Ashton J.K. and Pham K. (2007) 'Efficiency and price effects of horizontal bank mergers'CCP Working Paper 07–9 Available at SSRN: http://ssrn.com/abstract=997995

Barros, P.P., Berglof, E., Fulghierri, J., Gual, J., Mayer, C and, Vives, X., (2005). *Integration of European Banks: The Way Forward*. Centre for Economic Policy Research, London

Battese, G.E. and Coelli, T.J. (1995). 'A model for technical inefficiency effects in a stochastic frontier production function for panel data'. *Empirical Economics* 20, 325–32

Bauer, P.W., (1990). 'Recent development in the econometric development estimation of frontier'*Journal of Econometrics*, 46, 39–56

Bauer, P.W., Berger, A.N., Ferrier, G.D. and Humphrey, D.B. (1997). 'Consistency Conditions for Regulatory Analysis of Financial Institutions: A Comparison of Frontier Efficiency Methods'. The Federal Reserve Board, Finance and Economics Discussion Series, no. 1997–50

BBC News (2008a). 'HBOS shareholders back takeover', 12–12-2008, available at http://news.bbc.co.uk/1/hi/business/7778914.stm.

BBC News (2008b). 'HBOS confirms Lloyds merger talks', 17–09-2008, available at http://news.bbc.co.uk/1/hi/business/7621151.stm.

Becher, D.A., (2000), 'The valuation effects of bank mergers'. *Journal of Corporate Finance* 6, 189–214

Behr, A. and Heid, F. (2008) 'The success of bank mergers revisited – an assessment based on a matching strategy', Deutsche Bundesbank Discussion Paper Series 2: Banking and Financial Studies, No 06/2008

Beitel, P. and Schiereck, D., (2001). 'Value creation at the ongoing consolidation of the European banking market'. Working Paper 05/01 (University of Witten/Herdecke). Presented at the X edition international conference of banking and finance. Tor Vergata University Rome, December 5–7

Beitel, P., Schiereck, D. and Wahrenburg, M., (2004). ,Explaining M&A success in European banks'. *European Financial Management*, 10, 109–39

Berger, A.N., (1993). 'Distribution-free estimates of efficiency in the US banking system and tests of the standard distributional assumptions'. *Journal of Productivity Analysis*, 4, 261–83

Berger, A.N., (2003). 'The efficiency effects of a single market for financial services in Europe', *European Journal of Operational Research*, 150, 466–81

Berger, A.N. and Dick, A.E. (2007) 'Entry into banking markets and the early-mover advantage', *Journal of Money, Credit and Banking*, 39: 775–807

Berger, A.N. and Humphrey, D.B., (1992). ,Megamergers in banking and the use of cost efficiency as an antitrust Defense', *The antitrust bulletin* 37, 541–600

Berger, A.N. and Humphrey, D. B., (1997). 'Efficiency of financial institution: international survey and directions for future research'. *European Journal of Operational Research* 98, 175–212

Berger, A.N. and Mester, L.J (1997). 'Inside the black box: what explains differences in the efficiency of financial institutions'. *Journal of Banking and Finance* 21, 895–947

Berger, A.N. and Mester, L.J., (2003). 'Explaining the dramatic changes in performance of US banks: technological change, deregulation, and dynamic changes in competition'. *Journal of Financial Intermediation* 12, 57–95

Berger, A.N., Demsetz, R.S. and Strahan, P.E., (1999). 'The consolidation of the financial services industry: Causes, consequences and implications for the future'. *Journal of Banking and Finance*, 23, 135–94

Berger, A.N., DeYoung, R. and Udell, G., (2001). 'Efficiency barriers to the consolidation of the European financial services industry'. *European Financial Management* 7, 117–30

Berger, A.N., Buch, C.M., De Long, G. and DeYoung, R., (2004). 'Exporting financial institutions management via foreign direct investments mergers and acquisitions'. *Journal of Money and Finance*, 23, 333–66

Berger, A.N., Dai, Q., Ongena, S. and Smith, D., (2003). 'To what extent will the banking system become globalized? A study of bank nationality and reach in 20 European countries'. *Journal of Banking and Finance* 27, 383–415

Berger, A.N., DeYoung, R., Genay, H. and Udell, G.F., (2000). 'Globalization of Financial Institutions: Evidence from Cross-border Banking Performance', Brookings-Wharton Papers on Financial Services 3: 23–158

Berger, A.N., Saunders, A., Scalise, J.M. and Udell, G.F., (1998). 'The effect of bank mergers and acquisitions on small business lending', *Journal of Financial Economics* 50, 187–229

Berger, A.N., Clarke, G.R.C., Cull, R., Klapper, L. and Udel, G.F., (2005). 'Corporate governance and bank performance: A joint analysis of the static, selection, and dynamic effects of domestic, foreign, and state ownership'. *Journal of Banking and Finance*, 29, 2179–221

Bos, J.W.B., Koetter, M., Kolari, J.W. and Kool, C.J.K., (2008). 'Effects of heterogeneity on bank efficiency scores'. *European Journal of Operational Research*, doi:10.1016/j.ejor.2008.01.019

Brown, S.J. and Warner, J.B.,(1980). 'Measuring security price performance'. *Journal of Financial Economics* 8, 205–58

Bruner, R.F., (2004). *Applied Mergers and Acquisitions*, Wiley & Sons, Inc, Hoboken, New Jersey

Buch, C.M. and De Long, G., (2004). 'Cross-border bank mergers: What lures the rare animal'. *Journal of Banking and Finance* 28, 2077–102

Buch, C.M., Driscoll, J.C. and Ostergaard, C. (2005) Cross-border diversification in bank asset portfolios, European Central Bank Working Paper No. 429 January

Cable, J.R. and Wilson, N. (1989). 'Profit sharing and profitability: An economic analysis of UK engineering firms'. *Economic Journal*, 99, 366–75

Campa, J.M. and Hernando, I. (2006) 'M&As performance in the European financial industry', *Journal of Banking and Finance* 30: 3367–92

Carbo-Valverde, S. and Humphrey D.B. (2004). 'Predicted and actual costs from individual bank mergers'. *Journal of Economics and Business*, 56, 137–57

Carbo-Valverde, S., Gardener, E.P.M., Molyneux, P. and Williams, J., (2000). *Adaptive strategies by European savings banks, in Strategic Challenges in European Banking*, London: Macmillan Press, pp. 181–210

Carletti, E., Hartmann, P. and Ongena, S. (2007) 'The economic impact of merger control: What is special about banking?' European Central Bank Working paper No 786, July

Carretta, A., (2001). *Il Governo del cambiamento culturale in banca*. Bancaria Editrice, Roma, Italia

Carretta, A., (2008). 'Introduzione. Creazione di valore nel governo dei processi di fusione e acquisizione nel sistema finanziario'. In Carretta A., Schwizer, P. (2008, pp. 9–30)

Carretta A. and Schwizer, P. (2008). *Le fusioni in banca. Gestire l'integrazione per creare valore*. Bancaria Editrice, Rome, Italy

Cartwright, S. and Cooper, C.L. (1993). 'The psychological impact of merger and acquisition on the individual: a study of building society managers'. *Human Relations*, 46, 327–47

Cecchini Report, 1988. *The Cost of Non-Europe*. European Commission, Brussels

Coelli, T. Prasada Rao, D.S. and Battese, G.E., (2005). *An introduction to efficiency and productivity analysis*. Springer Publisher, New York, U.S.

Cornett, M.M. and Tehranian, H., (1992). 'Changes in corporate performance associated with bank performance'. *Journal of Financial Economics*, 31, 211–34

Cornett, M.M., McNutt, J.J. and Tehranian, H. (2006) 'Performance changes around bank mergers: Revenue enhancements versus cost reductions', *Journal of Money, Credit, and Banking* 38: 1013–50

Cornett, M.M., Hovakimian, G., Palia, D. and Tehranian, H., (2003). 'The impact of the manager-shareholder conflict on acquiring bank returns'. *Journal of Banking and Finance* 27, 103–31

Cuesta, R.A. and Orea, L. (2002), 'Time varying efficiency and stochastic distance functions: the effect of mergers on Spanish savings banks,' *Journal of Banking and Finance*, 26, 2231–47

Cummins, J.D. and Weiss, M.A., (2004). 'Consolidation in the European insurance industry: Do mergers and acquisitions create value for shareholders?' Brookings – Wharton Papers on Financial Services, 217–58

Cybo-Ottone, A. and Murgia, M., (1996). 'Mergers and acquisitions in the European banking market', Working Paper, Università di Pavia

Cybo-Ottone, A. and Murgia, M., (2000). 'Mergers and shareholder wealth in European banking', *Journal of Banking and Finance*, 24, 831–59

Davy, J.A., Kinicke, A., Kilroy, J and, Scheck, C. (1988). 'After the merger: Dealing with people's uncertainty'. *Training and Development Journal*, 57–61.

De Guevara, J.F. and Maudos, J. (2007) 'Explanatory factors of market power in the banking system', The Manchester School 75: 275–296

De Larosiére, J. (2009), 'The high-level group on financial supervision in the EU', Brussels, 25/02/2009. Available at www.ec.europa.eu/internal_market/finances/docs/de_larosiere_report_en.pdf

Debreu, G. (1951). 'The coefficient of recourse utilisation'. *Econometrica*, 19, 273–92

Defourney, J., Estrin, S., Jones, D.C., (1985). 'The effects of worker participation on enterprise performance'. *International Journal of Industrial Organization* 3, 197–217

DeLong, G.L., (2001). 'Stockholder gains from focusing versus diversifying bank mergers', *Journal of Financial Economics* 59, 221–52

DeLong, G.L. and DeYoung, R. (2007) 'Learning by observing: Information spillovers in the execution and valuation of commercial bank M&As', *Journal of Finance* 62: 181–216

Dermine, J., (2003) 'Banking in Europe: Past, present and future'. In: Gaspar, V., Hartmann, P., Sleijpen, O. (eds), *Proceedings of the 2nd ECB Central Banking Conference on the Transformation of the European Financial System*. ECB Frankfurt

Dermine, J., (2006). 'European banking integration: Don't put the cart before the horse'. *Financial Institutions, Markets and Money* 15, 57–106

DeYoung, R., (1993). 'Determinants of cost efficiencies in bank mergers'. Working paper 93–1. Office of the Comptroller of the currency

DeYoung, R., Evanoff, D., Molyneux, P., (2009). Mergers and Acquisitions of Financial Institutions: A Review of the Literature, *Journal of Financial Services Research*, forthcoming

Di Antonio, M. (2002). *Creazione di valore e controllo strategico nella banca*, Bancaria Editrice, Roma

Diaz, B., Olalla, M. and Azorfa, S. (2004) 'Bank acquisitions and performance: Evidence from a panel of European credit entities', *Journal of Economics and Business* 56: 377–404

Dietsch, M. and Lozano-Vivas, A., (2000). 'How the environment determines banking efficiency: a comparison between French and Spanish industries.' *Journal of Banking and Finance* 24, 985–1004

Dodd, P. and Warner, J.B.,(1983). 'On corporate governance. A study of proxy contest', *Journal of Financial Economics* 11, 401–38

Duso, T., Gugler, K. and Yurtoglu, B., (2007). 'Is the Event Study Methodology Useful for Merger Analysis? A comparison of Stock Market and Accounting Data'. WZB Markets and Politics Working Paper No. SP II 2006–19

Ekkayokkaya, M., Paudyal, K. and Holmes, P.R., (2009) 'The euro and the changing face of European banking: Evidence from mergers and acquisitions', *European Financial Management*, 15, 451–476

Elkington, W. (1993), 'Bancassurance', *Chartered Building Societies Institutions Journal*, March, pp. 2–3

European Central Bank, (2005). 'Consolidation and diversification in the Euro area banking sector'. *ECB Monthly Bulletin*, May, pp. 79–87

European Central Bank, (2007a). EU banking structures, October

European Central Bank,(2007b). *Financial Stability Review, December*

European Central Bank, (2007c). Review of the Lamfalussy framework Eurosystem contribution,

European Central Bank, (2008a). MFI statistical report update, April

European Central Bank, (2008b). Statistics Pocket Book, April

European Central Bank, (2008c). Financial Stability Review, October

European Commission (2004). Mergers & Acquisitions Note, N.1, October

Feldman, M. L. and Spratt, M.F., (1999). *Five Frogs On A Log: A CEO's Field Guide to accelerating the transition in Mergers, Acquisitions, and Gut Wrenching Change*. Harper-Collins, New York, NY

Financial Stability Institute (2006). 'Implementation of the new capital adequacy framework in non-Basel Committee member countries: Summary of responses to the 2006 follow-up Questionnaire on Basel II implementation'. Bank for International Settlements, Occasional Paper, n.o 6

Fiordelisi, F., (2007). 'Shareholder value efficiency in European Banking'. *Journal of Banking and Finance*, 31, 2151–71

Fiordelisi, F. and Molyneux, P.,(2006). *Shareholder value in banking*, Palgrave-Macmillan, U.K

Fixler, D.J. and Zieschang, K.D., 1993. An index number approach to measuring bank efficiency: an application to mergers. Journal of Banking and Finance, 17, 437–450

Focarelli, D. and Pozzolo, A.F., (2001). 'The patterns of cross-border bank mergers and shareholdings in OECD countries'. *Journal of Banking and Finance*, 25, 2305–37

Focarelli, D., Panetta, F. and Salleo C., (2002). 'Why Do Banks Merge?'. *Journal of Money Credit and Banking*, 34, 1047–66

Forbes (2008), The global 2000 Special report, available at http://www.forbes.com/lists/2008/18/biz_2000global08_The-Global-2000_MktVal.html

Francis, B., Hasan, I. and Wang, H. (2008) 'Bank consolidation and new business formation', *Journal of Banking and Finance* 32: 1598–612

Fried, H.O., Lovell, C.A.K., and Schmidt, S.S., (1993). *The measurement of productive efficiency*. Oxford University Press, New York

Fried, H.O., Lovell, C.A.K. and Yaisawarng, S., (1999.) 'The impact of mergers on credit union service provision'. *Journal of Banking and Finance*, 23, 367–86

Frieder, L.A. and Apilado, V.P., (1983). 'Bank Holding Company Expansion: A Refocus on Its Financial Rationale'. *Journal of Financial Research*, 6, 67–81

Gandolfi, G., (2008). 'Le concentrazioni bancarie e gli effetti sulla struttura del sistema bancario italiano'. In Carretta A., Schwizer, P. (2008, pages 133–67)

Gewertz, K., 1997. 'Merton Wins Nobel Prize in Economics'. *Harvard Business School Gazette*, 16/10/1997, available on www.hno.harvard.edu/gazette/1997/10.16/MertonWinsNobel.html

Goddard, J., Molyneux, P., Wilson, J.O.S. and Tavakoli, M., (2007). 'European banking: An overview'. *Journal of Banking and Finance*, 31, 1911–35

Greene, W.H., (1993). 'The econometric approach to efficiency analysis'. In Fried et al., (1993, 68–119)

Gugler, K., Mueller, D.C., Yurtoglu, B.B. and Zulehner, C., (2003). 'The Effects of Mergers: An International Comparison'. *International Journal of Industrial Organization*, 21, 625–53

Gupta, A. and Misra, L. (2007) 'Deal size, bid premium, and gains in bank mergers: The impact of managerial motivations', *Financial Review* 42: 373–400

Hamilton, R., (1777), *An introduction to merchandize*. Edinburgh

Hannan, T.H. and Wolken, J.D.,(1989). 'Returns to bidders and targets in the acquisition process: evidence from the banking industry'. Finance and Economics Discussion Series 64, Board of Governors of the Federal Reserve System

Haspeslagh P. and Jemison, D., (1991). *Managing Acquisitions*, Free Press, New York

Haynes, M. and Thompson, S., (1999). 'The productivity effects of bank mergers: Evidence from the UK building societies'. *Journal of Banking and Finance* 23, 825–46

Henock, L. (2004) 'The cost of using bank mergers as defensive mechanisms against takeover threats', *Journal of Business* 77: 295–310

Hjalmarsson, L., Kumbhakar, S.C., and Heshmati, A., (1997). 'Temporal patterns of technical efficiency: Results from competing models', *International Journal of Industrial Organization*, 15 , 597–616

Houston, J.F. and Ryngaert, M.D., (1994). 'The overall gains from large bank mergers'. *Journal of Banking and Finance* 18, 1155–76

Hughes, J.P., Lang, W., Mester, L.J. and Moon, C.G., (1999). 'The dollars and sense of bank consolidation'. *Journal of Banking and Finance*, 23, 291–324

Huizinga, H.P., Nelissen, J.H.M. and Vander Vennet, R., (2001). 'Efficiency effects of bank mergers and acquisitions in Europe', Tinbergen Institute Discussion Paper 2001–088/3

Humphrey, D.B. and Vale, B., (2004). 'Scale economies, bank mergers, and electronic payments: A spline function approach'. *Journal of Banking and Finance*, 28, 1671–96

Ismail, A. and Davidson I., (2005).' Further analysis of merger and shareholder wealth effects in European banking'. *Applied Financial Economics*, 15, 13–30

Jones, D.C. and Kato, T., (1995). 'The productivity effects of employee stock ownership plans and bonuses: Evidence from panel data'. *American Economic Review* 85, 391–414

Kiymaz, H., (2004). 'Cross-border acquisitions of US financial institutions: Impact of macroeconomic factors'. *Journal of Banking and Finance*, 28, 1413–39

Knapp, M., Gart, A. and Chaudhry, M. (2006) 'The impact of mean reversion of bank profitability on post-merger performance in the banking industry', *Journal of Banking and Finance* 30: 3503–17

Koetter, M. (2005). 'Evaluating the German Bank Merger Wave'. Deutsche Bundesbank, Discussion Paper, Series 2: Banking and Financial Studies, no. 12

KPMG (2000), 'The new art of the deal: How leading organizations realize value from transactions', White paper, available at: http://www.kpmg.ca/en/services/advisory/ta/newArtDeal.html

Kruse, D.L., (1992). 'Profit sharing and productivity: microeconometric evidence from the United States'. *Economic Journal*, 102, 24–36

Kwan, S.H. and Wilcox, J.A., (2002)'. Hidden cost reductions in bank mergers: accounting for more productive banks'. *Research in Finance*, 19, edited by Andrew H. Chen, Elsevier Press: 109–124

Lang, G. and Welzel, P., (1999). 'Mergers among German cooperative banks: a panel-based stochastic frontier analysis'. *Small Business Economics* 13, 273–86

Langan-Fox, J. and Tan, P., (1997). 'Images of a culture in transition: Personal constructs of organizational stability and change'. *Journal of Occupational and Organizational Psychology*, 70, 273–95

Lepetit, L., Patry, S. and Rous, P. (2004) 'Diversification versus specialization: An event study of M&As in the European banking industry', *Applied Financial Economics* 14: 663–9

Linder, J.C. and Crane, D.B., (1992). 'Bank mergers: integration and profitability'. *Journal of Financial Services Research*, 7, 35–55

Lloyds TSB (2008). Result of general meetings, available at http://www.investorrelations.lloydstsb.com/media/pdf_irmc/ir/2008/2008Nov19_LTSB_GM_Poll_Results.pdf

Maccario, A., Sironi, A. and Zazzara, C., (2002). 'Is banks' cost of equity capital different across countries? Evidence from the G10 countries major banks'. SDA Bocconi working papers, n.77

Madura, J. and Wiant, K.J., (1994). 'Long-term valuation effects of bank acquisitions'. *Journal of Banking and Finance* 18, 1135–54

Marshall, A., (1890). *Principle of economics*. The McMillan Press Ltd. London, New York

Masera, R. (2009), 'La crisi finanziaria e I modelli di corporate governance delle banche: implicazioni e prospettive', *Bancaria*, 65, issue 1, pages 3–19

Moeller, S.B., Schlingemann, F.P. and Stulz, R.M., (2004). 'Firm size and the gains from acquisitions'. *Journal of Financial Economics*, 73, 201–28

Nohria, N., Groysberg, B. and Lee, L.E., (2008). 'Employee Motivation- A Powerful New Model'. *Harvard Business Review*, 86, p.78–84

Olson, G.T. and Pagano, M.S. (2005) 'A new application of sustainable growth: A multi-dimensional framework for evaluating the long run performance of bank mergers', *Journal of Business Finance and Accounting* 32: 1995–2036

Padoa Schioppa, T., (2001). 'Bank Competition: A Changing Paradigm'. *European Finance Review*, 5, 13–20

Papademos, L., (2005). 'Banking supervision and financial stability in Europe'. Speech delivered to a Conference on Supervision of International Banks, European Banking Federation, Brussels, 28 October

Penas, M.F. and Unal, H. (2004) 'Gains in bank mergers: Evidence from the bond market', *Journal of Financial Economics* 74: 149–79

Petmezas, D., (2008). 'What drives acquisitions? Market valuations and bidder performance'. *Journal of Multinational Financial Management*, doi:10.1016/j. mulfin.2008.05.001

Pilloff, S.J. and Santomero, A.M., (1997). 'The value effect of bank mergers and acquisitions'. Wharton working Paper 97–07

Pilloff, S.J. and Santomero, A.M., (1998). 'The Value Effect of Bank Mergers and Acquisitions'. In Amihud, Y., Miller, G (eds). *Bank Mergers and Acquisitions*, Boston: Kluwer Academic Publishers

Quagliarello M. (2004), 'La bancassicurazione: profili operativi e scelte regolamentari', *Il Risparmio* n. 3/2004

Rappaport, A., (1998). *Creating shareholder value*. The free press, New York

Reichers, A.E. and Schneider, B., (1990). 'Climate and culture: An evolution of constructs'. In B. Schneider (ed.), *Organizational climate and culture*. San Francisco, CA: Jossey-Bass, pp. 5–39

Rentsch, J.R., (1990). 'Climate and culture: Interaction and qualitative differences in organizational meanings'. *Journal of Applied Psychology*, 75, 668–81

Resti, A., (1998). 'Regulation can foster mergers, can mergers foster efficiency? The Italian case'. *Journal of Economics and Business*, 50, 157–69

Resti, A., (2006). *Le fusioni bancarie. La lezione dell'esperienza*. Bancaria Editrice, Roma, Italia

Resti A. and Sironi, A., (2007). *Risk management and shareholder value in banking*, John Wiley and Sons, Chichester, UK

Rhoades, S.A., (1986). 'The Operating Performance of Acquired Firms in Banking before and after Acquisition'. Staff Studies 149. Washington: Board of Governors of the Federal Reserve System, 1986. A version with alternative statistical tests is, 'The Operating Performance of Acquired Firms in Banking,' in Robert Wills, Julie A. Caswell, and John D. Culbertson, (eds), *Issues after a Century of Federal Competition Policy*, Lexington Press, U.S., 1987

Rhoades, S.A., (1993). 'Efficiency effects of horizontal (in-market) mergers', *Journal of Banking and Finance* 17, 411–22

Rhoades, S.A., (1998.). 'The efficiency effect of bank mergers: an overview of case studies of nine mergers', *Journal of Banking and Finance* 22, 273–91

Rose, P.S., (1987a).'Improving Regulatory Policy for Mergers: An Assessment of Bank Merger Motivations and Performance Effects'. *Issues in Bank Regulation* (Winter), pp. 32–39

Rose, P.S., (1987b). 'The Impact of Mergers in Banking: Evidence from a Nationwide Sample of Federally Chartered Banks'. *Journal of Economics and Business*, 39, 289–312

Ruozi, R., (2001). La cultura aziendale e I processi di fusione e acquisizione. In Carretta A., 2001

San Paolo and IMI (2006). Merger by incorporation of sanpaolo IMI S.P.A. with and into Banca intesa S.P.A, notice pursuant to Art. 84 of consob regulation No. 1971/99 and subsequent amendments and integrations, available at: http://www.group.intesasanpaolo.com/

Sathye, M., 2001. 'Cost efficiency in Australian banking: an empirical investigation'. *Journal of Banking and Finance* 25, 613–30

Schmautzer, D. (2008) 'Cross-border bank mergers: Who gains and why?'. European University Studies Series V: Economics and Management/ Eurasische Hochschulschriften. Reihe 5: Volks- Und Betriebswirtschaft). Peter Lang Publishing; 1 edition

Scholes, M. and Williams, J., (197)7. 'Estimating betas from nonsynchronous data', *Journal of Financial Economics* 5, 309–327

Schwizer, P., (2008). 'Concentrazioni e ristrutturazioni bancarie: benefici ricercati e risultati ottenuti. Le "colpe" dei manager'. In Carretta A., Schwizer, P. (2008, pp. 171–218)

Smircich, L., (1983). 'Studying organizations as cultures'. In G. Morgan (ed.), *Beyond method*. Beverly Hills, CA: Sage Publications, pp. 160–172

Spindt, P.A. and Tarhan, V., (1993). 'The impact of mergers on bank operating performance', Working paper, Tulane university

Srinivasan, A. and Wall, L.D., (1992). 'Cost saving associated with bank mergers', Working paper 92 – 2, Federal reserve bank of Atlanta

Stewart, B.G. (1991), *The quest for value*, HarperBusiness, New York, U.S.

Sudarsanam, S., (2003). Creating Value from Mergers and Acquisitions, FT Prentice Hall

Sudarsanam, S., 2003. *Creating value from mergers and acquisitions -The challenges*. Prentice Hall, London, U.K.

Sutton, J., (1991). *Sunk Costs and Market Structure*. MIT Press, London

Swiss, R.E. (1994). 'Bancassurance', *Sigma* n.1/1994

Thomson Financial (2007). *Mergers & Acquisitions Review*, Fourth Quarter 2007, available at http://banker.thomsonib.com

Thomson Financial (2008). *Mergers & Acquisitions Review*, Fourth Quarter 2007, available at http://banker.thomsonib.com

Thu Nguyen, H. and Yung, K., (2007). 'Mergers and Acquisitions: Evidence of Three Motives'. Paper presented to the Eastern Finance Association, 3rd Annual Meetings, April 18–21, New Orleans, U.S.

Unicredit and Capitalia (2007). 'Strengthening a Key Market: Merger Between UniCredit and Capitalia', 21 May 2007, available at http://www.unicredit-capitalia.eu

Uyemura, D.G., Kantor, G.C. and Pettit, J.M., (1996). 'EVA for banks: value creation, risk management and profitability measurement', *Journal of Applied Corporate Finance*, 9, 94–105

Vander Vennet, R., (1996). 'The effect of mergers and acquisitions on the efficiency and profitability of EC Credit institutions', *Journal of Banking and Finance* 20, 1531–58

Vestring, T., King, B., Rouse, T., Critchlow, J., (2003). 'Merger integration: why the "soft issues" matter most,' *EBF*, 13, 69-71

Wadhwani, S. and Wall, M., (1990). 'The effects of profit-sharing on employment, wages, stock returns and productivity: Evidence from UK microdata'. *Economic Journal*, 100, 1–17

Walkner, C. and Raes, J.P., (2005). 'Integration and consolidation in EU banking – an unfinished business European Commission, Directorate-General For Economic And Financial Affairs', Economic Papers, N226, April

Wang, J.C., (2003). 'Merger-Related Cost Savings in the Production of Bank Services'. Federal Reserve Bank of Boston, Working Paper 03–8

Webb, Q., (2009), 'Crisis sparks 33 percent drop in first-quarter M&A', Reuters news on the March 26, 2009 8:08pm, available at http://www.reuters.com/article/euPrivateEquityNews/idUSTRE52Q3Y520090327

Wheelock, David C. and Wilson, P.W., (2004). 'Consolidation in US banking: Which banks engage in mergers?'. *Review of Financial Economics*, 13, 7–39

Zhang, H., (1995). 'Wealth effects of U.S. Bank takeovers', *Applied Financial Economics* 5, 329–36

Index